Increase Your Web Traffic In a Weekend

Fourth Edition

Jerry Lee Ford, Jr.
and
William R. Stanek

THOMSON

COURSE TECHNOLOGY ™

Professional ■ Technical ■ Reference

ISBN: 1-59863-108-X

Library of Congress Catalog Card Number: 2005931907

Printed in the United States of America

06 07 08 09 10 PH 10 9 8 7 6 5 4 3 2 1

Thomson Course Technology PTR,
a division of Thomson Course Technology
25 Thomson Place
Boston, MA 02210
http://www.courseptr.com

Publisher and General Manager,
Thomson Course Technology PTR:
Stacy L. Hiquet

Associate Director of Marketing:
Sarah O'Donnell

Manager of Editorial Services:
Heather Talbot

Marketing Manager:
Cathleen Snyder

Senior Acquisitions Editor:
Emi Smith

Senior Editor:
Mark Garvey

Marketing Coordinator:
Jordan Casey

Project Editor:
Jenny Davidson

Technical Reviewer:
John Gosney

Thomson Course Technology PTR
Editorial Services Coordinator:
Elizabeth Furbish

Interior Layout Tech:
Shawn Morningstar

Cover Designer:
Mike Tanamachi

Indexer:
Sharon Shock

Proofreader:
Sandi Wilson

Jerry Lee Ford, Jr.

To my wife, Mary, and my three children,
Alexander, William, and Molly.

William R. Stanek

To my children, Jasmine, William Jr., and Jennifer.
Thanks for the joy, the laughter, and the light.
Always chase your dreams…

ACKNOWLEDGMENTS

There are a number of individuals who deserve credit for their work on the fourth edition of this book. Special thanks goes out to Emi Smith, who served as the book's Senior Acquisitions Editor and the book's Project Editor, Jenny Davidson. Other major contributors that deserve to be acknowledged include the book's Technical Editor, John Gosney, as well as everyone else at Thomson Course Technology PTR for all their hard work. Thanks also go out to those individuals who made signification contributions to the three previous editions of this book.

ABOUT THE AUTHORS

Jerry Lee Ford, Jr. is an author, educator, and IT professional with over 16 years' experience in Information Technology, including roles as an automation analyst, technical manager, technical support analyst, automation engineer, and security analyst. Mr. Ford has authored 16 other computer books, including *Visual Basic 2005 Express Programming for the Absolute Beginner, VBScript Professional Projects, Microsoft Windows Shell Scripting and WSH Administrator's Guide, Learn VBScript in a Weekend, Microsoft Windows Shell Scripting for the Absolute Beginner, Learn JavaScript in a Weekend,* and *Microsoft Windows XP Professional Administrator's Guide.*

Mr. Ford has a master's degree in Business Administration from Virginia Commonwealth University in Richmond, Virginia, and has over five years' experience as an adjunct instructor teaching networking courses in Information Technology.

William R. Stanek is a leading network technology expert and an award-winning author. Over the years, his practical advice has helped programmers, developers, and network engineers all over the world. He is also a regular contributor to leading publications like *PC Magazine.* He has written, co-authored, or contributed to numerous computer books, including *Microsoft Windows 2000 Administrator's Pocket Consultant, Microsoft SQL Server 7.0 Administrator's Pocket Consultant,* and *Windows 2000 Scripting Administrator's Guide.*

Mr. Stanek has a master's degree in Information Systems, with distinction, and a bachelor's degree in Computer Science, magna cum laude. Mr. Stanek has been involved in the commercial Internet community since 1991. He has experience in developing server technology, encryption, Internet development, and a strong understanding of e-commerce technology and its development.

CONTENTS

Introduction

These days, everyone seems to have a home page or a Web site. However, just because you create and publish a Web page doesn't mean anyone will visit it. Competition to attract visitors is extreme. The reality is that of the millions of Web pages out there, only a handful actually attract a steady readership; and these same Web pages are the ones that attract advertisers. In order to compete, you need to develop and implement a Web site promotion plan.

What can you do when you build a home page that no one visits? What can you do to earn money on your Web site? Is there an easy way to attract readers and advertisers without spending a fortune? There are low-cost ways to attract readers and advertisers to your home page or Web site, and *Increase Your Web Traffic In a Weekend, Fourth Edition* shows you how.

What's This Book About?

With users from countries around the world, the Web has an extremely diverse audience. Trying to tap into the tremendous potential of the Web can be a daunting task. Enter *Increase Your Web Traffic In a Weekend, Fourth Edition*. The goal of this book is to lay out a cost-effective, comprehensive plan that both Web beginners and experts can use to build an audience for a home page or Web site.

This book has gathered together low-cost Web-promotion and advertising techniques collected from years of practical experience. These secrets could save you thousands of dollars. Now that's something to think about!

How Is This Book Organized?

This book is designed to be easy to follow and understand. Anyone, regardless of skill level or work schedule, will be able to learn the secrets of successful Web promotion and advertising.

This book is divided into five sessions. Session one begins with a Friday evening preview of what is ahead for the weekend. Saturday is broken down into morning and afternoon sessions designed to help you understand the following concepts:

- Where to publicize your home pages for free
- How to tailor your pages for search engines
- How to use <META> tags to increase Web traffic
- How to register with search engines
- How to submit your site to directories, guides, and lists
- How to use specialized directories, such as community guides
- How to get your home page listed as the Cool Site of the Day
- How to use registration services

Sunday is also divided into morning and afternoon sessions designed to help you understand the following ideas:

- The right way to sell your site through e-mail
- Techniques that you can use to attract masses
- How to create, track, and manage banner advertising
- How to place ads on other sites without spending a dime
- Who is currently visiting your home page
- How to track and analyze visitor statistics
- How to put those statistics to work
- How to direct visitors to popular areas of your Web site
- How to gain readers who otherwise would be lost because they used the wrong URL

Who Should Read This Book?

Anyone who wants to learn how to attract visitors to a home page or a Web site should read this book. Consider the following questions:

- Are you disappointed with the results that you've achieved through Web publishing?
- Have you created wonderful Web pages, yet receive only a few visitors?
- Do you think that the lack of visitors means that your ideas, interests, or products aren't interesting?
- Do you want to reach a larger audience?
- Do you want to learn how to attract a steady readership to your Web site?
- Do you want to learn the secrets of Web promotion and marketing?

- Do you want to attract advertisers to your Web site?

- Do you want to learn how to tap into the tremendous potential of the Web?

- Do you want to learn the secrets of marketing without spending a dime?

If you answered yes to any of these questions, this book is for you.

What Do You Need to Use This Book?

The most important ingredients for using this book are a connection to the Internet and a home page or Web site that you want to promote. You'll also need to set aside a little time to implement some of the Web site promotion techniques that you will learn about in this book. A major goal of this book is to present you with free and low-cost Web site promotion techniques. Depending on how eager you are to quickly see increased Web traffic, you may want to set aside a small budget, anywhere from $50 to a few hundred dollars, to support your Web site promotion plan. However, 99 percent of the Web site promotion techniques that you will learn about as you go through this book can be implemented at no cost. So, setting aside a small budget is optional.

What Do You Need to Know?

Increase Your Web Traffic In a Weekend, Fourth Edition guides you through everything you need to successfully promote your Web site or home page. It is assumed that you already have a Web site that you are ready to promote. Although you certainly don't need to be an HTML expert, you should know at least the basics of HTML. If you don't know HTML, a good how-to guide is Premier Press's *Learn HTML 4 In a Weekend, Fourth Edition* (ISBN: 1-59200-059-2). Finally, you should also know the basics of Web browsing. If this is all true, you're on the right track.

Conventions Used in This Book

This book uses a number of conventions to help make it easier for you to work with, including:

Notes. Enhance a discussion in the text by drawing your attention to a particular point that needs emphasis.

Tips. Offer helpful hints or additional information.

Italics. Used to highlight new terms and emphasize key pieces of information.

Promoting Your Web Site to the World

➤ Promoting Your Web Site without Spending a Fortune

➤ Making the Web Work for You

➤ Getting Your Web Site Noticed

Thousands of Web publishers have created home pages to sell products and services or to simply share ideas. Often they are disappointed with the results. They create wonderful pages and yet receive only a few visitors. These publishers might think that their ideas, interests, and products aren't interesting, but nothing could be further from the truth. Capitalizing on available resources and knowing how to promote your site are the keys to increasing your Web traffic. By the end of this weekend, you'll know a great deal more about how to do that.

So go ahead—get started. It's Friday evening (at least if you're following the schedule). This evening's session provides an overview of what you need to get started, and it gets you acquainted with crucial issues and resources you'll focus on to get your Web site noticed by the masses.

Increase Your Web Traffic In a Weekend, Fourth Edition is designed as a guide to everything you need to successfully promote your Web site or home page. In this book, promotion encompasses publicizing, marketing, advertising, and all the other techniques that help bring traffic to a Web site. Although promotion is 35 percent inspiration and 65 percent perspiration, promoting your Web site can be an awful lot of fun.

You Built It, But Will They Come?

As incredible as it might seem, cyberspace contains hundreds of millions of Web pages. As if this competition wasn't stiff enough, there are no Web maps—and there are relatively few signposts—to guide readers anywhere. So how can anyone find your Web site? Unfortunately, no easy answer to this question exists.

After you've spent hours of your time and possibly hundreds or thousands of dollars creating a home page, it is certainly disheartening when no one visits your site—or the traffic is so minimal that it might as well be non-existent.

Usually, the next step for many Web publishers is to launch their own promotion campaign. They register with all the search engines they can find, blanket newsgroups and mailing lists with information about their home pages, tell everyone they know to visit their site—in order words, they explore all the promotion avenues they've heard and read about.

You could register with search engines till your fingers won't type any more, but unless you truly understand how search engines work and how to use their indexing features, you are wasting your time. You could send out tons of e-mail through mailing lists and news-groups, but unless you know what you are doing, you will get so much hate mail that you will truly wish you had never published a home page in the first place.

In the end, when the euphoria over getting a new Web page noticed wears off, many Web publishers wake up to the cruel reality that creating a Web page doesn't automatically draw visitors to it. Fortunately, there are reliable, low-cost and free ways to get your Web site noticed, as well as to substantially increase traffic to your Web site. By the end of this book, you will have everything you need to successfully attract a following to your Web site, gain an audience for your ideas, and promote your Web site to the world.

Can You Really Promote Your Web Site without Spending a Fortune?

Invariably, people ask "How much will it cost?" If you've been publishing on the Web for a while, or if you have done some considerable browsing, you have probably come across sales pitches like these:

- Get 325 e-mail addresses for the top magazine, newspapers, and e-zines—only $325
- We'll submit your site everywhere for $275
- Send e-mail promotions to millions for pennies apiece!
- Get listed in 1,500+ search engines and directories for $99.95

Unfortunately, whether these types of pitches sell you on a pennies-apiece concept or a flat-fee-per-use concept, they are usually nothing more than cleverly designed ways to get you to open your pocketbook. For example, out of the list of 325 top magazines, newspapers, and e-zines, usually only a handful are really interested in the topic that your site covers, and you could get these e-mail addresses simply by visiting the related Web sites yourself. So why pay $325 for a few e-mail addresses that you could get yourself in less than an hour?

 NOTE Most of the techniques or concepts presented in this book are cost-free. That said, the Web is constantly changing and what may be free or low-cost today may not be tomorrow.

Making the Web Work for You

Making the Web work for you means conducting your Web promotion campaign. As with any campaign, your promotion efforts start with careful planning—such as Web site promotion through search engines. Few people truly understand how search engines do what they do. Now it is time to make these search engines work for you. Rather than visit

Google's Web site (**www.google.com**), shown in Figure 1.1, to find other Web sites, you will use Google to bring visitors to your Web site.

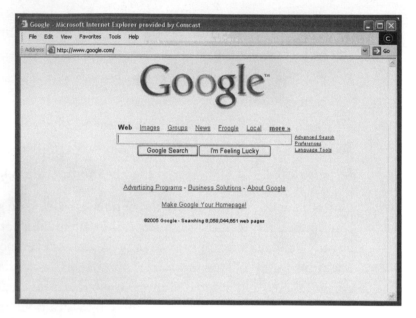

Figure 1.1

Google—one of the top search engines.

You start by learning to take advantage of the way search engines find and retrieve information. Although the inner workings of search engines aren't exactly state secrets, each search engine does things differently, which is why you should use many different techniques to make your Web pages more search-engine friendly. Web pages that are optimized for search engines using the techniques covered in the Saturday Morning session "Capitalizing on Search Engine Fundamentals" will help put your Web site on the map. These techniques ease the burden of obtaining references to your Web pages.

After you gain a firm understanding of how search engines work, you should register your Web site with the search engines used by the majority of Web users. Although your promotion efforts begin with search engines, you don't stop there. Afterward, you move on to Web guides, lists, and directories, such as the Open Directory (**dmoz.org**), shown in Figure 1.2.

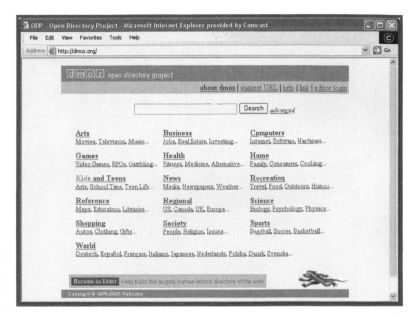

Figure 1.2

Open Directory—
one of the top
Web directories.

Just as few people understand how search engines work, few people take the time to plot out how to get the most out of Web guides, lists, and directories. You will create your own personal plan of attack in the Saturday Morning session, in the section called "Submitting Your Web Site to the Top Guides, Lists, and Directories."

The reason for targeting the best directories is to encourage you to use your time and resources wisely. Why waste your time registering with every single search engine and directory on the planet when 90 percent of Web users find what they are looking for by using the top 10 percent of the Web search and directory sites?

You will find many other search sites and directories that focus on specific types of information. These include Yellow Pages directories, category-specific directories, and specialty directories. Although these search and directory sites generally have narrow focuses, they are popular and frequently used to find information. For example, anyone looking for a business listing can use a Yellow Pages directory, such as INFOGROUPdirect (**www.infogroupdirect.com/english/search.asp**), as shown in Figure 1.3.

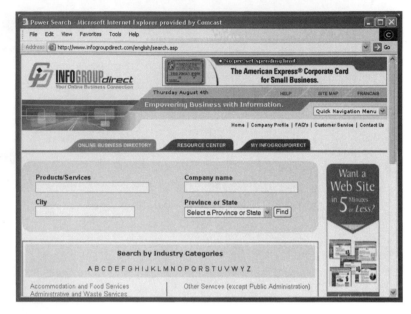

Figure 1.3

INFOGROUPdirect
—a Yellow Pages
directory.

Leveraging the Power of Search Engines and Directories

One of the major themes in any successful Web site promotion campaign is leveraging the search engines and directories to your advantage. However, because there are literally hundreds of search engines and directories out there, it is important that you choose wisely when selecting which search engines and directories you choose to work with. As you work your way through this book, you'll be introduced to the best search engines and directories.

Crawler-Based Search Engines

A search engine is a tool that assists people in locating Web sites on the Internet. Search engines seek out and locate new Web sites and then index their contents, storing the results in a search engine database. Search engine databases are repositories where search engines store information about the Web sites that they discover.

There have been many changes on the Internet since the first edition of this book was published. New search engines, such as Google, have appeared on the scene while many others are no longer available. Rather than try to find and register your Web site with every search engine on the Internet, you will be better served by focusing your attention on the major search engines presented in this book.

Today, Google and Yahoo! are by far the two most popular search engines on the Web. In fact, these two search engines handle over 65 percent of all searches. Microsoft's MSN search engine is quickly growing in its importance. Beyond these three search engines, there are plenty of other significant search engines that you may wish to work with. These search engines include: AOL, Netscape, Excite, Ask Jeeves, AllTheWeb, AltaVista, MetaCrawler, WebCrawler, and Lycos.

Many search engine sites no longer maintain their own search engine databases. Instead, they retrieve their search engine results from other search engines. For example, AllTheWeb and AltaVista are actually owned by Yahoo!. Search results retrieved at either of these two Web sites are actually pulled from the Yahoo! search engine database. So if you get your Web site registered with Yahoo!, your Web site will also appear in the search results retrieved from AllTheWeb and AltaVista.

Part of the mission of this book is to help you wade through the complex set of interrelationships that have been established between search engines in order to identify the key search engines with which you will want to register your Web site.

Human-Powered Directories

Like search engines, there are many directories on the Web that people visit when looking for information. Human-powered directories are created and maintained by editors who manually review and add Web sites to the directory, as opposed to search engines, which use automated tools to locate and collect information about Web sites. Of the directories on the Web, Yahoo!, Open Directory, and LookSmart are the three biggest.

Yahoo! now operates its own search engine from which main results are retrieved when someone performs a search. However, Yahoo! still maintains its directory. The Open Directory is a vast directory, created and maintained by a global community of volunteers. LookSmart is a somewhat smaller but still important directory.

Getting listed in a directory is important, because once listed there you'll find that some search engines will automatically discover your Web site and add you to their search engine database.

Hybrid Sites

The differences between search engines and directories have become blurred over the years. That's because many search sites pull information from search engines as well as directories. For example, Excite, MetaCrawler, and WebCrawler are all able to pull results back from LookSmart. Similarly, AOL and Netscape retrieve their primary search results from Google. In addition, AOL and Netscape also pull results from the Open Directory.

In addition, there is a new breed of search sites known as *meta search engines* that retrieve their results by passing queries on to multiple search engines and then combining all the results that are returned back into a single listing. Examples of popular meta search engines include Mamma and DogPile.

Paid Inclusion and Paid Placement

A primary focus of this book is to show you how to register for free with all the major search engines and directories. Generally speaking, it can take somewhere between 4 to 6 weeks for your Web site to appear in a search engine's listings once you initially register with it.

However, every major search engine on the Web also provides an option for *paid inclusion* and *paid placement*. These two options will cost you a few dollars but can be important when you are in a hurry to get your site noticed on the Web. Paid inclusion is a service in which you are guaranteed a high ranking for your Web site for certain search keywords. Paid placement is a service that guarantees you a place in a search engine's listings but does not guarantee you a high ranking. These two services can be very useful because they provide you with the ability to get your Web site registered and noticed within a few days.

Promoting Your Web Site to Joe Surfer

Joe Surfer is your average person browsing the Web. He's been there and done that. Now he's out looking for a bit of excitement or trying to find something—gasp!—useful. He's looking for a site like yours. He just doesn't know it yet. Well, to help Joe on his way, you have to give him a bit of prodding and grab his attention.

In the real world, you could grab Joe's attention by putting up a flashing neon sign that says, "Hey, Joe, over here!" In cyberspace, you grab Joe's attention using the tools of the Web promotion trade.

If Joe is looking for something cool, you grab his attention by getting your site listed as the Cool Site of the Day. Although Cool Site of the Day is one of the key awards that will get your Web site noticed, many other awards exist that will get him to notice your site as well. He may be looking for sites like those featured as Bizarre, Strange, Unusual, or Weird, such as the site shown in Figure 1.4 (**www.webweirdness.com**).

 NOTE　You'll find more information on these and other awards in the Saturday Afternoon session, under "Getting Your Site Listed as the Cool Site of the Day."

If Joe is looking to get something for nothing, you grab his attention with freebies, such as a giveaway. Then again, Joe may be interested in some other type of freebie, such as a contest, sweepstakes, or treasure hunt. Catching his eye when he's looking for freebies is covered on Sunday Morning under "Attracting the Masses with Giveaways, Contests, Sweepstakes, and More."

Figure 1.4

Definitely not a
guide to the
ordinary.

Other ways to grab Joe's attention include using straightforward Web advertising. Most Web users have a newsgroup or mailing list they like to follow, and Joe is no exception. So to get to Joe where he lives, you have to visit the discussion groups and forums where he hangs out. If Joe is interested in topics similar to those covered at your Web site, chances are good that you will find him hanging out in a like-minded newsgroup or mailing list. Web site promotion through newsgroups and mailing lists is featured on Sunday Morning under "Selling Your Web Site through E-mail."

Sometimes, the best way to get Joe's attention is to use good old-fashioned advertising. On the Web, this means using a banner advertisement. You have to admit that sometimes you do click on them, and so does Joe. If something grabs his eye, he's going to click on it, and when he does, you want it to be your site that he visits. To help Joe on his way, you can use the free advertising techniques that you'll explore on Sunday Morning under "Free Banner Advertising: No Joke."

Determining Who Is Visiting Your Web Site

Increasing your Web site traffic means taking a closer look at your Web site to understand the big picture—who is visiting your Web site and why. Trying to promote your Web site without understanding the big picture is like trying to play baseball without a ball—you just can't do it.

To get your hands on the "big picture," you will need to collect and analyze statistical data regarding who is visiting your Web site, which you will learn how to do on Sunday Afternoon's session "Discovering Who's Visiting Your Site and Why." With this data in hand, you will be able to examine your Web site with an honest eye and take a look at problem areas within your Web site. By examining your Web site's statistical data, you will see firsthand the pages at your Web site that get the most visitors and those that don't get any visitors.

When you examine your site's traffic, you will move beyond tracking file accesses and zero in on the things that matter, such as page views and the actual number of visitors. When you look at page views and visitor counts, you can answer many of the following questions about your Web site.

- What are the busiest days of the week?
- What are the busiest hours of the day?
- What are the most requested pages?
- Where do visitors live and work?
- What is the average number of page views per day?
- What is the average number of visitors per day?
- What is the average number of page views per visitor?
- What is the length of the average visit?
- What is the total number of visitors?

You will use stats not only to understand who is visiting your Web site right now and why, but also to help put together a promotion campaign for your Web site. By digging deeper through the stats, you can find out whether people like what they see or are just racing through. You also can discover problem areas at your Web site that may cause you to lose visitors who otherwise might come back to your Web site repeatedly.

After you develop a clear understanding of your Web site, you will learn how to put your Web site's stats to work. The first step is to summarize the stats and transform them into meaningful data. Then you will use the stats to make your Web site a better place to visit by taking care of

- Cleaning up unused pages
- Clearing out dead ends
- Fixing errors

You can use the stats to build cross-traffic to attract users to popular areas of your Web site.

Wrapping Up and Looking Ahead

Registering with search engines is a terrific way to build Web site traffic, especially when you consider that millions of people use search engines to find information every day. Guides, lists, and directories can also help get your Web site noticed. Of course, to make the best use of your available time, the best approach is to make sure that you focus your attention on the best search engines, guides, lists, and directories. Although you aren't guaranteed a listing in a guide to the best of the Web, your time is still well spent when you consider that a single award could bring thousands of visitors to your site.

That's enough for this evening. It's time to put this book down and relax your mind and body. Tomorrow you'll learn how to start registering with search engines and how to submit your Web site for inclusion in the major guides, lists, and directories. You'll also learn about a number of specialty directories and how to get listed in What's New? directories and what steps to take to get your Web site listed as Cool Site of the Day. So, watch a little TV and get a good night's sleep. Tomorrow will be a busy day.

Putting the Motion in Promotion

➤ **Search Engine Fundamentals**

➤ **Registering with the Top Search Engines**

➤ **Submitting Your Web Site**

Registering with search engines is a terrific way to build traffic to your Web site, especially when you consider that millions of people use search engines to find information every day. Guides, lists, and directories can also help your Web site get noticed. Although you aren't guaranteed a listing in a guide to the best of the Web, your time is still well spent when you consider that a single award could bring thousands of visitors to your site.

Capitalizing on Search Engine Fundamentals

Finding Web sites would be nearly impossible without sites that let you quickly and easily search for information. These so-called search engines provide a service that puts all the resources of the Web within reach. Search engines allow Web publishers to register their pages so that they will be added to the list of resources the search engine knows about. Search engines also allow Web users to find pages using keywords and keyword phrases that identify the information the users want to find.

Although search engines provide a great tool that you can use to get your Web site noticed by users around the world, few people truly understand how they work. That is, people rarely get the most out of the search engine and often waste their time and resources when they register their site with search engines. In this session, you will learn how search engines do what they do and how you can make the most of the techniques that search engines use to index and reference your Web site.

Millions of Users Are but a Search Away

Millions of people are just a click away from your Web site. They just need to follow the references that lead to you. The only problem is that your Web site probably doesn't show up in the results retrieved by the search engine they are using. Or on the rare occasion when the results show your site, users lack the information necessary to make the decision to visit your site. At that point, they head off to some other site. Day in and day out, this is the scenario at hundreds of search engines on the Web. The result is that your Web site doesn't get the level of traffic it deserves.

Because few people truly understand how search engines work, Web site publishers often get frustrated when they try to attract visitors using search engines. Usually, the Web site publisher will register the site with a few search engines, then sit back and wait for visitors to come. When visitors don't come, the Web site publisher registers with more search engines. Eventually, the Web site publisher might even turn to commercial services that promise to bring visitors to the Web site.

Search engines are one of the least understood Internet tools, and a lack of understanding can be a golden opportunity for someone to make a buck at your expense. You'll find services trying to sell you the Holy Grail for hundreds of dollars. These services tell you that they will register your site with every search engine available, get your site listed in the top 10 search results every time, or trick search engines into displaying your site more often. Don't buy whatever they're selling unless you've got money to burn. Instead, take the time to learn how search engines work, and use this information to get your site noticed by millions of Web users.

Indexers, Spiders, Crawlers, and Other Web Beasties

In the Web's early days, search engines were simply tools for finding information using indexes. Much like the index of your favorite computer book, the purpose of the index was to make finding information possible by using keywords. Rather than page references used in traditional indexes, Web indexes have hypertext links that you click on to access the information at Web sites around the world.

Over the years, search engines evolved. Today, the best search engines are complex applications that use advanced techniques to put millions of Web pages at the fingertips of Web users.

Working with Search Engines

No matter what label you use to identify a search engine, the fundamental purpose of a search engine is to index Web sites in a way that allows people to use keywords to find Web pages that interest them. To do this, search engines rely on a computer called an indexer, spider, or crawler to ferret out the pages at your site and then create indexed references to those pages in the search engine's database. After the pages are indexed, anyone can use the front-end search process to find the pages.

If you jaunt over to Excite at **www.excite.com**, you will find that the main page has an area called Search. As shown in Figure 2.1, Search contains an input field for entering the keywords or keyword phrases you want to search on. When you click on the Search button, the search engine uses the parameters you've entered to find matching references.

When you search using the keyword "CentralDrive" and click on the Search button, you get a list of results like those shown in Figure 2.2. Typically, the results of a search are displayed according to their relevance to the search parameters that you entered. The search engine believes the first document listed is the best match for your search.

Most search engines display reference to the top 10 or 20 pages that match your search parameters. Successive groups of matching pages are also available, but you have to follow a link to another results page. At Excite, you can click on the Next link found at the bottom of the results page to see additional pages that might be matches for your search.

Figure 2.1

Using a search engine.

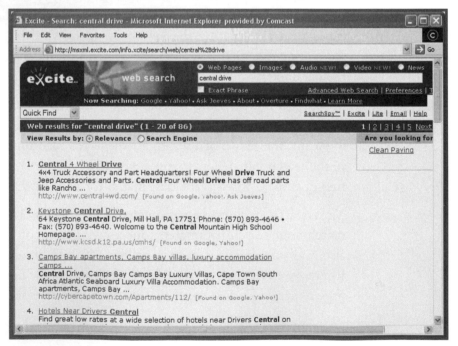

Figure 2.2

The results of a search.

Often, the matching pages are described using the page title and a brief description taken from the page itself. Most commercial search engines allow you to customize the search and results displayed. The search engine at Excite lets you customize the search in many different ways. For example, you can specify the number of results that are listed at a time or filter out adult content.

Comparing Search Engines and Directory Lists

Search engines and directory lists are very different. When you look for information with a search engine, you use keywords. When you look for infor-mation at a directory listing, you search by following links to pages within the directory site. You start your search by clicking on a broad category, such as entertainment, and eventually drill down to a very specific subject, such as movie reviews. One of the best-known directory lists is maintained by Yahoo! (**dir.yahoo.com**).

When you visit Yahoo's Directory page (shown in Figure 2.3), you are greeted by a listing of top-level categories of information available at the site. Under the top-level categories are more focused categories of information. If you select the News and Media category, you jump to the page shown in Figure 2.4. As you can see, this page shows many different broad categories of news. By selecting another link, you can get to a more narrowly focused category, such as business news or technology news.

Directory lists are covered extensively later in this session under the heading, "Submitting Your Web Site to the Top Guides, Lists, and Directories."

Who Powers Whom?

In order to make the best use of your time, it is important for you to know which search engines people use the most. This way you can target your efforts at the search engines that will help get your Web site noticed by the largest number of people.

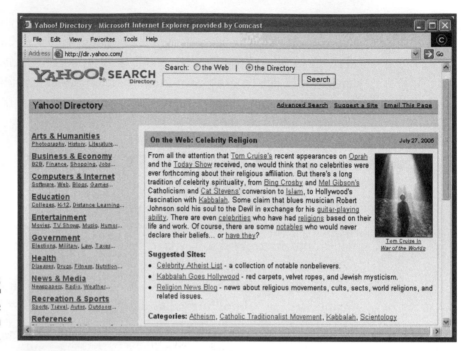

Figure 2.3

Directory sites are
different from
search sites.

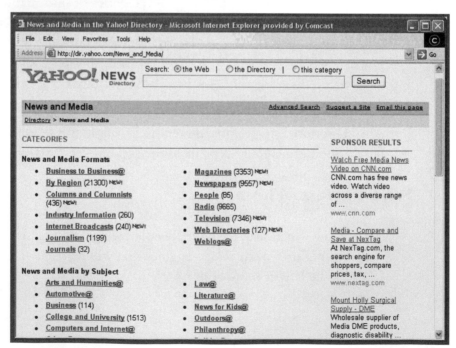

Figure 2.4

Accessing a
broad range of
information.

Today, the three most popular general-purpose search engines are Google (**www.google.com**), Yahoo! (**www.yahoo.com**), and Microsoft MSN (**www.msn.com**). Together these three search engines account for over 80 percent of all search engine queries. Perhaps even more importantly, many other search engines retrieve at least part of their results from Google and Yahoo!.

In addition to providing its own search results, Yahoo! provides search results to AllTheWeb (**www.alltheweb.com**) and AltaVista (**www.altavista.com**), both of which are owned by Yahoo!. Google is also a major source used by numerous search engines, including AOL (**www.aol.com**), Netscape (**www.netscape.com**), and Excite (**www.excite.com**).

There are plenty of other good search engines out there that you need to be aware of. In addition, there are a number of special purpose search engines, such as children-oriented search engines, that may also fit well into your Web promotion plan. You'll learn about these other search engines later in this session in the section named "Increasing Your Web Traffic with the Top Search Engines."

Search Engine Fundamentals

Before you run off and start registering your Web site with the different search engines, it is important that you understand exactly what search engines are and how they work. Although we've come to think of search engines as giant applications that find information, a search engine is really three different applications that work together to find and retrieve information. The applications are

- **An indexer.** The back-end application that finds and indexes pages for inclusion in a database; other names for this type of application include *spider*, *crawler*, and *robot*.

- **A database.** The application that stores the index references to Web pages.

- **A query interface.** The application that handles the queries submitted by users.

Search engines can't find or index your Web site without a little help, which is why people register their sites. Another way for a search engine to find your Web site is through a link to one of your pages from someone else's site. After a search engine finds your Web site, it uses the links within your pages to find additional pages at your site. In this way, the search engine navigates its way through your Web site one link at a time and adds the information from your Web site into its database.

What Do Search Engines Look For?

Search engines don't store all the data in your Web pages. Instead, they create indexed references to your pages. Most of the time, such an indexed reference contains the following information.

- **Page title**. From the <TITLE> tag element of your Web page.

- **Page URL**. The absolute URL to your Web page.

- **Summary description**. A description taken from the page itself.

- **Keyword list**. A list of keywords taken from the page itself, accompanied by a relevancy index that explains how relevant each indexed word is to other indexed words and how relevant the indexed words are to the page title as well.

Most search engines create indexed references to your Web pages, although almost every search engine gathers this information from different areas of your Web page. Whereas one search engine might gather the summary description for your Web page from the first few hundred characters, another search engine might look for common words or phrases in the page to use in the summary description.

The various search engines use the summary information in different ways as well. Some search engines make all the information available to user queries. Other search engines store all the information categories, yet user queries are performed only against specific categories of data, such as the page title and keyword list.

What Does the Indexed Reference Look Like for a Real Page?

To get a better understanding of what indexers do, look at the code shown in Listing 2.1. As you examine the sample Web page, note the title and the use of the <META> tag to describe the page and identify keywords. Also, note that the page contains lots of text.

Listing 2.1   A Sample Web Page

```
<HTML>

<HEAD>

<TITLE>Writer's Gallery: Resources for Writers and
Readers</TITLE>

<META NAME=description" CONTENT="Writer's Gallery is a place
for anyone who loves the written word. You'll find links to
hundreds of writing-related resources as well as new works of
fiction published at our site. ">

<META NAME="keywords" CONTENT="writing, reading, write,
   read, book, author, story, fiction, nonfiction, literary,
   mythology, medieval, biblical, renaissance, library,
   Dante, Dickens, Faulkner, Shakespeare, news, world news,
   entertainment news, business news, current events,
   publishing, dictionary, encyclopedia, bookshelf">

</HEAD>

<BODY BGCOLOR="#000080" text="#ffff00" link-"#fffbf0"
vlink="#808000" alink="#ff0000"


<IMG SRC="wgtt12.jpg" ALT="Writer's Gallery" BORDER=0
   ALIGN=LEFT>

<CENTER>

<H1>A place for anyone who loves the written word!</H1>

<H3>Over 250 New Resources!</H3>

</CENTER>
```

```
<FONT SIZE=-1<P><A HREF="vpspons.html">We're looking for
   sponsors.</A>
<P>Brought to you by the Original Virtual Press - - Fine
   Publications, Community Service and Much More Since March,
   1994.
If you'd like more information about <A HREF="vpbg.html">The
Virtual Press</A> or would like to post information to the
Writer's Gallery:  Send e-mail to
   <A HREF="mailto:wg@tvpress.com">wg@tvpress.com</A>
   </FONT></P>
<P><IMG SRC="bboard.gif" ALIGN="BOTTOM" ALT="* ATTN *">Put a
bookmark here. Come back and visit!</P>
<BR CLEAR=ALL>
<H2><A HREF="vpwfeat.html">Writer's Gallery Features</A></H2>
<P>Find hundreds of zines, thousands of books and links to
all good things related to writing!</P>
<H2><A HREF="vpwlite.html">Writer's Gallery Literary
   Resources</A></H2>
<P>If you need a literary reference look here. From Greek
mythology to the Renaissance. From medieval to biblical.
From the 9th century to the 19th century. This page covers
it all.</P>
<H2><A HREF="vpwauth.html">Writer's Gallery Great Authors
   </A></H2>
<P>If you are looking for information on great writers from
history, look here. You'll find information on writers from
Dante, Dickens, Faulkner, Shakespeare and more!</P>
<H2><A HREF="wcurrent.html">Writer's Gallery Guide to Current
   Events
</A></H2>
```

```
<H3><A HREF="http://tvpress.comhttp://www..tvpress.com/idn/"
TARGET="_parent">Internet Daily News</A> ||
<A HREF="wcurrent.html#usnews">US News</A> ||
<A HREF="wcurrent.html#worldnews">World News</A> ||
<A HREF="wcurrent.html#busnews">Business News</A> ||
<A HREF="wcurrent.html#entnews">Entertainment News</A> ||
<A HREF="wcurrent.html#finnews">Finance News</A></H3>


<H2><A HREF="vpwcomp.html">Writer's Companions</A></H2>
<P>Dictionaries, encyclopedias & more! All the reference
works you wish were on your bookshelf.</P>
<H2><A HREF="vpwresou.html">Writer's Resources</A></H2>
<P>A comprehensive resource list for writers! The Writer's
 Resource includes Virtual Libraries, Meta Indexes, Web
Databases and more! Dozens of them . . . </P>
<H2><A HREF="vpnewgp.html">Newsgroups for Writers</A></H2>
<P>Looking for a great way to meet fellow writers?
Join a discussion group!</P>
<H2><A HREF="vppubl.html">Who's in Publishing on the
WWW&#153;</A></H2>
<P>Find publishers on the Web</P>
<H2><A HREF="vpwart.html#art">Art</A></H2>
<P>Interested in finding art resources> Try these
  resources.</P>
<H2><A HREF="vpwart.html#movies">Movie &amp; Industry
Information</A></H2>
<P>Movie reviews & great movie information</P>
<HR SIZE=4>


<FORM METHOD="POST" ACTION="mailto:wg@tvpress.com">
```

```
<P>Help us grow, add a link to Writer's Gallery!</P>
<P><TEXTAREA NAME="Writer's gallery links" COLS="40" ROWS="1">
</TEXTAREA></P>
<P>Please describe the link.</P>
<P><TEXTAREA NAME="Writer's gallery description" COLS="40"
  ROWS="1"
</TEXTAREA></P>
<P><INPUT TYPE="SUBMIT"> <INPUT TYPE="RESET"></P>
</FORM>
<HR SIZE=4>
<P>Questions or comments pertaining to the TVP Web site can be
directed to <A HREF="mailto:webmaster@tvpress.com">
<IMG SRC="mail.gif" ALIGN="MIDDLE" ALT="*.e-mail*"
webmaster@tvpress.com</A></P>
<P>This page, and all contents, are <A HREF="vpcopy.html">
Copyright © by The Virtual Press, USA.</A>
<P>
</BODY>
</HTML>
```

When retrieving results, search engines follow a set of rules known as an algorithm. Each search engine has its own unique algorithm, which is kept secret. As a result, when different search engines index this Web page, they will come up with different results. For search engine A, an indexed reference to the page could look like this:

○ **Page title**. Writer's Gallery: Resources for Writers and Readers.

○ **Page URL**. **http://www.tvpress.com/vpwg.html**

○ **Summary description**. A place for anyone who loves the written word! Over 250 new resources. We're looking for sponsors.

- **Keyword list**. Author, biblical, books, bookshelf, business news, comment, community, companion, current events, database, entertainment news, events, finance news, gallery, Greek mythology, history, index, industry, information, library, literary, medieval, movie, mythology, news, newsgroup, press, publication, question, reference, renaissance, resource, service, sponsor, virtual, word, world news, writer, writer newsgroup, writing, written word.

Here, the search engine takes most of the information it needs directly from the body of the Web page. Because of this, each word in the page is weighed for relevancy and inclusion in the keyword list. You learn more about relevancy later in this session. Also, note that the summary description for this page is truncated at a preset number of characters, which means that the last sentence isn't complete in this case. For search engine B, an indexed reference to the page could look like this:

- **Page title**. Writer's Gallery: Resources for Writers and Readers.

- **Page URL**. http://www.tvpress.com/vpwg.html

- **Summary description**. Writer's Gallery is a place for anyone who loves the written word! You'll find links to hundreds of writing-related resources as well as new works of fiction published at our site.

- **Keyword list**. Author, biblical, book, bookshelf, business news, current events, Dante, Dickens, dictionary, encyclopedia, entertainment news, Faulkner, fiction, fiction works, library, literary, medieval, mythology, news, nonfiction, publishing, read, reader, reading, renaissance, resource, Shakespeare, story, world news, write, writer, writing, written word.

Here, the search engine obtains the page description from a <META> tag, and then combines the keyword information provided in another <META> tag with words used in the page to come up with a keyword list. Although this technique might seem unusual, many search engines that take advantage of meta-information combine the description and keywords that you provide with information taken from the body of the page.

NOTE You will learn more about the <META> tags and meta-information later in the session. Look for the heading, "Getting the Most from Keywords and Meta-Information."

For search engine C, an indexed reference to the page could look like this:

○ **Page title**. Writer's Gallery: Resources for Writers and Readers.

○ **Page URL**. http://www.tvpress.com/vpwg.html

○ **Summary description**. A place for anyone who loves the written word! Over 250 new resources. We're looking for sponsors.

Here, the search engine only makes use of the page title and a summary description obtained from the first 100 characters of text found in the page. Although the streamlined entries in the database aren't desirable for the Web page publisher, the search engine designers probably chose this format because it drastically reduces the size of the database, which in turn reduces overhead and speeds up database queries.

What Happens After Your Web Site Is Indexed?

Indexing a Web site is not a one-time deal. After a search engine initially indexes your site, your site is usually scheduled for reindexing at periodic intervals. By reindexing Web sites, search engines keep up with the ever-changing face of the Web. That said, not all search engines automatically reindex your site, and some search engines reindex your Web site so infrequently that you end up with outdated references.

Additionally, the way that a search engine reindexes your Web site might not be what you expect. Some search engines simply check to see whether the page still exists but don't update the actual reference to the Web page. Other search engines check the page header to see whether the page has changed, so if you changed text at the bottom of the page, the search engine won't reindex the page. Still other search engines use the modification date on the page to determine whether the page should be reindexed. The search engine then either reindexes the page immediately or schedules the page for reindexing at a later date.

Another problem with search engines is that Web pages you deleted months ago might still be listed. Although some search engines let you remove outdated references from the database, the best way to solve these and other problems you might encounter is to periodically resubmit your Web site to the search engine. For problems related to pages you've moved to different locations, you might also want to use placeholder documents and the redirection techniques examined in the Sunday Afternoon session under "Redirecting Lost Readers." In this way, you direct readers from the old page to the new page, and eventually the search engine will pick up on this and update the references to your Web site.

Determining Popular Keywords

Keyword selection is an important consideration in the preparation of your Web pages for search engine registration. People surfing the Web using search engines enter keywords or keyword phrases in order to generate lists of links related to the topics they are looking to find information about. The better the keywords and keyword phrases on your Web pages match up against the keywords or keyword phrases entered by the people you are trying to attract, the more your Web site will get noticed.

Keyword Creation Tips

There are a number of different things that you need to think about when determining what keywords to use on your Web pages. For starters, think about the search words or phrases you think people will use when searching for the topic covered on your Web pages. These words and phrases should be your keywords and keyword phrases. For example, if you have a Web page that covers rock climbing, then "rock climbing" should be one of your keyword phrases.

TIP A good way to come up with good keyword phrases is to think of magazine and newspaper headlines. A good headline helps attract your attention and guides you to articles that are of interest to you. A good headline is short, to the point, and descriptive.

In fact, it is better to use keyword phrases made up of two to three words than to specify single word keywords. For one thing, lots of sites specify single word keywords, making competition for these keywords intense. Instead, by creating phrases specific to your topic, you greatly increase the chances that your keyword phrases will be viewed by the search engines as being more relevant.

TIP If your Web site covers a number of different topics, then you will want to generate different keywords and keyword phrases for each unique Web page.

Some search engines are case-sensitive. Therefore, searches on "Rock Climbing" and "rock climbing" may generate different results from the same search engine. One way around this is to specify different variations of capitalization when specifying your Web page keywords, such as "Rock Climbing," "Rock climbing," "rock Climbing," "rock climbing," or even "ROCK CLIMBING." However, since almost everybody searches the Web using lower case typing, it is usually not worth the trouble trying to come up with every possible keyword variation. In addition, by attempting to anticipate every possible keyword capitalization variation, you run the risk of accidentally spamming search engines, as discussed in the next couple pages.

Researching Popular Search Engine Keywords

Another way to come up with good keywords is to take a few minutes and visit each of the major search engines to see what keywords are being used most often by people. Google provides a listing of top search engine queries on a weekly basis at **www.google.com/press/zeitgeist.html**, as shown in Figure 2.5.

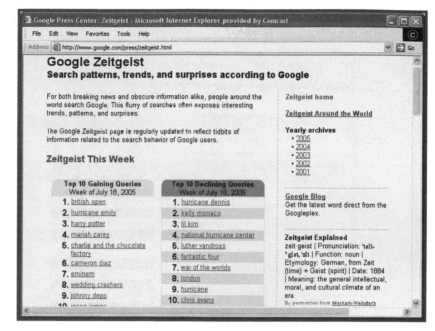

Figure 2.5

Examining popular
keywords used by
people searching
on Google.

The following list shows where you can go to research popular keywords
for other major search engines.

- **Yahoo!. buzz.yahoo.com**

- **Ask Jeeves. sp.ask.com/docs/about/jeevesiq.html**

- **MSN. www.imagine-msn.com/insider/**

- **AOL. hot.aol.com/hot/hot**

Free Keyword Generation Tools

If you are still uncertain as to what keywords you want to create for your
Web pages, you might want to try two keyword generator tools provided
by Google and a Yahoo! owned company named Overture. Both of the
tools are designed to help paying customers select keywords for ads.
However, these services are free and you can use them to help you generate
your own keywords.

You can find the Google AdWords Keyword Tool at **adwords.google.com/ select/main?cmd=KeywordSandbox** as shown in Figure 2.6.

You can find the Overture Keyword Selector Tool at **inventory.overture. com/d/searchinventory/suggestion/.**

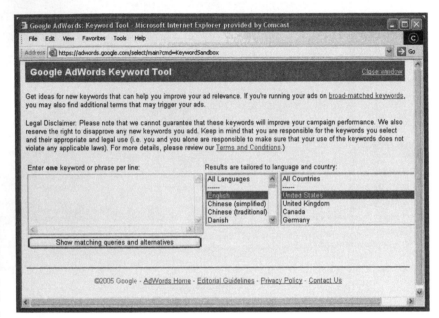

Figure 2.6

Using the Google AdWords Keyword Tool to generate your own keywords.

Be On Guard Against Accidental Spamming

Keywords are an important tool used to help attract visitor to your Web pages. However, it is important that you do not get too overzealous. If, for example, you repeat the same keywords, search engines may pick up on it and identify your Web page as attempting to spam the engines in an effort to achieve a high relevancy for certain keywords. If this happens, then either your Web page's ranking may be reduced or your Web page may even be removed from the search engine's index. So tread carefully in regards to how many times you repeat your keywords.

Boosting Visits with Ordinary Descriptions

To a search engine, text is the most important part of the page. Search engines use ordinary text to describe the page, build the keyword list, and determine the relevance of the page to particular subjects. Although search engines treat text in different ways, they share some common themes concerning how text is indexed and referenced.

Understanding Summary Descriptions

Whenever a search engine displays results, the main thing that sells your page to the reader is the summary description, which usually comes from the first 100 to 200 characters in the Web page. When you look at your Web page to see what the description might look like, be sure to include all text in headers, paragraphs, and other text elements on the page.

Search engines have very specific parameters for obtaining the summary description. Text at the top of the page is usually given more weight than text at the bottom of the page. Thus, if you have a short description at the top of your page followed by several graphic elements, tables, or linked lists, the search engine might not use text from later sections of the page. You can see why some page descriptions are short and others fill out the full 100 to 200 characters used by the search engine.

To help your Web site get noticed, create clear summary statements for your key Web pages, which include the home page and top-level pages at your Web site. The summary statement should be the first text element in the page, perhaps directly following your graphical banner. If you keep the summary statement short but descriptive, it will usually flow well with the rest of the page.

 NOTE Whenever possible, try to end your summary statement with proper punctuation. Believe it or not, a few search engines look for complete statements. Phrases without punctuation are considered ambiguous; phrases with punctuation are considered relevant.

Understanding Relevancy

The position of text in your Web page often determines its relevancy. Because of the variations in how search engines use text, relevancy is one of the hardest search engine terms to pin down. In general terms, the relevancy of text describes

○ How a word relates to other words.

○ The proximity of one word to another.

○ The position of the word within the page.

○ Whether the word is presented as part of a complete statement.

○ How many times the word is used in the page.

The concept of relevancy explains why some of the techniques that publishers use to get their pages listed at the top of search results lists have little effect, as well as why a technique might work for one search engine and not for others. In the end, the varying definition of relevancy makes optimizing your Web pages for each and every search engine almost impossible. In fact, you'd probably be wasting your time if you tried to optimize your Web pages for all the search engines.

Have you ever come across a Web page that repeated a word over and over again? Well, the Web site publisher was probably trying to get the page listed as the top choice for searches using this keyword. Although this technique might work for a particular search engine, most other search engines will completely ignore the repeated use of the word, which causes the page to appear lower in their search results lists.

Have you ever come across a Web page that used phrases that didn't seem to fit in the Web page, yet the phrases were there just the same? Here, the Web site publisher was probably trying to get the page to show up when someone searched for a hot topic, such as news, entertainment, or sports. Again, this technique might work for a particular search engine, but other search engines will give the entire page lower relevancy because it's full of ambiguous phrases and doesn't seem to have a common thread.

Rather than haphazardly repeat keywords or use ambiguous phrases in your Web page, use sound organizational techniques that bolster the relevancy of your page's theme. Focus your attention on your home page and your top-level pages first. When you look at your home page or top-level page, ask yourself these questions:

- Is the subject of the page clear?

- Can I weave the main subject(s) of the page throughout the main text in such a way that it builds relevancy?

- Does the page build the relationship between the main subject and related topics?

- Can I add descriptions to lists of links to clearly define what the link points to?

- Are the statements made in the page clear and complete?

- Can I transform ambiguous phrases into clear statements that relate to the main theme on the page?

Using Page Titles to Your Advantage

A good Web page title will bring visitors to your Web site. Most search engines display Web pages according to their titles, making the page title one of the most important elements for bringing visitors to your Web site. Additionally, your browser displays the title at the top of its window, as demonstrated in Figure 2.7, and when you bookmark a Web page, the title is used to differentiate the Web page from other Web pages that you've marked, as shown in Figure 2.8.

Beyond its job of grabbing the reader's attention, the title also plays an important role in determining the relevancy of the Web page to the reader's search parameters. Specifically, the keywords in the title often receive greater emphasis than other keywords on the page.

Figure 2.7

A Web page's title is automatically displayed in the browser's titlebar.

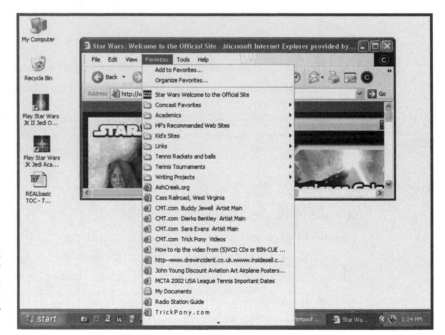

Figure 2.8

A Web page's title is also used to label browser bookmarks.

The best titles describe the subject of the page in a clear and meaningful way. Instead of a title that says, "Welcome to my home page," use a title that says "Bill's Home Page: Find Sports Memorabilia, Sports Records, & Player Stats." In this way, search engines that use the page title to determine relevance will have a clear understanding of the page's subject and the most important keywords.

Getting Your Frame-Enhanced or Graphics-Intensive Page Noticed

Pages with frames, scripts, tables, and lots of graphics present special problems to Web site publishers and search engines. With frame-enhanced Web pages, the main document usually contains only references to the files that a browser loads into each frame. With scripts, the code is often located at the top of the code for the Web page in the place of the all-important descriptive text. With graphics-intensive pages, room for text on the page is limited.

Although some search engines are smart enough to understand and properly handle frame-enhanced pages, scripts, and graphics-intensive pages, such search engines are more the exception than the rule. Fortunately, you can get your Web page noticed without eliminating frames, scripts, or your wonderful graphics. One way for you to try to do this is through use of meta-information, which is discussed in a couple pages. However, there are a few element-specific tricks that you may want to consider as well, including:

✿ Dealing with frame issues

✿ Dealing with scripts

✿ Managing your tables

✿ Keeping graphics under control

NOTE Not every search engine provides the same level of support for meta-information. So while helpful, meta-information alone may not be enough to accommodate for your frames, scripts, tables, and graphics on every search engine.

Handling Problems with Frames

Frames present a bit of a challenge for many search engines. When you create a Web site based on frames, you define a frameset and frames. The frameset specifies the location and dimension of each frame. However, some search engines are unable to see past the frameset page, meaning that they cannot locate the associate frame pages. At this point the rest of your Web site becomes effectively invisible to the search engine.

One way to deal with frames is to always remember to include a <NOFRAMES> tag. Using this tag, you can specify text that search engines and visitors with old browsers can see. The <NOFRAMES> tag allows browsers and search engines that can't understand frames to display other text so the page doesn't become a dead end. An example of how to apply the <NOFRAMES> tag is shown in Listing 2.2.

Listing 2.2   Using a <NOFRAME> Area in a Web Page

```
<HTML>

<HEAD>

<TITLE>Las Vegas Virtual Tour Guide</TITLE>

</HEAD>


<FRAMESET ROWS="25%,*" BORDER=0>

    <FRAME SRC="side.htm" NORESIZE>

    <FRAME SRC="main.htm" NORESIZE>

</FRAMESET>

<NOFRAMES>

<BODY>

    Add text and links here for version of Web page without
frames.

</BODY>

</NOFRAMES>

</HTML>
```

If you include links along with the descriptive information, you can provide search engines with the ability to view the other pages in your Web site. Unfortunately, this approach opens up the possibility that a visitor may arrive at one of your frame pages, and because it is not presented within the overall context of your frameset, things begin to break down. However, you can easily fix this using just a few lines of JavaScript as demonstrated here:

```
<SCRIPT LANGUAGE= "JavaScript"
  <!-
    If (top == self) self.location.href = "frameset-url"
  //->
</Script>
```

All that you have to do is to modify this code by replacing the frameset-url parameter with the name of your frameset page and then copy and paste the code into the HEAD or BODY section of your HTML for each of your frame pages. If a visitor attempts to directly access any of your frames pages, this code will automatically execute and load your frameset page as you intended.

Working Around Scripts

Embedding large scripts into your Web pages presents another problem for search engines. Since most people place their scripts at the top of their Web pages, the script pushes the content for the rest of the Web page down. Unfortunately, many search engines don't scan your entire page when indexing your Web site. This can result in the search engine missing out on most of your Web page's content.

One way to deal with this issue is to move your scripts, when possible, further down in your Web pages. Another option to consider is to externalize your scripts and call them from within your HTML Web pages.

Preventing Problems with Your Tables

Tables present search engines with a similar obstacle to that presented by scripts. For example, you may include a table about rock climbing equipment at the top of your Web page that visually displays like the one shown in Table 2.1.

TABLE 2.1 ESSENTIAL ROCK CLIMBING EQUIPMENT	
Equipment	**Description**
Boots	To protect your sore feet
Gloves	To prevent blisters and other injuries
Rope	To tie yourself down and prevent falling
Radio	To call for help in the event of an emergency
First Aid Kit	To deal with cuts, bruises, and other minor injuries

To a search engine, this table might look like

Equipment
Boots
Gloves
Rope
Radio
First Aid Kit

Description
To protect your sore feet
To prevent blisters and other injuries
To tie yourself down and prevent falling
To call for help in the event of an emergency
To deal with cuts, bruises, and other minor injuries

As you can see, any text on the Web page occurring after the table will be pushed much further down from a search engine's point of view, potentially pushing your content out of view.

The best way to deal with this situation is to try and move your tables further down in your pages and to make sure that, where possible, your tables include references to your keywords and phrases.

Working Around Your Graphics and Image Maps

As if frames, scripts, and tables weren't enough, search engines also have trouble with graphics. From a search engine's point of view, the only thing that matters on your Web pages is text. Graphics are ignored. You can create stunning Web pages that present all sorts of information in the form of graphics and search engines won't see a bit of it.

Consider the importance of balancing presentation with content when you are designing your Web pages, because it's the text-based content that search engines see and use to rate the relevancy of your Web pages. One way to help mitigate the effectiveness of graphics is to always supply a descriptive <ALT> tag that includes your keyword phrases for every graphic on your Web pages. This way search engines will be able to read and index alternative information regarding the content of your Web pages.

If you make use of image maps as a navigation tool for providing access to your Web pages, you are presenting another problem for search engines. Once again, the search engine won't be able to view links that you've established via your image map and therefore will not be able to locate and index your other Web pages. One good way of working around this problem is to provide a text-based set of links to your Web pages at the bottom of each of your Web pages. As Figure 2.9 demonstrates, the text links don't need to be anything fancy. The important thing is to give search engines a way to find your other Web pages.

Text-based
navigation links

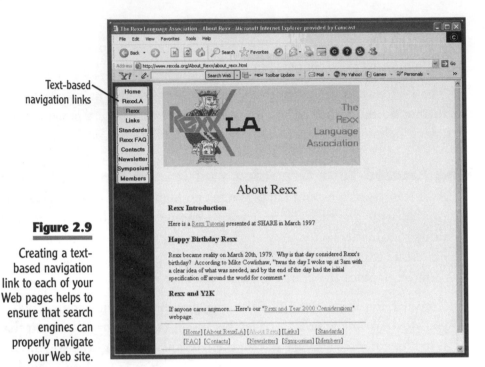

Figure 2.9

Creating a text-
based navigation
link to each of your
Web pages helps to
ensure that search
engines can
properly navigate
your Web site.

One other technique that you may want to consider is to create a site map
for your Web site and to submit the site map to each search engine along
with your main Web pages. A site map is a Web page that contains links to
every Web page that makes up your Web site. By creating and submitting a
site map, you ensure that the search engines will be able to locate every page
on your Web site.

TIP

Graphics take time to load. They take even longer for people that visit your Web site
using a dial-up connection. Many visitors will leave your Web site if it takes too long for
your graphics to load. To prevent this from happening, try keeping the total size of your
main page and any other high-level pages below 50 KB.

Getting the Most from Keywords and Meta-Information

Meta-information is data that is included in a Web page header but is hidden from the reader. Usually, meta-information contains instructions or special notes for Web clients, such as your browser or the indexer used by a search engine. To provide meta-information to a Web client, you use the <META> tag. The information that you can provide to search engines with the <META> tag includes a very specific description of the page as well as additional keywords for the page.

<META> tags alone are not enough to guarantee that your Web pages will get a top-10 ranking with any search engine. However, when used properly, they can help give you some control over the manner in which search engines describe your Web site.

Working with Meta-Information

Before you add meta-information to your Web pages, you should know that not all search engines make use of the <META> tag. A search engine that doesn't use the meta-information simply ignores the information. For example, Google ignores the <META> description tag and generates its own description of your Web page based on the content that it finds. Additionally, most of the search engines that use meta-information still index the entire contents of your Web page. Thus, you use the <META> tag to give search engines additional information, not to replace the information that they've already gathered from the Web page.

You use the following two main attributes when you use the <META> tag:

- NAME: Used to describe the type of meta-information that you are providing, such as NAME="description" or NAME="keywords".

- CONTENT: Used to supply the actual meta-information, such as the description of your Web page or a list of keywords for the Web page.

You can add a description to your page using meta-information as follows:

```
<META NAME=description" CONTENT="Writer's Gallery is a place
    for anyone who loves the written word. You'll find links to
    hundreds of writing-related resources as well as new works of
    fiction published at our site. ">
```

You can add a keyword list to your page using meta-information as follows:

```
<META NAME="keywords" CONTENT="writing, reading, write, read,
    book, author, story, fiction, nonfiction, literary,
    mythology, medieval, biblical, renaissance, library, Dante,
    dickens, Faulkner, Shakespeare, news, world news,
    entertainment news, business news, current events,
    publishing, dictionary, encyclopedia, bookshelf">
```

 NOTE Most search engines ignore the `<META>` keywords tag. However, some don't, so this tag is still worth including in your Web pages.

In a Web page, the meta-information is always added to the page header inside the `<HEAD>` and `</HEAD>` tags, as in this example:

```
<HTML>
<HEAD>

<TITLE>Writer's Gallery: Resources for Writers and
Readers</TITLE>
<META NAME=description" CONTENT="Writer's Gallery is a place
    for anyone who loves the written word. You'll find links to
    hundreds of writing-related resources as well as new works of
    fiction published at our site. ">
```

```
<META NAME="keywords" CONTENT="writing, reading, write,
    read, book, author, story, fiction, nonfiction, literary,
    mythology, medieval, biblical, renaissance, library,
    Dante, Dickens, Faulkner, Shakespeare, news, world news,
    Entertainment news, business news, current events,
    publishing, dictionary, encyclopedia, bookshelf">


</HEAD>
<BODY
.  .  .
</BODY>
</HTML>
```

 NOTE If you do not use words located in your <META> keywords tag elsewhere in your Web page, you won't see any boost in your search engine ranking, and if you repeat your keywords too many times in your <META> keywords tag of your Web page, you run the risk of hurting your ranking or getting removed from the search engine's database.

Using Meta-Information in Your Web Page

The description of your page in the <META> tag can be every bit as important as the summary description in the main text of the page. The advantage to describing a page in the <META> tag is that you provide the exact description you want to use, rather than have the search engine extrapolate the description from the main text of the page. A good <META> tag description summarizes the main selling points of the page in 200 characters or less. Because some search engines use page descriptions that are fewer than 200 characters, try to put the most relevant information first.

When it comes to finding your Web page in a search engine, a <META> tag keywords list may give your Web page a definite edge over a page that doesn't use meta-information (for search engines that support it). The main thing to remember is that the <META> tag keywords list is normally used in addition to the keywords that the search engine gathers from the main text of the page. Thus, rather than simply repeating keywords that appear in the main text, you might want to concentrate on related topics or variations of the primary keywords. For example, if the keyword is *writer*, you can use variations such as *write, writing,* and *written*.

TIP

It is better to create keywords that are two or more words long. This makes them more relevant to your Web site.

You can also create various combinations of keywords or phrases in the keyword list. This doesn't mean that you should repeat the keyword several times. Instead, create working combinations, such as business news, entertainment news, and sports news. Keep in mind that some search engines penalize you for repeating specific keywords too many times. In fact, the search engine might disregard the keyword list entirely if you repeat keywords too many times, as in the following example:

```
<META NAME="keywords" CONTENT="news, news, news, news,
   news, news, news, news, news, news,
   business, business, business, business, business, business,
   business, entertainment, entertainment, entertainment,
   entertainment, entertainment, entertainment, sports, sports,
   sports, sports, sports, sports, sports">
```

The following example instead uses word combinations and variations of the topic for the keyword list.

```
<META NAME="keywords" CONTENT="news, business, entertainment,
   sports, current events, business news, entertainments news,
   sports news">
```

Just as the length of your description is important, the length of your keyword list is important as well. Generally speaking, limit the keyword list to fewer than 1,000 characters. Further, try to restrict the number of times that you repeat any word in the keyword list. A good rule of thumb is to use a keyword or a word combination that uses the keyword no more than seven times. In the previous example, the keyword "news" was repeated four times.

After you update your home page and top-level pages with meta-information, consider adding meta-information to the rest of your Web pages. Although this might be a mammoth undertaking, the payoff makes the time investment worthwhile. Also, tailor your meta-information to each individual page rather than the site as a whole.

Meta Tag Generators

If you want a little help in the generation of your <META> tags to ensure that they have the correct syntax, help is just a few clicks away. There are a number of Web sites where you can go for assistance. You'll still have to supply the actual description and keywords that you wish to use for your Web site. These sites will take this information and generate <META> tags, which you can then copy and insert into your Web pages. For example, take a look at the Meta Manager page provided at **www.siteowner.com/system/meta.cfm** as shown in Figure 2.10.

There are plenty of other <META> tag generator Web sites that you might also want to give a try, including

○ SiteUp Networks Meta Tag Generator—
www.siteup.com/meta.html

○ SiteAnnounce.com ABC Meta Tag Generator—**www.siteannounce.com/tools/meta-tag-generator/**

○ KlickonUSA.COM FREE Meta Tags Builder—
www.klickonusa.com/metatagbuilder/htm

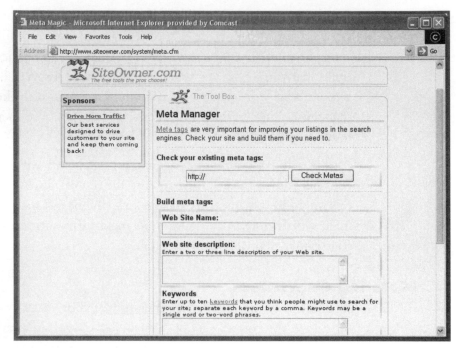

Figure 2.10

Use the free
<META> tag
generator at
**www.siteowner.
com** to create
<META> tags for
your Web pages.

Analyzing Your Meta Tags

If you have already created your own <META> tags, it might be worth
taking a few extra seconds to get an impartial third party's opinion of how
good your tags are. You can do this by visiting any number of Web sites
that provide free <META> tag analysis, such as the Meta Tag Analyzer provided at **www.submitexpress.com/analyzer/** (shown in Figure 2.11).

If you still want some additional feedback regarding the quality and construction of your <META> tags, you can visit the following Web sites.

- ✿ SiteOwner.com Meta Manager—
  www.siteowner.com/system/meta.cfm

- ✿ Widexl.com Meta Tag Analyzer—**www.widexl.com/remote/
  search-engines/metatag-analyzer.html**

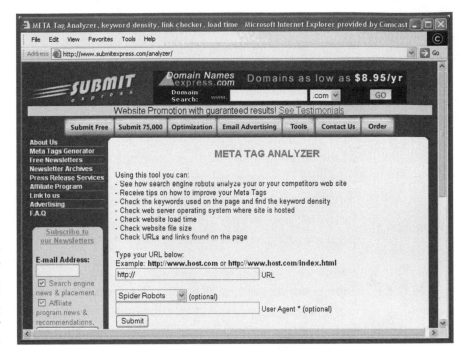

Figure 2.11

Just key in your
Web page's URL
and click on Submit
for an instant
analysis of your
<META> tags.

Leveraging Your ALT Tags and Comments

As has already been stated, search engines cannot read or gain information
from graphics embedded in a Web page. Therefore, it is important to add
an <ALT> tag for each image that is displayed. Obviously, each <ALT> tags
should provide a description of its associated image. Search engines read
<ALT> tags. Therefore, you can use them to help you increase your ranking
for specific keywords and keyword phrases. To avoid accidental spamming,
it's a good idea to limit the number of keywords used in your <ALT> tags to
3-5 instances.

Search engines also read any HTML comments that you embed in your
Web pages. HTML comments provide you with another opportunity to
present your keywords and keyword phrases. Just don't go overboard and
abuse them.

Inspecting Your Web Page's Body Text

Adding keywords and keyword phrases to your <TITLE> and <META> tags is an important step in your effort to achieve a high search engine ranking for your Web pages. However, in order for your keywords and keyword phrases to have their full effect, you must also include them in the text located in the body of your Web pages.

Many search engines add extra weight to keywords found at the beginning of a Web page over those found at the end of the Web page. Therefore, it's a good idea to make sure that you make the integration of keywords and keyword phrases at the beginning of your Web page a primary objective.

 NOTE   Some search engines build all or part of the description for your Web site from the text that it finds at the beginning of your Web pages. Therefore, it's a good idea to consider making the first sentence on your Web page match the text that you added to your <META> tag description statement. This will increase the chances of you getting the description you want with some of the major search engines.

If the design of your Web page depends on the use of graphics at the beginning of your page, that's okay too. Just make sure that you find a way to include some text just above, below, or beside your graphics and that you remember to include your keywords and keyword phrases.

A Last Look at Search Engine Fundamentals

As you have seen, you can do many things to improve the odds of someone finding your Web page through a search engine. The idea here is not to trick the search engine into displaying references to your pages. Instead, you are structuring your pages so the search engine can clearly identify the subjects your pages cover and index the appropriate keywords for those subjects. You are also using techniques that make it easier for your readers to identify the subjects covered in your pages. Figure 2.12 shows the main design concepts to follow when you optimize your Web pages for search engines.

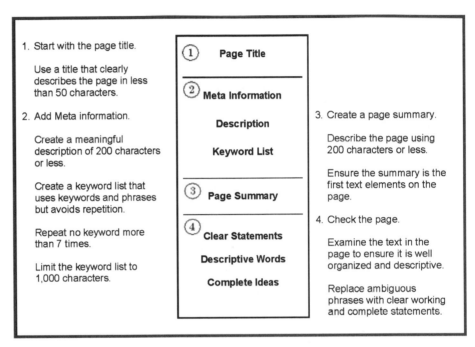

Figure 2.12

Optimizing your Web page for search engines, step-by-step.

1. Start with the page title.

   Use a title that clearly describes the page in less than 50 characters.

2. Add Meta information.

   Create a meaningful description of 200 characters or less.

   Create a keyword list that uses keywords and phrases but avoids repetition.

   Repeat no keyword more than 7 times.

   Limit the keyword list to 1,000 characters.

① **Page Title**

② **Meta Information**

   Description

   Keyword List

③ **Page Summary**

④ **Clear Statements**

   Descriptive Words

   Complete Ideas

3. Create a page summary.

   Describe the page using 200 characters or less.

   Ensure the summary is the first text elements on the page.

4. Check the page.

   Examine the text in the page to ensure it is well organized and descriptive.

   Replace ambiguous phrases with clear working and complete statements.

If you haven't done so already, create descriptive blurbs for your Web site. Start by identifying the most popular areas at your Web site, and then use the subjects covered in these areas to come up with a brief description that identifies your site's niche. Next, create separate descriptions for each popular area at your Web site. When you finish this, take a few minutes to apply the concepts discussed in the search engine fundamentals section to your home page and other top-level pages at your Web site. This will prepare you to register with search engines of all types.

Take a Break

Okay, this is a good place to take a quick break. You've already covered a lot of ground. Stretch. Relax for a moment and let things soak in. Go get a cup of coffee or tea and when you return you will take a look at some additional search engines and directories where you may also want to register your Web site.

Registering with the Top Search Engines on the Planet

Once you have optimized your Web pages for indexing, you are ready to submit your Web pages to search engines. Although hundreds of search engines are out there, trying to submit your Web site to every single one of them is not practical or worthwhile. Instead, you should start by registering your site with the major search engines. Because the search engines covered in this section index tens of millions of Web pages, they are the ones used most often to search the Web, and you can make the most of your time and resources by focusing your efforts on these search engines.

Submitting Your Site to a Search Engine

When you register with a search engine, you let the search engine know that your Web site exists. Many search engines take a preliminary look at your site immediately after you submit your site and verify that the address you provided is valid. Afterward, the search engine schedules your site for indexing.

Although several days might pass before the indexing begins, the actual time you have to wait to get into the database depends on the backlog of new sites waiting to be entered into the database and the efficiency of the indexer. Some search engines might index your Web site within hours, while others might not index your site for weeks.

How Does Indexing Work?

Most search engines use the URL you submit to find other pages at your Web site. Give the search engine the URL to your home page in this form: **http://www.your_isp.com/~you/**.

The indexer uses this page as a launching pad to all the other pages at your Web site. Generally, the indexer creates an indexed reference to the current page and then searches all the links on the page one by one. If the first link the indexer finds is to a page called background.html, the indexer accesses the background.html page, creates an indexed reference, and then searches all the links on this page one by one. Eventually, the indexer crawls through every page at your Web site.

 NOTE If an area of your Web site is not linked to a main page that the indexer can find, that area will not be indexed. The solution is to add a link on a top-level page that the indexer can find or to register the area separately.

How Can You Exclude Directories and Pages?

Although indexing your site is a good thing, sometimes you might not want the search engine to index your entire site. There are a couple of different ways that you can control what pages are indexed and what pages aren't indexed. One option is to use a robot exclusion file. The exclusion file is a plain-text file placed in the top-level directory for your Web server. In the exclusion file, you specify the directories or pages that search engines are not allowed to index. The name of the exclusion file must be robots.txt.

Because you will generally want the exclusion to apply to all search engines, the first line of the file should read as follows:

```
User-agent: *
```

Here, user-agent refers to the search engine accessing the file, and the asterisk (*) is a commonly used symbol that means *all*. After telling the search engine to make the exclusions, you specify the directories or pages to exclude. Alternatively, you can exclude an entire directory as follows:

```
Disallow: /cgi-bin/
```

Or

```
Disallow: /images/
```

TIP There is an online Robots.txt analysis tool located at **http://www.searchengineworld.com/ cgi-bin/robotcheck.cgi** that you can use to scan and verify the contents of your Web servers Robots.txt file.

If you prefer, you can exclude an individual single page as follows:

```
Disallow: /prg/webstat.html
```

You can put all these entries into an exclusion file as follows:

```
User-agent: *
Disallow: /cgi-bin/
Disallow: /images/
Disallow: /prg/webstat.html
```

TIP If you publish a large Web site or publish your Web site as part of a larger domain, you should strongly consider using an exclusion list. With so many Web pages, search engines are finding it harder and harder to index everything at a Web site. For this reason, some search engines index only 500-700 pages per domain.

Another option available to you is the Robots <META> tag. By placing an instance of this tag in the HEAD section of a Web page, you can specify whether it should be indexed and whether the search engine should follow any links that it might find in the page. This option is particularly useful when you don't have access to the robots.txt file.

The Robots <META> tag supports four different parameters (or directives), as listed below.

- **index.** Instructs the search engine to index the page.

- **noindex.** Instructs the search engine not to index the page.

- **follow.** Instructs the search engine to follow any links that it finds on the page.

- **nofollow.** Instructs the search engine not to follow any links that it finds on the page.

The following example shows a Robots <META> tag that instructs the search engine not to index the Web page's content or follow any of its links.

```
<META Name="Robots" Content="noindex,nofollow">
```

Similarly, the following example instructs the search engine to index the page but not to follow any of it links.

```
<META Name="Robots" Content="index,nofollow">
```

How Often Is Your Site Reindexed?

Indexing your Web site is not a one-time deal. Most search engines periodically reindex your pages. By reindexing your pages the search engine can verify that the pages still exist and update the database reference to your page if necessary.

In an ideal world, search engines would rapidly remove references to Web pages that no longer exist and just as rapidly create references to new Web pages that you build. In reality, search engines do not remove Web pages or find new Web pages as quickly as we would like. Whenever your site is busy, down, or can't respond to a request, the search engine simply marks the Web pages and moves on. If the server can't find the Web page on several occasions, the Web page is removed from the database.

Search engines don't add new Web pages as fast as one would like because they often don't reindex the entire site and all its contents. Instead, the search engine might check only for changes by comparing Web page headers or modifications dates. The result is that the search engine might need several visits to find and index a new area of your Web site.

Why Won't This Search Engine List Your Site?

Sometimes you register with a search engine only to find, days or weeks later, that you can't locate your site anywhere in the search engine's database. A search engine might not list your site for several reasons, but the main reason is usually that the URL you provided couldn't be read or used. To avoid this problem, ensure that you type the complete URL to your Web site. Because URLs can be case-sensitive (depending on the Web server), ensure that your URL uses the proper case. For example, some Web servers might consider the URLs **http://www.tvpress.com/HOME.htm** and **http://www.tvpress.com/ Home.htm** as being different Web pages.

You should also watch the syntax of the URL. Some search engines will not use a URL that includes reserved characters, such as:

=	The equals sign
$	The dollar sign
?	The question mark

Another reason for a search engine not to index your site is that you use frames and the search engine doesn't know how to deal with them. To ensure that the search engine can find your page links, add a `<NOFRAME>` tag that contains the text and links to the Web page.

Scripts and graphics-only pages can also present problems for search engines. To ensure that your Web page has a description and keywords, use the techniques discussed previously this morning under "Capitalizing on Search Engine Fundamentals."

Additionally, if you don't have your own domain, a Rotots.txt file might be the cause of your problems. As discussed previously, the Robots.txt file can be used to keep search engines out of specific directories. To check the contents of the Robots.txt file for your domain, use this URL:

http://www.your-domain.com/robots.txt

in which "your-domain" is your actual domain. If the Robots.txt file excludes your directory or all public directories on the server, you've found the cause of the problem. If you find that your files are excluded in the Robots.txt file, ask the Web server administrator whether this can be changed.

Search Engine Tricks to Avoid

One of the goals of this book is to show you proven techniques for improving your standing in the search engines. There are other unconventional promotion tricks that you can also employ to try to trick search engines into giving your Web site a better standing. You may have seen some of these tricks applied at other Web sites or read about them on the Web. Use of these tricks is dubious at best and you should avoid using them.

Search engine developers consider these tricks to be a form of spam, and when you use spam, you have to expect a penalty. The penalty is often delisting from a search engine. Delisting means that none of your Web pages will be available in the search engine.

The next several sections point out some of these tricks (or traps) in order to make you aware of them so that you won't fall prey to using them on your Web pages.

Title Tricks

Page titles are a very important means of improving your standing with search engines. Some Web site publishers try to get more oomph out of their titles using a technique called *keyword loading*. Using a form of keyword loading, you add multiple instances of the `<TITLE>` tag to your Web pages and load them with keywords to try and improve keyword relevance. For example:

```
<TITLE>Daily News: finance news, business news, current
events</TITLE>

<TITLE>Sports Connection: baseball, football,
basketball</TITLE>

<TITLE>Book Nook: rare book, collector book, first print
book</TITLE>
```

While it might be temping to list lots of keywords in this manner, it is better to stick with the top 10 or so. This will give the keywords greater importance.

Having more than one `<TITLE>` tag isn't considered proper HTML, but it doesn't cause any errors. Another trick that you may come across is `<TITLE>` tag duplication. When you repeat a page title, you take a standard title (without keyword loading) and copy it several times. The thought here is that by repeating the same `<TITLE>` tag statement, Web site publishers may be able to give their site better standing on some search engines.

For example, instead of

```
<HEAD>
<TITLE>Daily News: Your news source</TITLE>
</HEAD>
```

You could use

```
<HEAD>
<TITLE>Daily News: Your news source</TITLE>
<TITLE>Daily News: Your news source</TITLE>
<TITLE>Daily News: Your news source</TITLE>
</HEAD>
```

Modern browsers are smart enough to look only at the first instance of a <TITLE> tag in a Web page and to skip over any duplicate tags that may follow. But just because your visitors cannot tell the difference, that does not mean that search engines won't identify the use of this trick and delist the offending Web site.

Hidden Text and Fields

Earlier, you read about adding descriptive summaries to your Web pages as a way of improving your standing. While this works in many cases, sometimes you don't want a summary paragraph in the midst of your polished page. Because of the importance of this text, you might be tempted to try and hide the text from visitors. You might also want to load up the page with additional descriptions or keywords that are all hidden from your visitors.

One way that some Web site publishers try to hide text from visitors is to add descriptions or keywords that use the same color as the background for the page. For example, if the background color is black they might add hidden text by setting the font color to black. In addition, to give this text as small a footprint as possible on the page, the Web site publisher might set the font size to 1 as demonstrated here.

```
<FONT COLOR ="#000000" SIZE="1"> Writer's Gallery is a
   place for anyone who loves the written word. You'll find
   links to hundreds of writing-related resources as well as
   new works of fiction published at our site.</FONT>
```

TIP To avoid the watchful eye of search engines, some Web site publishers try to use a color that is close to the background color but doesn't match it exactly. However, most modern search engines now look for these types of tricks and may delist Web sites that use the same or similar color for both the font and background. Another technique to avoid a penalty is to use a background image with colors that your hidden text can blend into.

HTML comments also let you hide text from readers. With HTML comments, you can place text on the page that the search engine can see but your readers can't:

```
<!- Entertainment news, business news, current events ->
<!- Rare book, collector book, first print book ->
```

While it is perfectly acceptable to add keywords into your HTML comment statements, avoid loading them up. Otherwise you'll run the risk that some search engines will view the comments as spam. Some search engines also read values associated with input fields. Some Web site publishers try to use hidden input fields to boost their standings, as demonstrated in the following example.

```
<INPUT TYPE="HIDDEN" VALUE="baseball, football, basketball, hockey">
```

Here, input type HIDDEN and its associated VALUE attribute were used to store additional descriptive text or keywords. Clearly, using hidden input fields in this manner puts any Web site that tries this trick at risk.

Setting Up Multiple Versions of Your Pages

Mirror sites have long been used to provide additional ways to access popular Web resources. What many Web site publishers have discovered is that if they mirror individual pages, they can drive additional traffic to their Web site. When you mirror a page, you create copies of a page.

To give the mirrored pages greater importance, the Web site publishers keep their mirrored pages short and stick with text descriptions and keywords. They use different descriptions and keywords to tailor the pages to specific audiences and search engines and then save the pages with unique names. For example, pages might be named sequentially, such as index1.htm, index2.htm, index3.htm, and so on. Once finished, each individual page is registered.

The idea here isn't to dazzle readers with these mirror pages, but rather to get the readers to visit the main Web site. Once at the door, readers will find a link that directs them to the main page or will automatically be redirected by a <META> tag.(Redirecting readers to a new page is discussed in the Sunday Afternoon session titled "Redirecting Lost Readers.")

Search engines and directories look unfavorable on any Web site that tries to manipulate things in this manner and visitors often don't appreciate being redirected like this. The bottom line here is not to use this trick.

Increasing Your Web Traffic with the Top Search Engines

Registering with the major search engines is one of the best ways to increase traffic to your Web site. If you've followed the techniques for optimizing your Web site for search engines as discussed previously under "Capitalizing on Search Engine Fundamentals," you should see marked improvements in your Web traffic simply by registering with the search engines listed in this section. Don't expect a flood of traffic the day after you register your Web site; rather, you should see a steady increase in the level of traffic your Web site receives over time. The actual increase you see will depend on the subject of your site, its size and quality, and your use of search engine optimization techniques.

Although you could use the techniques discussed here to register with hundreds of other search engines, the reward for all your hard work usually isn't worth the effort. Millions of people use only the major search engines to find what they need. Every day, these search engines collectively handle about 90 percent of the searches performed by general search engines. Obviously, this means that the hundreds of other general search engines handle only 10 percent of the search transactions. Do you really want to spend countless hours registering with hundreds of other search engines when you can potentially reach the vast majority of users simply by registering with the most-used search engines? Probably not.

When you register with a search engine, you generally provide the URL to your top-level page. The search engine uses this single URL to find all the other resources at your site. You should also register the URLs to the top-level pages that cannot be reached from your home page.

The material that follows is designed as a quick reference resource that you can use time and again. The idea is to provide only the information you need. With this in mind, you'll find the sections are organized alphabetically based on the name of the search engine. You'll also find the URL to the main page and the relevant registration page (if available). If you find that the URL for the registration page is no longer valid, go to the main page and follow the submission link to the appropriate page. Usually, the submission link is labeled "Add URL," "Add a Page," or something similar.

 NOTE Keep in mind that these are general search engines, not specialized or category-specific search engines. In upcoming sections, you will learn how to increase your traffic using other types of search engines. Note also that there are many popular alternatives to search engines, such as directories and guides, which are discussed later in the book as well.

AllTheWeb

Main Page: http://www.alltheweb.com

Submission Page: http://submit.search.yahoo.com/free/request

Instructions: Search results for AllTheWeb come from Yahoo!. New site submissions must be made to Yahoo!.

Figure 2.13

AllTheWeb is a search engine owned by Yahoo! that still maintains a loyal following.

AltaVista

Main Page: http://www.altavista.com

Submission Page: http://submit.search.yahoo.com/free/request

Instructions: Search results for AltaVista come from Yahoo!. New site submissions must be made to Yahoo!.

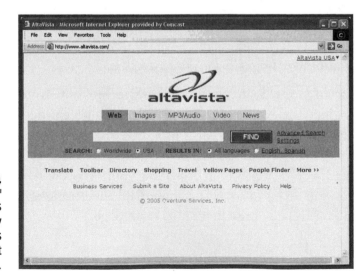

Figure 2.14

With millions of accesses every day, AltaVista is a major Internet search engine.

AOL Search

Main Page: http://www.aolsearch.com/aolcom/webhome

Submission Page: http://www.google.com/addurl/?continue=/addurl

Instructions: Search results for AOL Search come from Google. New site submission must be made to Google.

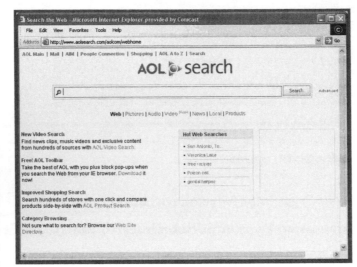

Figure 2.15

AOL Search is a search engine owned by America Online but available to everyone on the Web.

Ask Jeeves

Main Page: http://www.askjeeves.com

Instructions: Search results for Ask Jeeves come from the Teoma search engine. The Teoma search engine does not accept free URL submissions. Ask Jeeves does provide for paid advertising. However, chances are that over time the search engine will eventually discover and add your Web site if you do a good job of making your Web site search engine friendly. You can access information about paid advertising at Ask Jeeves by clicking on the Advertise link on its main page.

Figure 2.16

Ask Jeeves is unique in that you can do searches in the form of complete questions.

Excite

Main Page: http://www.excite.com

Instructions: Excite is owned by Ask Jeeves. Excite does not accept free URL submissions. You can, however, pay to ensure that your Web site is listed by visiting **help.excite.com** and clicking on the Submit Your Site link.

Figure 2.17

Excite pulls its search results from Ask Jeeves, but also adds in its own paid listings to its results lists.

Go.Com

Main Page: http://www.go.com

Submission Page: http://submit.search.yahoo.com/free/request

Instructions: Search results for Go.com come from Yahoo!. New site submission must be made to Yahoo!.

Figure 2.18

Go.com pulls its search results from Yahoo!.

Google

Main Page: http://www.google.com

Submission Page: http://www.google.com/addurl/?continue=/addurl

Instructions: Provide your URL and a comment about the content of your Web site before clicking on the Add URL button.

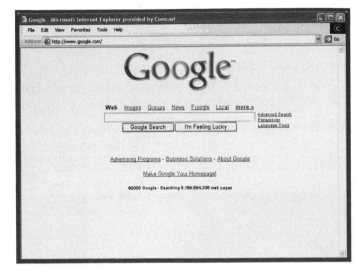

Figure 2.19

Google has become
one of the
most used and
well-known
search engines
on the Web.

HotBot

Main Page: http://www.hotbot.com

Instructions: HotBot can return results from Ask Jeeves and Google. To see
your Web site listed here, register with Google at **www.google.com/addurl/
?continue=/addurl**. Clicking on the Submit Site link on HotBot's main page
takes you to **inside.lycos.com** where you can pay to advertise your Web site.

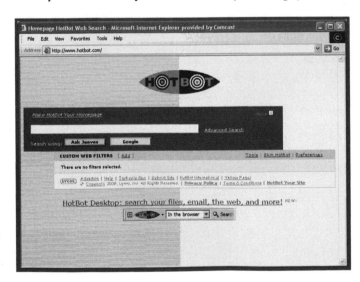

Figure 2.20

HotBot stormed
onto the scene in
1996 and quickly
became one of the
most popular
search engines
on the Web.

Lycos

Main Page: http://www.lycos.com

Instructions: Lycos retrieves its search results from Yahoo!. You can register with Yahoo! at **submit.search.yahoo.com/free/request**. Clicking on the Advertise link on Lycos' main page takes you to **advertising.lycos.com/ contactus.html** where you can pay to advertise your Web site.

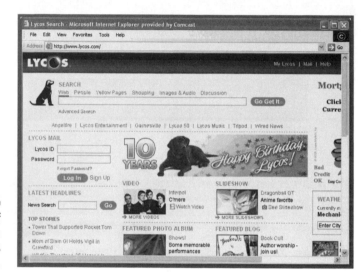

Figure 2.21

Lycos has one of the best-known search engines on the Web.

MSN Search

Main Page: http://search.msn.com

Submission Page: http://search.msn.com/docs/submit.aspx

Instructions: Submit your top level URL to the submission page.

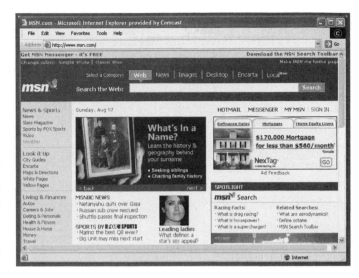

Figure 2.22

Microsoft's MSN search engine is rapidly gaining ground in the search engine business, surpassing many older search engines.

Netscape

Main Page: http://www.netscape.com

Submission Page: http://www.google.com/addurl/?continue=/addurl

Instructions: Search results for Netscape come from Google. New site submission must be made to Google.

Figure 2.23

Netscape's search results include its own paid listings combined with search results retrieved from Google.

whatUseek

Main Page: http://www.whatuseek.com/

Submission Page: http://www.whatuseek.com/addurl.shtml

Instructions: Key in your top-level URL and your e-mail address and click on the Submit URL button.

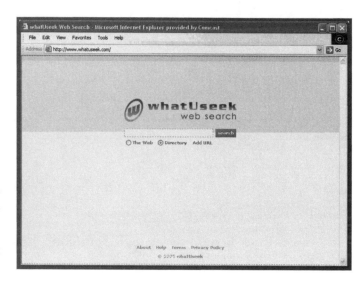

Figure 2.24

whatUseek is another growing search engine where you'll want to be listed.

Yahoo!

Main Page: http://www.yahoo.com

Submission Page: http://search.yahoo.com/free/request

Instructions: Key in your top-level URL and click on the Submit URL button.

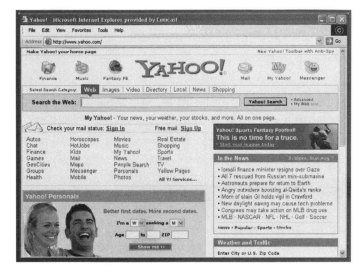

Figure 2.25

Yahoo! runs one of
the two most
popular general
search engines
on the Internet.

Metasearch Engines

In recent years a new type of Internet search Web site has emerged called a metasearch engine. A metasearch engine doesn't crawl the Internet looking for content to maintain its own database. Instead, metasearch engines retrieve search results by passing search queries on to a number of search engines and directories and correlating the results returned from each source into a single, combined results listing.

Metasearch engines are generally best used when performing general searches because they return a broad set of results from different sources. Web surfers like metasearch engines because they can save time when looking for information.

The Mechanics Going on Behind the Scenes

Metasearch engines collect user queries and format them as appropriate for various search engines and directories. After submitting a query, the metasearch engine collects results from each source in a virtual database, from which it then removes duplicate results. Some metasearch engines display their results in one consolidated list while other metasearch engines display results by category or by source. Regardless of how a metasearch engine chooses to display its results, the results are ultimately sorted according to relevance.

Dog Pile, Mamma, and Other Sites

Like search engines, not all metasearch engines are equal, some being more popular than others. In this section you will find information about some of the most commonly used search engines.

Metasearch engines do not maintain their own databases. Therefore, they are not able to accept free URL submissions. However, most offer paid listings. To help ensure that your Web site is listed in the results returned by a metasearch engine, make sure that you get listed with at least one of the search engines or directories that it retrieves results from.

DogPile

DogPile (**www.dogpile.com**), shown in Figure 2.26, sends queries to a number of search engines and directories, including Google, Yahoo!, MSN, Ask Jeeves, and LookSmart. The results returned from these sources are displayed in a single list according to relevancy. The name of the search engine or directory from which results were retrieved is also listed, showing the user where the results ultimately came from. DogPile offers paid listings, which you can learn about by clicking on the Submit Your Site link on the main page.

Mamma

Mamma (**www.mamma.com**), shown in Figure 2.27, sends queries to a number of search engines and directories, including Google, Yahoo!, MSN, Teoma, LookSmart, and Open Directory. Search results retrieved from these and other sources are displayed in a single list according to relevancy and the name of the search engines and directories from which results originated are also listed. Mamma offers paid listings, known as Mamma classifieds, which you can learn about by clicking on the Submit Your Site link on the main page.

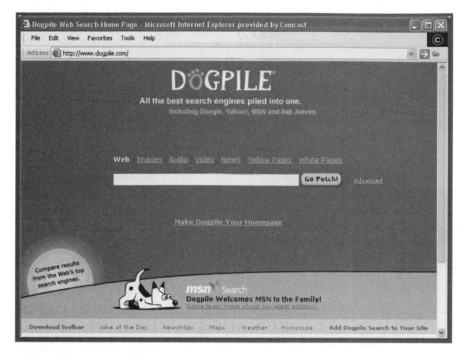

Figure 2.26

DogPile combs numerous search engines and directories in an effort to collect results for user queries.

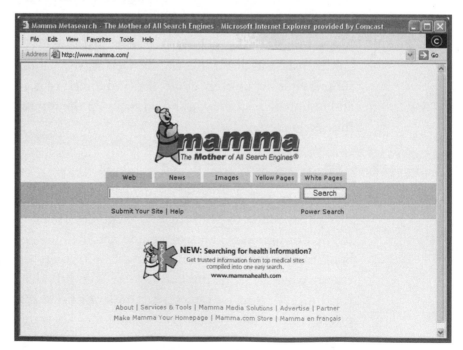

Figure 2.27

Mamma is one of the older and best known of the metasearch engines.

DogPile and Mamma are just a couple of the many good metasearch engines available on the Web. The following list shows a number of other metasearch engines that you might also want to look into a little further.

- **Vivisimo. http://vivisimo.com**
- **Kartoo. http://www.kartoo.com**
- **Planet Search. http://www.planetsearch.com**
- **WebCrawler. http://www.webcrawler.com**

Submitting Your Web Site to the Top Guides, Lists, and Directories

The phenomenal popularity of resource directories such as Open Directory ushered in a whole new era of guides, lists, and directories designed to help people find things on the Web. Whereas the focus of Web guides is usually on the top or best sites, lists and directories focus on categorizing information found on the Web.

Just as hundreds of search engines are available, you can find hundreds of guides, lists, and directories on the Web as well. Unfortunately, trying to submit your site to every guide, list, and directory is a waste of your time and resources. Instead, you should focus on the top resources you find in this section.

Submitting Your Site to Lists and Directories

Guides, *lists*, and *directories* are all terms used to describe Web resources that provide links to Web pages. Web guides usually provide pointers to the best or top sites. Think of a guide as something you might buy at the bookstore to help you learn about a country you are visiting. Lists are exactly what the name implies: Lists of Web sites that are usually organized into several major categories. Think of a list as something you might put together before you go grocery shopping. Beyond lists, you will find directories, which usually have rather extensive listings of Web sites divided into many categories. When you think of a directory, think of the Yellow Pages directory, that huge yellow tome that lists tons of businesses.

Although size is usually the major factor that distinguishes a list from a directory, don't get hung up on the terminology. Generally speaking, lists and directories serve the same purpose and often the terms are used interchangeably.

Web site listings in guides and directories are very different from the results returned by a typical search engine. Guides and directories do not index your Web pages at all; they simply use the information you provide to create a listing for your Web site.

When you submit your Web site to a list or directory, you submit the URL for your home page or other top-level pages at your site. Along with the page URL, you usually are asked to submit the Web page title, a brief description of the Web page, and a specific category for the Web page. The Web page category should always be tailored to the specific directory to which you are submitting your page. Some directory sites have hundreds of narrowly focused categories, such as entertainment news for kids and computer book reviews. Other directory sites have only a few broadly focused categories such as entertainment and travel.

Most directory sites screen all new submissions rigorously. If the same page has been submitted previously, the site usually disregards the submission. The site might also disregard the submission if the page was submitted to the wrong category.

Rather than place your listing in a category that you think is popular, you should place your listing in a category that strongly relates to the topic your site covers. Placing your site in a category that fits your content ensures that readers who are looking for a site like yours will be able to find it.

Trying to submit the same Web page to multiple categories will usually get you in trouble. Rather than submit the same Web page to multiple categories, examine the type of content that you publish to see whether different areas of your Web site fall into different categories. You could, for example, list your home page in one category, your writing area in another category, and your job center in yet another category. Whenever possible, list each of the major areas of your Web site separately in directories. This gives your Web site a better chance of getting noticed. And the more your Web site is noticed, the more your Web traffic will increase.

The Open Directory and Yahoo!

On the Internet, a directory is a human edited collection of information about Web sites. People all over the world regularly visit the major Web directories to look for information regarding specific subjects. This makes getting listed in a Web directory very important to any Web site publisher. Being listed in the major Web directories is even more important because just being listed in them is often all that it takes for your site to eventually get noticed by and then indexed by some major search engines.

While there are many Web directories out there, two are particularly well known and popular, the Open Directory and Yahoo!'s directory. As a result they merit a little extra attention.

The Open Directory is the only major directory that is and always has been 100 percent free. Some directories only accept paid inclusion while many others offer both free and paid inclusion. A global community of volunteer editors manages the Open Directory. One of the reasons that getting listed in the Open Directory is so important is because results from the Open Directory are retrieved by numerous search engines on the Internet, including Google, Netscape, and AOL. In addition, many search engines provide direct access to the Open Directory. For example, if you visit **www.google.com** and click on the Directory link, you'll be presented with a listing of the high-level categories that make up the Open Directory (**directory.google.com**). Simply click on a category to drill down into subcategories and ultimately to a list of Web site links.

Earlier in this chapter, you were told that Yahoo! was one of the Internet's largest search engines. This is true. However, before it switched over to retrieving its primary search results from its search engine, Yahoo!'s main source was its directory. Yahoo! still maintains its directory. Yahoo! provides for free registration for non-commercial submission. If you want to submit a URL for a business, Yahoo! requires that you pay a $299 fee (to Overture —a Yahoo! owned company), which you have to pay every year to keep your paid listing. Unfortunately, the $299 fee doesn't guarantee you a listing in Yahoo!'s directory; it only guarantees that Yahoo! will receive your Web site within seven days and provide you with a formal answer as to whether your site has been accepted for inclusion.

Like the Open Directory, Yahoo!'s directory serves as a feed for numerous search engines, making it all the more attractive. Even if your Web site is for commercial use, it may very well be worth the $299 registration fee for the first year to get listed in Yahoo!'s directory. Once your Web site is established and listed in other directories and search engines, you might later decide not to renew your yearly registration.

TIP Before you run out and start registering with the various directories, it's best to do a little preparation. For starters, prepare a well written description of your Web site that is around 25 words long and be sure to include at least a few of your keywords or keyword phrases.

Submitting Your Site to Web Guides

The focus on the top or best sites puts Web guides in a league of their own. When you submit your site to a guide, you are betting that the guide's reviewers will find your site useful, informative, or well presented. If the guide's reviewers count your site among the best, they will write a review of your site, and your site will show up in their database of the Web's top sites. If your guide's reviewers don't like your site for whatever reason, they will move on to the next site in their long list of sites to review.

Contrary to what you might think, the Web sites with the fancy graphics and multimedia don't always have the best ratings. In fact, some of the highest rated Web sites have mostly text.

You can improve your odds of getting your site reviewed by taking the time to learn what the guide looks for and what the guide's reviews look like. When you have gained a clear understanding of how the guide works, submit your site with descriptive information that will catch the eyes of the reviewers. Along with the summary information, you might want to include a rating for your Web site. If this rating is realistic, you might give the reviewer a reason to visit your Web site.

Another way to improve your odds with Web guides is to focus on the top-level areas of your Web site. For example, if your primary Web site publishes two key resources, Writers Gallery and Internet Job Center, you could submit entries for both of these areas rather than the Web site as a whole. The reason for this is that these areas have very different focuses—creative writing and jobs—and can't be realistically rated in the same review.

As a final note, remember that reviewers are real people. With thousands of Web sites to review, several weeks or even a month could elapse before a reviewer gets a chance to look at your Web site. If reviewers don't review your site, there isn't much point in inundating them with e-mail or repeated submissions. Instead, wait a few months and then try again.

How Do People Find Your Listing in a Guide or Directory?

Most guides and directories can be searched in two ways: by category or by keyword.

When you search by category, you follow links from a broad category to a progressively more focused category. In a category search, the categories themselves are the main elements driving users to your listing. Yet when users finally get to the detailed paged that shows your listing, it is the page title and summary description that will influence their decision to visit your Web site.

A keyword search in a guide or directory is handled in a very different manner. Rather than follow links, you use a search interface to find categories and list within the guide. If the keywords you enter lead to several categories, you see category headers. If the keywords you enter lead to a specific listing, you see either the listing itself or the page of which the listing is part.

How Often Is Your Site's Listing Updated?

Unlike search engines that periodically schedule your site for reindexing, most guides and directories rarely update their listings. The problem with updating listings is a logistical one. To update a list in a Web guide, a reviewer needs to take another look at the Web site. To update a listing in a directory, the directory site needs to have someone check the validity of the link and the description. Both actions require time and resources that could be directed at new listings.

Don't rely on someone from the guide or directory site to update your listing in six months or a year; take a proactive stance instead. If you move the furniture around a bit and add a new edition to your Web home, inform the folks who run the guide or directory site. Generally, you should send a message to the people who maintain the directory or guide. The key things to tell them are what the old information looked like and what the new information should look like.

Increasing Your Web Traffic with Guides and Directories

Getting your Web site listed in a popular guide or directory will definitely increase the traffic to your site. As with search engines, you will find that you get the most out of your time investment when you submit your site to the top guides and directories, which is why this session focuses on the best guides and directories.

Although you know that a Web page or area within your Web site will be listed in the directory, there is no assurance that you will get listed in a

Web guide. Still, submitting your site to the guides listed in this section is worthwhile, especially when you consider that getting your site listed in any one of these guides could bring thousands of visitors to your Web site every single day. For many Web sites, an extra thousand visitors a day would effectively double or triple the site's traffic. Doubling or tripling your Web traffic from a single listing might seem like a pipe dream, but the reality is that people often seek out the best that the Web has to offer. After all, do you settle for bronze, when silver, gold, and platinum are waiting in the wings?

As you read this section, you should submit your Web site to the featured guides and directories. As discussed earlier, directories often ask for detailed information, which can include page URL, page title, keywords, description, contact information, and categories/topics. Before you submit your listing, you should have this information plotted out.

Alcanseek

Main Page: http://www.alcanseek.com/

Submission Page: Visit the home page and click on the Add Your Site link.

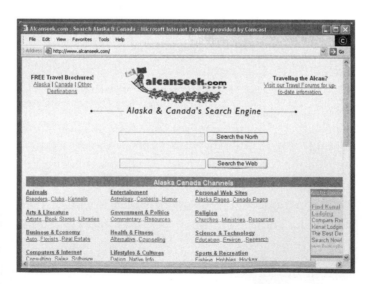

Figure 2.28

Alcanseek is a Web directory for Alaska and Canada.

CANLinks

Main Page: http://www.canlinks.net/

Submission Page: http://www.canlinks.net/addalink/

Figure 2.29

CANLinks is a Web directory for Canada.

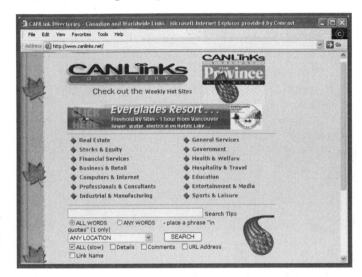

CentralDrive

Main Page: http://www.centraldrive.com/

Submission Page: Visit a specific topic area and follow the submission links.

Figure 2.30

CentralDrive is a growing online community that features topic-specific Web directories.

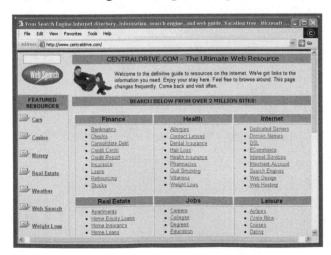

EuroSeek

Main Page: http://www.euroseek.net/

Submission Page: http://www.euroseek.net/system/show.cgi?item=adv2.html

Figure 2.31

EuroSeek is one of the most popular Web directories in Europe.

Galaxy

Main Page: http://galaxy.einet.net/

Submission Page: http://galaxy.einet.net/cgi-bin/annotate?/galaxy

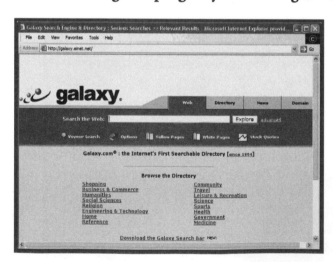

Figure 2.32

As one of the oldest Web directories, Galaxy has a lot to offer, and although it might take a while to get listed, it's worth the wait.

Gimpsy

Main Page: http://www.gimpsy.com/gimpsy

Submission Page: Click on the Suggest a Site link on the main page.

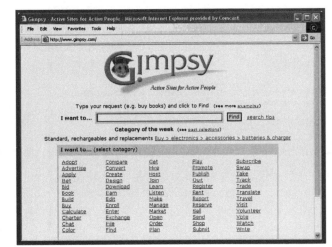

Figure 2.33

Gimpsy is small but very well maintained directory offering free and paid URL submission.

Illumirate

Main Page: http://www.illumirate.com/

Submission Page: Click on the Free Add URL link on the main page.

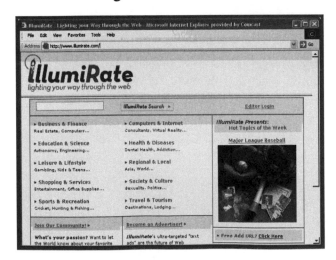

Figure 2.34

Illumirate is a small but well run Web directory.

Jayde

Main Page: http://www.jayde.com/

Submission Page: http://dir.jayde.com/cgi-bin/submit.cgi

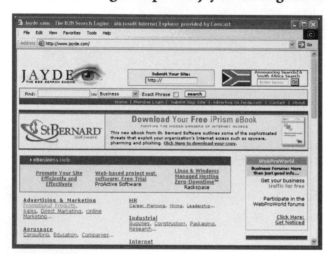

Figure 2.35

Jayde is a growing Web directory and guide that can help bring visitors to your Web site.

LookSmart

Main Page: http://www.looksmart.com

Submission Page: http://listings.looksmart.com/campaigns/submit/initial. jhtml?registerState=2&loginState=3

Figure 2.36

LookSmart maintains a hugely popular directory that is also used to feed results to a number of search engines.

Mavicanet

Main Page: http://www.mavicanet.com

Submission Page: Drill down into a subcategory and then click on the Add Site link.

Figure 2.37

Mavicanet is a multilingual directory that spans more than 20 languages.

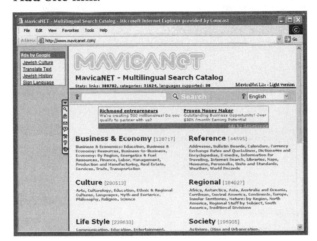

Nerd World Media

Main Page: http://headlines.nerdworld.com/modules.php?name=Top

Submission Page: http://headlines.nerdworld.com/modules.php?name =Web_Links&l_op=AddLink

Instructions: You must register before you are allowed to submit a new URL.

Figure 2.38

Nerd World Media is a stylish Web directory that heavily promotes the top 10 listings in various categories.

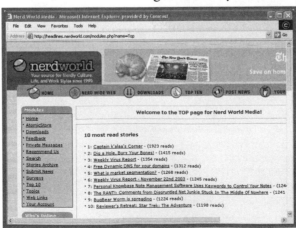

Open Directory

Main Page: http://dmoz.org

Submission Page: http://dmoz.org/add.html

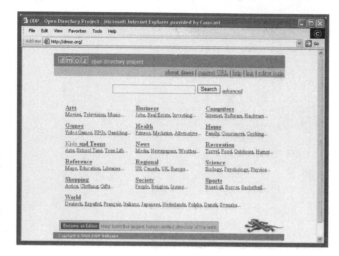

Figure 2.39

The Open Directory is the world's largest human-edited directory.

Scrub The Web

Main Page: http://www.scrubtheweb.com/

Submission Page: http://www.scrubtheweb.com/addurl.html

Figure 2.40

Scrub The Web is a small but growing Web directory.

Skaffe

Main Page: http://www.skaffe.com

Submission Page: Click on the Suggest URL link on the main page.

Figure 2.41

Skaffe is a small but very good volunteer-edited Web directory.

Yahoo!

Main Page: http://dir.yahoo.com/

Submission Page: Visit the category where your site fits and the click on the Suggest a Site link.

Figure 2.42

Yahoo! hosts one of the most popular Web directories on the planet; getting listed here can certainly bring visitors to your Web site.

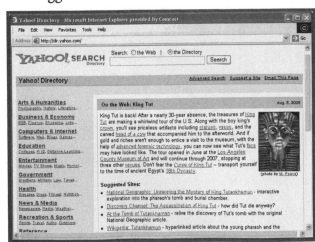

Wrapping Up and Looking Ahead

Millions of people use search engines to find information every day, and one of the best ways to build traffic to your Web site is to register with search engines. Guides, lists, and directories can also help your Web site get noticed. Keep in mind you aren't guaranteed a listing in a guide to the best of the Web. Still, your time is well spent if you manage to garner one or more such listings for your site.

This afternoon, you'll examine many different types of search engines and Web directories. You'll learn about the best directories and search engines for business-oriented Web sites, industry- and category-specific directories, getting more mileage from What's New? directories, and a whole lot more.

The Coolest, the Hottest, and the Best

- ➤ Business Search Engines and Yellow Pages Directories
- ➤ What's New? Directories
- ➤ Getting Your Site Listed as the Cool Site of the Day

Hundreds of business search and directory sites are currently available. The first part of this afternoon's coverage focuses on the best of these sites so that you can get the most exposure for your time investment.

If you have time, make use of these resources as you learn about them; that is, proceed with the registration process as you go through this section. If you don't have time to get them all now, come back when you do. It will be worth your while.

Later this afternoon, you'll find out how to vie for awards that will help your site get noticed by cyberspace travelers. Awards abound on the Web, and your site can sizzle as Hot Site of the Day or freeze out the competition as Cool Site of the Week. Some awards are more likely to increase your Web traffic than others, though, and this afternoon's session introduces you to some of the best.

The Best Business Search Engines and Yellow Pages Directories

Business search engines and Yellow Pages directories provide great resources for anyone who offers products, services, or business-related information on the Web. Most business-oriented search engines and directories provide much more detailed information than other search sites and directories. These detailed entries allow you to list your Web site and tout your products and services as well.

Submitting Your Site to Business Search and Directory Sites

Hundreds of thousands of businesses offer products and services on the Web. The sites that help Web users make sense of all these offerings are the business search engines and Yellow Pages directories. Because these search and directory sites are tailored for businesses, you can search for specific businesses by company name, location, industry, as well as by the products and services that the companies offer. Although they are similar to traditional search engines, most business search engines do not index your Web site or the pages that you submit for listing at the search site. Instead, these search engines create an indexed reference to your site based solely on the information you submit, which doesn't necessarily include the URL to your Web site. In this respect, this type of business search engine is more like a directory listing than a traditional search engine.

Because business search engines don't actually index your site, many business search sites are called Yellow Pages directories. Although some Yellow Pages directories are modeled after the Yellow Pages of your phone book, most Web-based Yellow Pages directories have features of both traditional directory sites and traditional search engine sites.

Due to their very direct focus, business search sites and directories often want a great deal of information from anyone registering with the site. For this reason, before you register with these sites, you should have all the following information at hand:

- What subject category you want to be listed under
- How you want company contact information to read
- Who you will list as the contact name at the company
- What keywords you want associated with your site
- What Web page's URLs you want listed
- What e-mail address you want to use for inquiries
- What description you will use for your company, products, and services

You should also know that, by their very nature, business search sites and directories are out to make a profit. The worst of these sites exist only to push paid services on unwitting souls who want to get listed at the site. However, there is no need to sign up for anything that will cost you money. Plenty of sites are happy just to have your listing and will list you without charge. These sites get their money from advertising rather than listings.

Increasing Your Web Traffic with Yellow Pages Directories

Just as the top search engines and directories receive millions of visitors every day, so do the top Yellow Pages directories. Accordingly, registering your Web site with Yellow Pages directories will increase the traffic to your Web site. That said, Yellow Pages directories generally don't drive thousands of visitors to a particular Web site; rather, you can reasonably expect relatively modest increases in your Web traffic over time.

The traffic depends, of course, on the types of products and services you offer. Right now you might be wondering if it's really worth the effort. The answer is yes—as long as you focus your efforts on the top Yellow Pages directories listed in this section.

Although Yellow Pages directories are popular and receive millions of visitors every day, they are business oriented. Visitors to these directories are usually looking for very specific types of information (for example, information on a management consulting service). Furthermore, because Yellow Pages listings contain addresses, phone numbers, and other contact information, people visiting the Yellow Pages directory might not visit your Web site at all. Instead, they might visit your physical storefront or contact you by phone, fax, or e-mail.

Whether visitors to a Yellow Pages directory go to your storefront, contact you, or visit your Web site, you have managed to bring in the all important consumers who are actively looking for a business that offers products or services like yours. With a listing in a traditional search engine or directory site, you simply cannot bring in this type of visitor on a consistent basis. Most businesses would much rather have 50 people browsing their aisles—virtual or otherwise—than have 500 people racing past the windows on their way to somewhere else.

NOTE As you follow along with the discussion, submit your Web site to the search engines and directories found in this section. If you are in a hurry and don't have time to register with all the sites, simply start with the first site and register with as many sites as you can.

BigBook

Main Page: http://www.bigbook.com/

Submission Page: New submissions are handled via Superpages.com.

Instructions: Click on the Add/Change Listing link to open a link to Superpages.com.

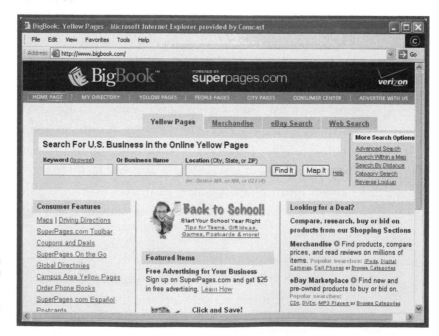

Figure 3.1

BigBook is one of the best-known Yellow Pages directories.

BizWeb

Main Page: http://www.bizweb.com/

Submission Page: http://www.bizweb.com/InfoForm/

Instructions: Read the information on the submission page and then submit your listing.

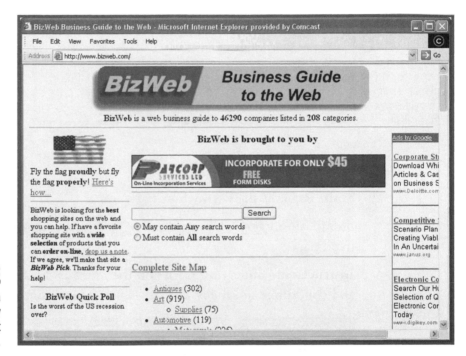

Figure 3.2

BizWeb is a popular directory for businesses that have Web sites.

Superpages.com

Main Page: http://www.superpages.com/

Submission Page: Click on the Add/Change Listing link at the bottom of the main page.

Instructions: To create a listing, you'll need to enter your business phone number and then follow the submission guidelines.

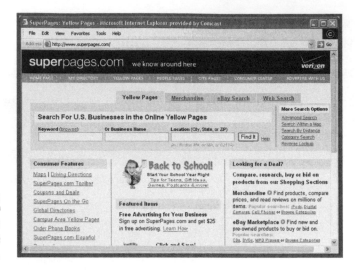

Figure 3.3

Superpages.com
provides free
basic listings.

Where2Go

Main Page: http://www.where2go.com/

Submission Page: Click on the List Your Site link at the bottom of the
main page.

Instructions: Enter your URL and then read and accept the site's terms
and conditions and follow the step-by-step submission process.

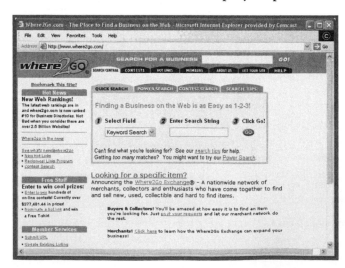

Figure 3.4

Where2Go is a
Yellow Pages
directory with
listings for
businesses
throughout
the world.

SMARTpages

Main Page: http://www.smartpages.com

Submission Page: http://www.smartpages.com/sp/contact/update.jsp

Instructions: Enter your contact information and descriptive information for your Web site, then submit the form. Be sure to enter a short description that accurately describes your site.

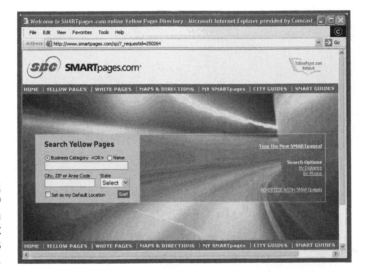

Figure 3.5

SMARTpages is a growing Internet Yellow Pages directory.

Yahoo! Local Yellow Pages

Main Page: http://yp.yahoo.com

Submission Page: http://dbupdate.infousa.com/dbupdate/yahoo1.jsp

Instructions: Yahoo! Local Yellow Pages does not accept listings to its database. Instead, you can register your listing at InfoUSA where you'll begin by providing your phone number and then follow the instructions that are provided.

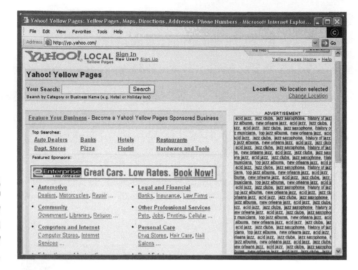

Figure 3.6

Yahoo! Local Yellow Pages lets you search by category or business name.

AnyWho

Main Page: http://www.anywho.com

Submission Page: New submissions are handled via Superpages.com.

Instructions: Visit **www.superpages.com/about/new_chg_listing.html**, click on the Business Listings link, enter your business phone number, and follow the instructions that are provided.

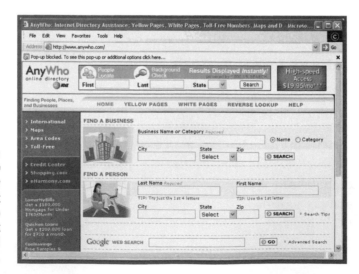

Figure 3.7

AnyWho is a Yellow Pages directory that provides access to information about businesses located all over the world.

TheYellowPages

Main Page: http://theyellowpages.com

Submission Page: http://www.superpages.com

Instructions: New submissions are handled via Superpages.com.

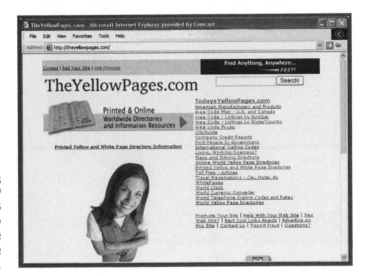

Figure 3.8

TheYellowPages provides access to printed and online worldwide directories.

AOL YellowPages

Main Page: http://yp.aol.com

Submission Page: http://yp.aol.com

Instructions: Click on the Add/Update a Listing link on the bottom of the main page. Click on Yes when asked if you own your own business and then follow the instructions that are provided.

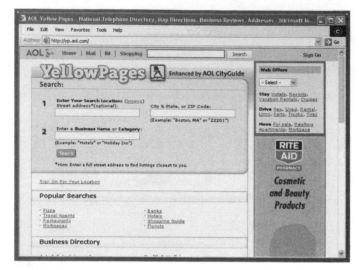

Figure 3.9

AOL YellowPages lets visitors browse or search its Yellow Page's listings.

MSN Yellow Pages

Main Page: http://yellowpages.msn.com

Submission Page: http://www.superpages.com

Instructions: New submissions are handled via Superpages.com.

Figure 3.10

MSN Yellow Pages lets visitors search by category or business name and filter search results down to a specific city or state.

Yellow Book

Main Page: http://www.yellowbook.com

Submission Page: http://www.yellowbook.com/ContactUs/?

Instructions: Select the option to Advertise with Yellow Book and then supply the information required to complete the submission form.

Figure 3.11

Yellow Book provides the ability to search by company name or by keyword phrases.

AskMrYellow

Main Page: http://www.askmryellow.com/home.php

Submission Page: https://www.todaysyellowpages.com/create_account_op.php

Instructions: You can submit a business listing for free and then choose from any number of optional paid advertising upgrades.

Figure 3.12

AskMrYellow lets visitors search by question, word, or phrase and can narrow search results based on ZIP code.

Directories by Industry and Category

The major search engines and directories are great for getting your Web site noticed by the masses, but you also want your site to be accessible to people looking for specific types of information. This is where industry- and category-specific directories come into the picture. Whether your site covers fine dining in Seattle, outdoor sports activities in Australia, or one or thousands of other topics, there are directories devoted to your subject. This section will show you how to find and use them.

NOTE Some of these directories have a fairly narrow focus. Be sure to read through the detailed descriptions before you submit a listing.

Getting the Most Out of Industry and Category Directories

Whereas industry directories focus on major industries, such as real estate or travel, category directories focus on specific topics, such as resources for writers or outdoor sports. People looking for specialized or tailored information seek out industry and category directories. This makes these directories the perfect place for your Web site to get noticed.

As with most directories, industry and category directories focus on pages rather than entire Web sites. Thus, you generally submit the URL of a specific page or area that strongly relates to the topic of the directory. Along with the URL, you usually submit the page title and a summary description. Although the description of your page might not be published with your listing, the directory maintainer uses the description to determine whether the page is appropriate for the directory.

Because industry and category directories have a very specific focus, they are great for increasing the traffic to your Web site. In a way, getting listed in these directories is like conducting an advertising campaign that targets readers who are interested in the exact type of Web site you publish.

Before you submit your Web site to industry or category directories, you should take a few minutes to plot out the industries or categories that fit your Web site. Although the first industry or category you think of is probably the best, a typical Web site will fit into several categories or industries. Your collection of articles on Spain would probably fit in perfectly with a travel or tourism directory. But, you could also look for metro or city guides that cover Spain. Additionally, your articles might cover the best restaurants in Madrid, making these pages suitable for a listing in a directory to restaurants, fine dining, or food.

Community Guides

Community guides are becoming increasingly popular. By focusing a directory on a specific city, state, or country, users can find information directly relating to an area of the world in which they are interested. If you want to find an Italian restaurant in Denver, you access a city guide featuring Denver. If you want to find a Web design firm in the Seattle area, you access a guide to the Seattle metropolitan area.

Every single Web site in cyberspace has a place in a community guide. After all, we all live somewhere. For this reason, you should register your site in a directory that covers your metro area, state, or country.

Unfortunately, only a few community guides actually let you submit listings. This section will highlight a number of excellent guides that accept submissions.

Creating a Listing in EscapeArtists

EscapeArtists (**www.escapeartist.com**) is a different kind of community guide. Instead of focusing on a particular city or state, EscapeArtists offers guides to a particular country or region.

EscapeArtists has hundreds of country and region specific guides. The easiest way to access these guides is to visit the main site and then follow the links to the guide with which you want to work. As shown in Figure 3.13, much of what you'll find at EscapeArtists is about travel and living in different countries. The listing for country-specific directories is organized alphabetically, while the listing for regional guides is organized into the following areas.

- Africa
- Asia-Pacific
- Canada
- Caribbean
- Central Europe & The Balkans
- Europe
- Mexico & Central America
- Pacific Islands
- South America

Figure 3.13

EscapeArtists provides access to information on a regional or country-by-country basis.

To submit a listing to EscapeArtists, visit the guide for the appropriate category and click on the Add URL link at the bottom of the page. Provide the required information and submit the form. There is a $5 charge for new registrations.

Submitting a Listing to the MetroGuide Network

MetroGuide (**www.metroguide.com**) is a community guide for Web sites located in the U.S. and around the world. Metro guides are organized into the following groupings.

- North America
- Caribbean
- Europe
- Africa-Middle East
- Asia-Pacific
- South America

You'll find individual directories for each state within the U.S. In addition to providing access to metro guides, you'll find other guides for hotels, retail, dining, and so on. As Figure 3.14 shows, listings in MetroGuide are displayed alphabetically by region.

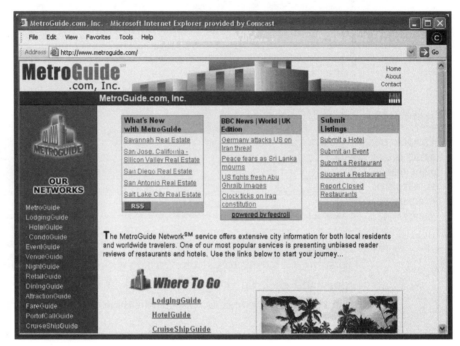

Figure 3.14

MetroGuide provides access to more than just a collection of metro guides around the world.

You can add a listing to MetroGuide by visiting its Link Exchange page (**metroguide-inc.com/link_policy.html**). In order to exchange links, you must agree to the terms and conditions specified on this page.

Yahoo! Country and Metro Guides

Millions of people are lost in the endless sea of the Web. They are looking for tailored information they can access easily and quickly, which is exactly what city guides provide. The growing trend to tailor information based on geographic boundaries is clearly evident when you visit the major search sites. Many of the major search engine sites have a city or metro guide. Yahoo! is no exception.

Yahoo! has set up separate areas for major metros and countries throughout the world. The Web site for Yahoo! Seattle (**seattle.yahoo.com**) is shown in Figure 3.15. If you want to register your Washington-based business or Web site in the Seattle metro guide, visit Yahoo! Seattle and go through the same submission process that you do for the main Yahoo! Directory. If you want to register your Web site in any other Yahoo! city guide, visit the city guide and go through the submission process as well.

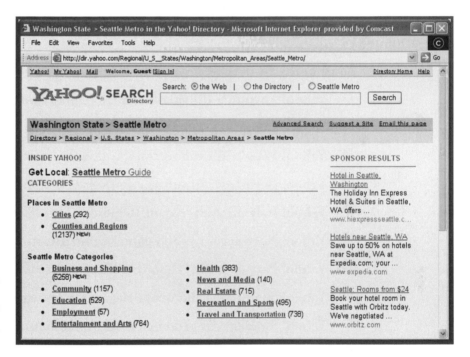

Figure 3.15

Yahoo! Metros provide a lot of area-specific information.

The Seattle metro guide is only one of many other Yahoo! Metro guides. Some of the other Yahoo! Metro guides include

⚙ **Yahoo! Atlanta: atlanta.yahoo.com**

⚙ **Yahoo! Austin: austin.yahoo.com**

⚙ **Yahoo! Boston: boston.yahoo.com**

⚙ **Yahoo! Chicago: chi.yahoo.com**

- Yahoo! Dallas/Fort Worth: dfw.yahoo.com
- Yahoo! Los Angeles: la.yahoo.com
- Yahoo! Miami: Miami.yahoo.com
- Yahoo! New York: ny.yahoo.com
- Yahoo! San Francisco: sfbay.yahoo.com
- Yahoo! Twin Cities: minn.yahoo.com
- Yahoo! Washington DC: dc.yahoo.com

Some of the Yahoo! country guides include

- **Yahoo! Australia: dir.yahoo.com/Regional/Countries/Austria/**
- **Yahoo! Denmark: dir.yahoo.com/Regional/Countries/Denmark/**
- **Yahoo! France: dir.yahoo.com/Regional/Countries/France/**
- **Yahoo! Germany: dir.yahoo.com/Regional/Countries/Germany/**
- **Yahoo! Italy: dir.yahoo.com/Regional/Countries/Italy/**
- **Yahoo! Norway: dir.yahoo.com/Regional/Countries/Norway/**
- **Yahoo! Portugal: dir.yahoo.com/Regional/Countries/Portugal/**
- **Yahoo! Spain: dir.yahoo.com/Regional/Countries/Spain/**
- **Yahoo! Sweden: dir.yahoo.com/Regional/Countries/Sweden/**
- **Yahoo! Zambia: dir.yahoo.com/Regional/Countries/Zambia/**

NOTE   To find a complete list of Yahoo! city and country guides and their URLs, visit Yahoo!'s main Web site at **dir.yahoo.com**.

Real Estate Directories and Guides

When you think of real estate, you probably think of real estate agents and brokers. Although agents and brokers are the cornerstones of real estate, the real estate industry encompasses many other professions and organizations. At one end of the spectrum are the construction companies, developers, engineers, planners, workers, and service organizations whose efforts create the homes in which we live and the office buildings in which we work. At the other end of the spectrum are the property mangers, asset managers, trust companies, and holding companies that manage the construction and the properties. In between are the financial institutions, the appraisers, the investors, and the property owners who make the construction possible.

With dozens of professions and organizations that make up the real estate industry, it is no surprise that this industry has a dominant presence in cyberspace. In fact, real estate directories are some of the best designed sites you'll find online. If your Web site or business covers any of the professions or organizations related to the real estate industry, you should add a listing to the directories in this section. Further, if you publish any information that relates to the real estate industry, you should consider adding a listing in the real estate directories as well.

Getting Listed at REALTOR.org

REALTOR.org (**www.realtor.org**), shown in Figure 3.16, is a real estate directory published by the National Association of Realtors. The directory covers many different aspects of the real estate industry. You'll find listings of real estate companies, retailers, products, and services. You'll also find listings of associations that are related to the industry.

REALTOR.org focuses on the U.S. real estate industry. It provides a built-in search capability for searching for real estate agents and offices. If your Web site has something to do with the real estate industry, you should consider registering with REALTOR.org. To do so, go to **resource. realtor.com/overview** and locate the right type of listing for your Web site and then call the phone number that is listed.

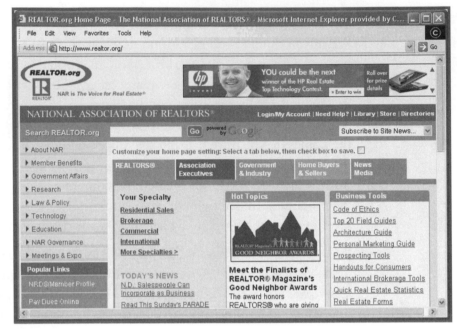

Figure 3.16

REALTOR.org is
one of the best
known and most
used real estate
Web sites.

Getting Listed in Estates Today

Estates Today (**www.estatestoday.co.uk**), shown in Figure 3.17, is a terrific directory for the commercial real estate industry. Its primary focus is on real estate services for the UK and Europe. Unlike some real estate directories that focus only on providing listings to companies, agencies, and brokers, Estates Today provides specific Internet services to the commercial real estate industry. In addition, it maintains two directories, CityOffices and BusinessParks.

The CityOffices directory provides links to information about commercial properties and is organized by major cities in the UK and Europe. Similarly, the BusinessParks directory provides access to links with information on business parks within the UK and Europe and is also organized by major cities.

Before you submit a listing to Estates Today, you should determine which directory best fits your Web site or company. Then submit an e-mail

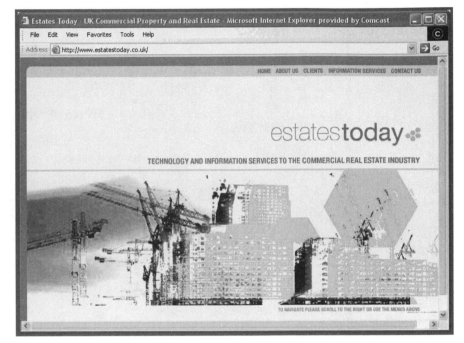

Figure 3.17

Estates Today provides access to information for commercial properties and business parks in the UK and Europe.

message to the e-mail address listed on the Web site's Contact Us page. The message should provide your company Web site title and the category in which you want your site listed.

Getting Listed in the International Real Estate Digest

The International Real Estate Digest (**www.ired.com**) is a comprehensive directory to the real estate industry. The goal of IRED is to be a one-stop shop for real estate information. As an actual online digest, the site features current news covering the real estate industry.

The International Real Estate Digest, shown in Figure 3.18, has thousands of listings from more than 85 countries. You can browse the listings in several ways, including by world region and by country. Individual listings appear with titles and summary descriptions. Most listings also have graphical icons that depict the kinds of information you will find at the Web site.

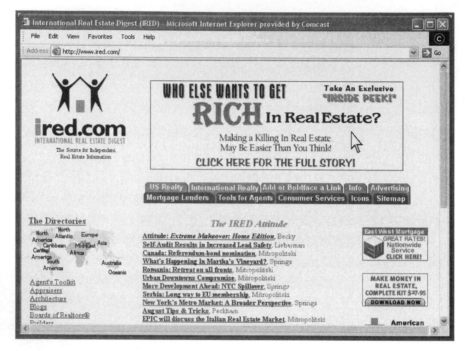

Figure 3.18

International Real
Estate Digest has
listings from
countries all
over the world.

The International Real Estate Digest accepts listings from many different types of organizations that relate to the real estate industry. Some of these organizations include agencies, appraisal companies, brokers, builders, construction services, education, inspectors, financial services, and legal services. You will find information about how to register your Web site with IRED at **www.ired.com/formpage.htm**.

To get the most out of your IRED listing, be sure to carefully consider the graphical icons that might pertain to your site. Each icon you select will be displayed with your listing. In the remarks sections, you should add a brief description of your Web site; doing so should ensure that your listing is displayed with a summary description.

Other Real Estate Directories

In addition to the real estate directories already discussed, many other real estate directories also exist. Some of the other real estate directories that you might want to consider include the Real Estate Cyberspace Society, Open House America, and Real-Estate-Agents.

The Real Estate Cyberspace Society (**www.recyber.com**) provides services for real estate professionals. You can submit your site to the Real Estate Cyberspace Society directory as **www.recyber.com/links/addform.html**.

Open House America (**www.openhouse.net**) is a site for homebuyers that includes directories for realtors, financial services, and general real estate related listings (see Figure 3.19). You can submit a listing to Open House America at **www.openhouse.net/realtor_register.html**.

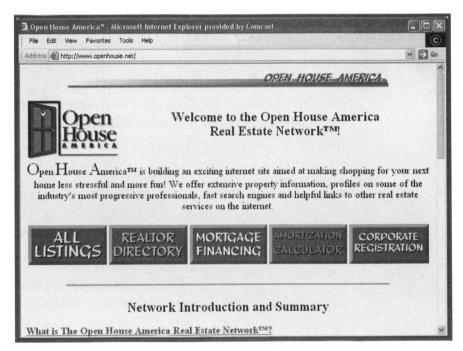

Figure 3.19

Real estate agents and agencies can submit listings to Open House America's real estate directory.

Real-Estate-Agents (**real-estate-agents.com**) maintains a comprehensive directory of commercial and residential real estate agents. Real estate agents can submit free listings by visiting the appropriate area within the directory and clicking on the Add Your Agency link.

Travel and Tourism: Guides and Directories

The travel industry covers many different professions and organizations. There are travel agents to book tickets and airlines, cruise lines, train companies, and bus companies to provide transportation. Hotels offer a place to stay, and car rental agencies give you flexible mobility. Recreation and amusement businesses provide entertainment.

Because travel and tourism is a big business, the industry is well represented online. As with the real estate industry, many high-profile travel directories can help you build traffic to your Web site. If your Web site covers any of the professions or organizations related to the travel industry, you should consider adding a listing to the directories in this section. If you publish any information that relates to travel and tourism, you should consider adding a listing in the travel directories as well.

Getting Listed in Hotels and Travel on the Net

Hotels and Travel on the Net (**www.hotelstravel.com**) is an international directory for the travel and tourism industry. This comprehensive directory contains hundreds of thousands of listings.

You can search Hotels and Travel by keyword or by following links to specific categories of information. Categories within the directory include hotels, airlines, airports, travel-related products, travel-related services, and travel references. Most of the major hotel chains have areas within the site as well.

Entries in Hotels and Travel cluster around hotels, airports, and airlines. Figure 3.20 shows listings for hotels whose locations are identified graphically on a map of the Tampa area.

If your site features travel-related information, you can add a listing to Hotels and Travel. The URL for this page is **www.hotelstravel.com/addsite.html**.

Fill out only the information that pertains to your Web site. If you are submitting a travel-related site, be sure to specify the city or country that your site services.

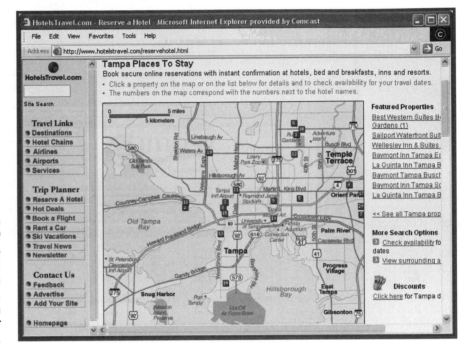

Figure 3.20

Hotels and Travel is easy to browse and search. You'll find a lot of resources, which makes it a good choice for your listing.

The Excite City Travel Guide

The Excite Travel Guide (**travel.excite.com**) is designed for travelers. The home page for Excite Travel is shown in Figure 3.21. When you visit the top-level page in the Excite Travel Guide, you see a listing of travel tools. You'll also see a section named Destination Guides. Click on a major area to visit areas within the travel guide dedicated to specific countries. By following the links, you will eventually end up on a page with listings dedicated to a specific city or metro area. Although you cannot place listings directly in the Excite Travel Guide, you can register your site with the Excite search engine, which then places you in the Excite database. (To learn more about Excite, see the Saturday Morning session under "Registering with the Top Search Engines on the Planet.")

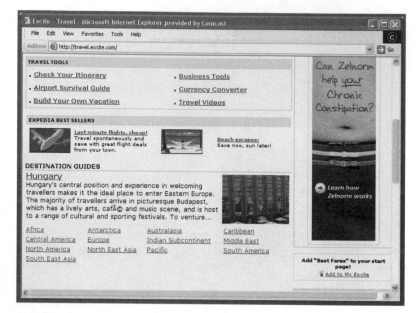

Figure 3.21

To get your listings in Excite's Travel Guide, you have to go through the main Excite site, **www.excite.com**.

Other Travel and Tourism Directories

After you submit listings to Hotels and Travel and Excite, you might want to try other travel directories as well. After all, you want to build traffic to your travel-related Web site, and the best way to do this is to spread the word about your Web site through the key directories for the travel industry. Some of the other travel directories to which you might want to submit your site include the Hotel Guide, HM USA Travel Guide, and TravelHub.

The Hotel Guide (**www.hotelguide.com**) provides a search interface to thousands of hotel listings. Versions of the site are available in English, French, Spanish, Italian, Japanese, and German. To submit a listing to this site, visit the free listing area at **www.hotelguide.com/html/businessservices/ hotelform.cfm**.

HM USA Travel Guide (**www.ht-usa.com**) provides a directory to travel resources in the United States. Areas of the Web site focus on trip planning, hotels, restaurants, car rental, national parks, theme parks, local weather, and more. You can submit related sites on the submission page at **www. hm-usa.com/mailcom.html**.

TravelHub (**www.travelhub.comwww.travelhub.com**) is a directory of travel agencies. If you are a travel agent, TravelHub provides a number of free services that can help you build traffic and boost your company's bottom line. To find out how you can get listed in this directory, visit **www.travelhub.com/admin/listing/signup.html**.

More Guides and Directories by Category

Company-specific guides and directories are great ways to get your site noticed. The usefulness of category guides is apparent when you want to find specific types of information without having to wade through search engine results. Because category guides are so useful, they are also extremely popular. The Web contains thousands of category-specific guides covering every imaginable topic. If you are looking for a very specific category guide, one of the best places to find it is Yahoo! (**dir.yahoo.com/ Business_and_Economy/Directories/Companies/**), shown in Figure 3.22.

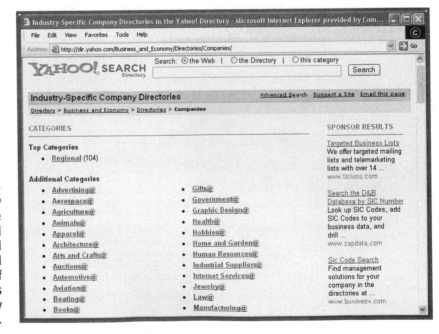

Figure 3.22

Yahoo! is the place to go to find additional directories. You'll find listings of specialty directories organized by category.

Before you go on to the next part in this section, look for additional directories that relate to topics or industries discussed at your site. Rather than try to submit your site in dozens of categories, focus on the top three. After you've identified these categories, submit your site to the best directories related to them.

Take a Break

Now that you've raced through most of Saturday afternoon, it is time to take a break. Crank up the radio. Grab an ice-cold drink and get something to eat. When you return, you'll learn how to hook up with a number of different specialty directories, including What's New? directories and Cool Site of the Day guides.

Children's Directories: Getting Noticed by One of the Web's Biggest Audiences

The Internet is as popular with young people as it is with adults. If your Web site in any way caters to children, then you ought to take advantage of the major kids' directories. These directories are different from other Web directories in that their content is filtered to weed out potentially objectionable sites. Their primary focus is to provide kids with a safe but still fun and interesting experience.

Unlike search engines, which provide tools that parents can use to attempt to block out objectionable material, kids' directories are much safer places. One of the best known of the kids' directories is Yahooligans (**www.yahooligans.com**), as shown in Figure 3.23.

Just like the regular Yahoo! directory, Yahooligans organizes everything into major high-level categories which kids can drill down into to find Web sites with specific information. You can submit your Web site to Yahooligans by clicking on the Suggest a Site link located at the bottom of the main page. You'll be asked to pick a category and then to supply a title, URL, and a 25 or less word description of your Web site.

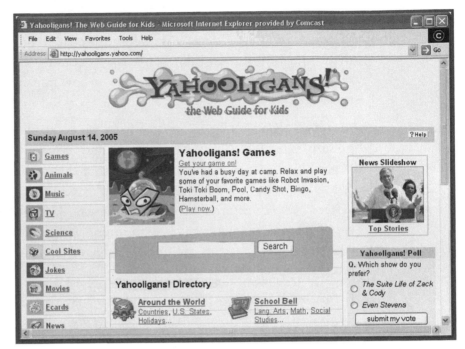

Figure 3.23

Yahooligans is one of the oldest and best run kids' directories and is primarily designed for children between ages 7 and 12.

There are a number of other online directories dedicated exclusively to kids that you might want to investigate further. These sites include

- ☼ **Ask Jeeves For Kids—www.ajkids.com**
- ☼ **KidsClick!—www.kidsclick.org**
- ☼ **Dibdabdoo—www.dibdabdoo.com**

Getting More Mileage out of What's New? Directories

Announcement sites are an effort to capture the euphoria surrounding the exponential growth of the Web, and simultaneously tap into the usual excitement over things that are new and fresh. One of the first What's New? directories was maintained by NCSA (National Center for Supercomputing Applications)—the same folks who gave the world the Mosaic browser. At its peak, the list received thousands of submissions for new Web sites every day. Today, it is no longer updated, but NCSA maintains the list for its historical value. After all, by reading the list archives, you can roll back time and truly get a sense of how fast the Web grew in the early days.

Although NCSA no longer updates its What's New? list, many other sites publish extensive What's New? directories. When you visit the major What's New? directories, you will find that these Web sites are tremendously popular. This popularity will help drive visitors to your Web site. What's New? directories are organized much like other directories, with specific broad categories such as business and entertainment. Listings within a specific category are usually arranged alphabetically by title and often chronologically as well.

By nature, What's New? lists are guides to new sites. Still, if you've never submitted your site to a specific list before, your site is new to the list and therefore you can certainly submit a listing.

When you register with What's New? directories, you will generally see short-term increases in your Web traffic. The reason for this is that your site usually will be featured in the What's New? directory for only one or two days. Afterward, your listing will appear only in the site's archive files—provided that the site has archive files. If you are interested in short-term increases in Web traffic, What's New? directories are definitely for you. Considering that people often bookmark sites they like, a listing in a What's New? directory can provide a modest increase in traffic over the long haul as well.

Exploring the Starting Point Directory

Starting Point (**www.stpt.com**) is a directory service that has reinvented itself several times over the years. Whereas Starting Point once strove to become a major directory a la Yahoo!, the service now focuses on providing a guide to the best Web sites. Despite the change of focus, Starting Point still maintains one of the top guides to new sites. The Starting Point

What's New? list is organized into 13 categories that range from business to Health and Fitness.

Within each category, listings are organized chronologically, with the most recent listings displayed first. Because Starting Point receives so many submissions, the directory displays only the most recent listings.

Each listing has a page title and a summary description (see Figure 3.24). To get the most out of your listing, be sure to select a category that fits your Web site. You should also provide a descriptive title and a clear summary for the listing.

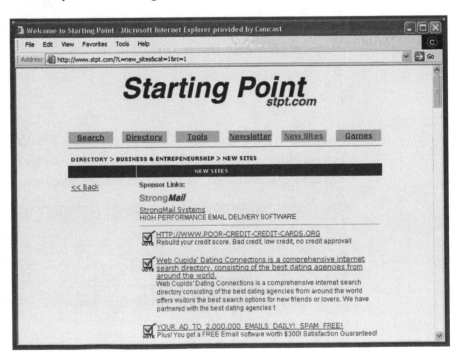

Figure 3.24

Your listing should provide a descriptive title and a clear summary for the listing.

You can submit your site to Starting Point by clicking on the New Sites link located in the New Sites area. When you examine the Starting Point submission form, the first thing that you might notice is that the site requests a great deal of information. Most of this information isn't used in the directory. So, you may want to only enter the mandatory information.

Finding Out What's New at NerdWorld

NerdWorld (**www.nerdworld.com**) is a Web site that has been around for a long time. Despite its name, NerdWorld is really for everyone. It provides insights to the latest and greatest gadgets and computer hardware. NerdWorld also maintains an extensive search engine and a list of what it considers to be the top 50 coolest and most interesting Web sites on the Internet.

NerdWorld also places a lot of emphasis on communications. Its services include

○ Chat bulletin boards

○ Shared surveys

○ News submissions

○ Nerd dating

NerdWorld also maintains one of the best What's New? lists (**www. nerdworld.com/whatsnew.html**) on the Web (see Figure 3.25). Here visitors can find out about the newest Web sites on the Internet.

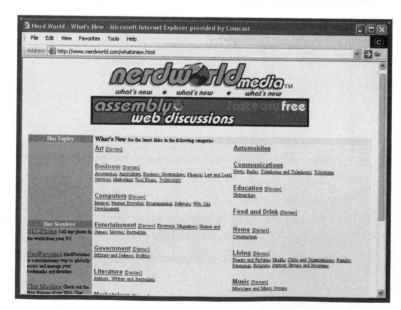

Figure 3.25

NerdWorld maintains a What's New? list organized into different topic categories.

In order to get listed in NerdWorld's What's New? listing, you must first register with NerdWorld and create a user account. Go ahead, it is free. Once you have created and activated your new account, you can click on the Web Links link on the main page to go to the Web Links page where you can submit a listing for your Web site by clicking on Add Link. You'll need to supply a title and your URL and then select a category and description. Next, type in your e-mail address and click on the Add this URL button.

Other What's New? Directories

Finding the new and the interesting is what announcement directories are all about. Two additional What's New? directories for you to consider submitting your Web site to are NewWebListings.com and Yahoo!'s What's New? area.

NewWebListings (**www.newweblistings.com**), shown in Figure 3.26, only lists new Web sites that most likely haven't made their way into the major search engine listings yet. What's nice about this site is that your Web site may be kept in the listing for a few months before it is removed, giving your Web site additional exposure while you wait for the major search engines to list your Web site. You can register with NewWebListings at **www.newweblistings.com/newweblistings/submit.asp**.

Yahoo!'s What's New? area (**dir.yahoo.com/new**) lists new Web sites that are added to Yahoo!'s directory. Listings are organized into groups. To submit your Web site, click on the Suggest a Site link at the top of the page. To see if your site has been listed in the What's New? area, drill down into the category for which you submitted your Web site. If it is not there yet, come back later. Yahoo! always has a backlog of submissions.

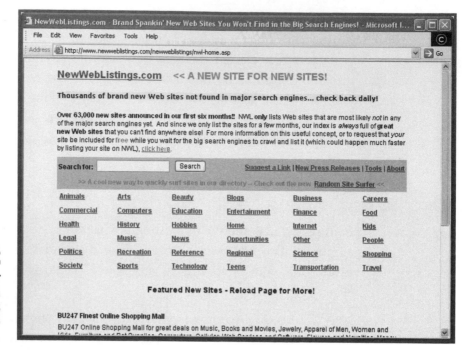

Figure 3.26

Register your Web site with NewWebListings and get your Web site noticed fast.

Getting Your Site Listed as the Cool Site of the Day

One of the most famous awards on the Web is the Cool Site of the Day award. Getting named the Cool Site of the Day is an accomplishment that gets your Web site noticed. But the Cool Site of the Day award is only the icing on the cake as far as awards go. There are dozens of other awards that range from the fleeting to the everlasting. Making sense of all these awards and finding the ones that truly make a difference is what this section is all about.

Nothing makes your Web site stand out from the crowd like an award. Awards are stamps of approval that tell the masses your site is worth their time. Not just any old award will do, though. The Web has more than a thousand different types of site awards. These awards range from somebody's individual Web site's Cool Site of the Day award to the Web 500 Best of the Web. Bunches of small awards might do wonders for your ego but the actual awards themselves may do very little for your Web site's traffic. On the other hand, an award like the Web 500 Best of the Web can dramatically increase traffic to your Web site.

Wandering in the Maze of Web Awards

Awards can work miracles when it comes to building traffic to your Web site, but they can also be mere self-serving trophies that you place in a glass case to brag about your achievements. The simple truth is that displaying your awards prominently doesn't build traffic to your Web site, no matter what the sites granting the awards want you to think.

TIP When your Web site wins an award, you are usually required to display an icon representing the award somewhere on your Web site. This icon contains a link to the Web site that granted you the award. You might want to consider placing the icon for the award somewhere other than your main Web page because the icon is, after all, a link away from your Web site. If your Web site wins multiple awards, why not create an awards page?

The number of awards doesn't matter, either. You could have hundreds of small awards and it wouldn't make much of a difference as far as your Web site's traffic is concerned. The reality is that these days it seems everyone is offering a Web award of some type or another. There are dozens of variations of Cool Site of the Day awards. These awards are for Cool Site of the Moment, Cool Site of the Hour, Cool Site of the Week, Cool Site of the Month, and Cool Site of the Year as well. Beyond the cool site awards, there are the Hot Site of the Day, Hour, Week, Month, and Year awards. Next comes the Crazy Site of the Day, Hour, Week, Month, and Year awards. There are so many awards that Web neophytes have started offering backward awards such as the Mediocre Site of the Day, Ugly Site of the Day, and the Bottom 95 percent of the Web.

NOTE Another way to get your Web site noticed is to create your own award. That way, the more sites that you give your award to the more links there will be pointing back to your Web site and the higher your Web site's ranking will become. However, creating and managing an awards site is a lot of work. You have to come up with formal criteria for judging Web sites and add supporting Web pages to your Web site to manage the award process. In addition, you have to be prepared to handle all of the entries that you may receive. In the event that the entries don't measure up, you may need to be prepared to set aside time to go surfing and looking for sites that you can offer the award to.

If displaying your awards or the number of awards doesn't matter, you are probably wondering what does matter. Well, the true equalizers are the underlying meaning of the award and the strength of the award giver's announcement medium. When an organization such as PC Magazine recognizes your Web site as one of the Top 100 of the year, you can expect your traffic to skyrocket. Again, the reason for this isn't so much the award itself as the significance of the award and the channels through which it is announced.

PC Magazine is well respected in the industry. The Top 100 of the Year award is bestowed upon sites only after thorough research and extensive review. The list of recipients of the Top 100 is published in PC Magazine, which has several million readers. After publishing the list in its print edition, PC Magazine publishes the list in its online edition (see Figure 3.27), where it is available to the Web community throughout the year. The longevity of the print edition coupled with the continued traffic to PC Magazine's Web site and Top 100 list itself are what drives traffic to the Web sites of the recipients.

Finding the Right Award

The right award can make all the difference in the world when it comes to increasing traffic to your Web site. To find the right award, you really need to visit the home of the organization or person granting the award.

Figure 3.27

PC Magazine Top 100 award can place your Web site in front of millions of potential visitors.

When you get to the Web site, spend some time reviewing the site and the techniques used to display awards.

Ideally, current awards are showcased at the site for at least a day and then later put into an archive that can be searched. Because the popularity of the award site is also important, you should try to gauge the level of traffic at the Web site. The busier the award site, the better the chances that it will increase traffic to your Web site.

All this talk of finding the right award might seem strange. After all, these sites are giving away an award! Unfortunately, with more than a thousand different organizations offering awards of one type or another, you really do need to make sure the award is meaningful and worthwhile before you take the time to submit your Web site. Fortunately, you don't have to look too far; this section already identifies some of the best awards sites.

Submitting Your Site

Receiving an award depends largely upon the personal tastes of the reviewer and the philosophy of the award site as a whole. Some award sites look for truly cool sites based on graphic design or coverage of zany issues. Other award sites look for great resources, with no consideration going to whether the site uses mostly text or a cutting-edge graphic design. Because personal opinion weighs heavily in the decision, truly great sites are sometimes passed by.

To improve your odds of being selected, take the time to get to know the types of sites that the reviewers prefer. If they review mostly entertainment sites and you have a business-oriented site, the odds are high that you will get passed by. So rather than submit the URL of your main business page, submit the URL for that fun area where you let customers interact with your products online, or highlight this area in the summary description you supply with the submission.

You can also improve your odds of winning by submitting each of the key areas within your Web site separately. If your site has three different areas, you might submit each of these areas. Ideally, these areas would cover unrelated topics, such as sports memorabilia, music singles from the '50s, and multi-media CD-ROMs for the Mac. In this way, you are truly submitting something different.

The adage, "If at first you don't succeed, try, try again," certainly applies to awards. Don't abuse the submission process by submitting your site every few days or weeks, though. Instead, wait a few months before submitting your site again. In the interim, you might also want to work on the design, flow, and content of your Web site.

Cool Site of the Day

Cool Site of the Day is one of the most popular awards. To help you make sense of the many offerings, you will find the top Cool Site of the Day awards in this section. These sites are the best of the best when it comes to the Cool Site of the Day award because they follow guidelines for a good award, discussed previously. For the most part, the awards are showcased for at least a day. Then, because they are archived, the awards can continue to generate traffic to your site over the long haul. The sites are also popular, which will help to improve your chances of increasing your Web traffic.

One of the best Cool Site of the Day awards is the original Cool Site of the Day award at **www.coolsiteoftheday.com**. Along with the Cool Site of the Day award, this site has many other features that make the site a great destination (see Figure 3.28). All sites that receive the Cool Site of the Day award are showcased on the day of the award. Afterward, they move the reference to the Web site to an archive featuring all past awards.

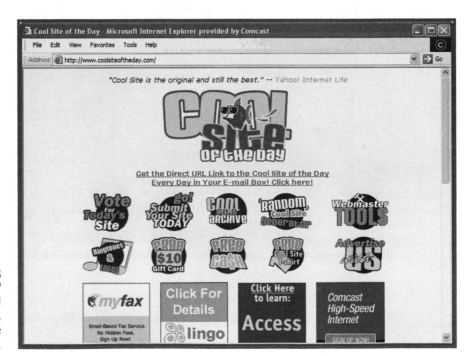

Figure 3.28

If you are looking to get noticed, Cool Site of the Day can help.

You can submit your Web site by clicking on the "Go! Submit your site today" icon at the top of the site's main page.

Another Cool Site of the Day award that you may want to try for is Cool-Stop's daily Cool pick (**www.coolstop.com**), shown in Figure 3.29. CoolStop features a daily selection of the best non-commercial Web sites. CoolStop looks for:

✪ Honest personal expression

✪ Excellence in Web design

✪ Original creative content

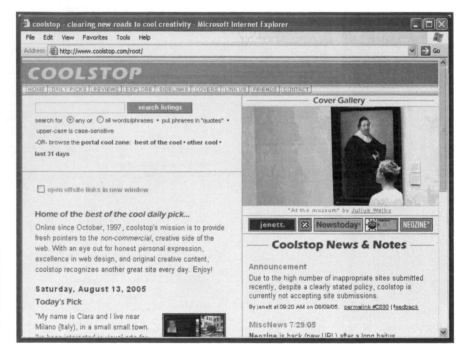

Figure 3.29

CoolStop provides links to the best non-commercial Web sites on the Web.

In addition to the current day's Cool pick, visitors to CoolStop can search the archives or browse any of the following categories:

✪ Portal cool zone

✪ Best of the cool

✪ Other cool

✪ Last 31 days

To submit your Web site to CoolStop, click on the Submit link located on the main page.

Still another popular and respected Cool site is CoolPick (**www.coolpick. com**). CoolPick selects a new cool site every day, as shown in Figure 3.30. The site also allows visitors to go back a full week to look at previous cool pick of the day selections. In addition, CoolPick provides access to its historical archive, going back to 1999. You can also search the archive using a keyword search. As of the writing of the Fourth Edition of this book, CoolPick was not accepting online Web site submissions. However, keep checking. Hopefully by the time this book is published, CoolPick will be accepting online submissions again.

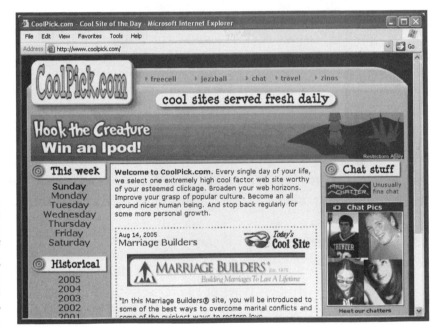

Figure 3.30

CoolPick displays a brief description of its daily cool pick and includes a link to the selected site's main Web page.

In addition to Cool Site of the Day, CoolStop, and CoolPick, there are a number of other Web sites that focus on picking cool Web sites that fit within with the particular scope of the award Web site. Once such example is AskMen (**www.askmen.com/cool_site/current**), as shown in Figure 3.31.

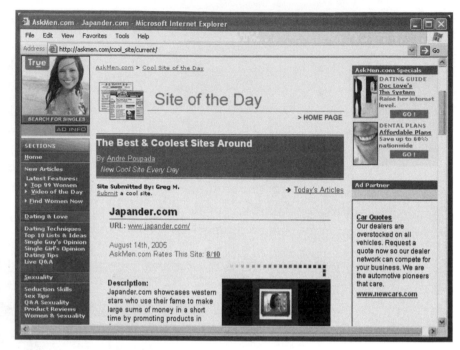

Figure 3.31

AskMen selects a
cool site of the day
that it thinks its
target audience
will appreciate.

At AskMen you will find a new Web site highlighted each day that is of interest to its patrons. If you think that your Web site fits in with the content of AskMen, you can submit your Web site as a cool site candidate by clicking on the Submit a Cool Site link on **www.askmen.com/cool_site/current/**.

Wild, Hot, and Zany Awards

Take a walk on the wild side with the wild, hot, and zany site awards. Although these types of awards are offshoots of the original Cool Site of the Day concept, this category has several terrific award sites.

One such Web site is HotSpots Today (**www.browsertune.com/flanga/ hotspots.htm**), as shown in Figure 3.32. HotSpots Today publishes a list of HotSpots with a new HotSpot added every day. This Web site gets a lot of visitors every day, making the HotSpot award something that will definitely increase traffic to your Web site.

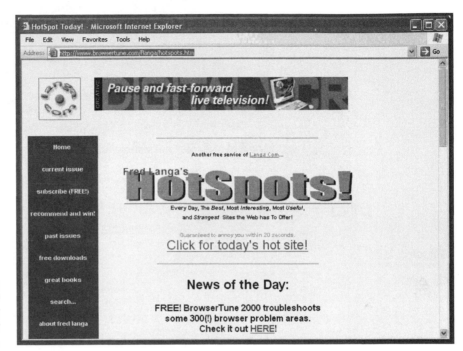

Figure 3.32

HotSpots Today
publishes a daily
HotSpot selection.

You can get your Web site listed here by participating in a link exchange program (**www.langa.com/code.htm**).

USA Today's Hot Sites (**www.usatoday.com/tech/webguide/front.htm**), featured in Figure 3.33, is an award for new and notable Web sites. New sites are featured each weekday with an expanded weekend edition featuring multiple sites. Submit your site by sending an e-mail to **cyber@usatoday. com**.

Another great award site is the Yahoo! Picks page (**docs.yahoo.com/picks**). The Yahoo! Picks page, shown in Figure 3.34, is a daily list of cool sites. Daily picks are listed by title with a description and picture of the daily cool Web site.

You can submit a page to Yahoo!'s Picks page by completing the Suggest a Site form at **add.yahoo.com/fast/help/us/picks/cgi_feedback**.

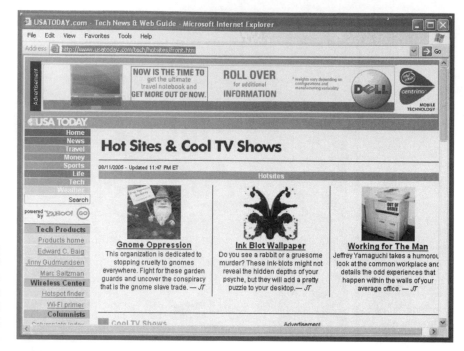

Figure 3.33

Submit your site to USA Today and see if you can get listed as the hot site of the day.

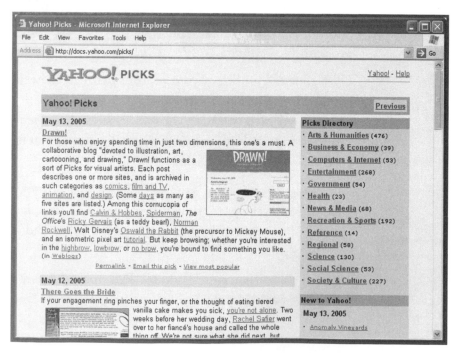

Figure 3.34

Yahoo! offers daily and weekly awards for cool sites.

Best of the Web

Truly great sites are designated as the best of the Web. Many Web guides offer insights into the best sites on the Web. Three in particular are worth taking a look at. These three are NerdWorld, World Best Websites, and the Webby Awards.

NerdWorld's Nifty-Fifty

Despite its name, NerdWorld (**www.nerdworld.com**) is in fact one of the coolest Web sites on the Internet. NerdWorld maintains a listing of what it considers to be the 50 coolest, most interesting, thought provoking, unusual, and most functional Web sites on the Internet. NerdWorld calls this list the Nifty-Fifty. You'll find this list published at **www.nerdworld. com/ww_nifty_fifty.html**, as shown in Figure 3.35. Getting listed in the Nifty-Fifty will go a long way towards driving Web traffic to your Web site.

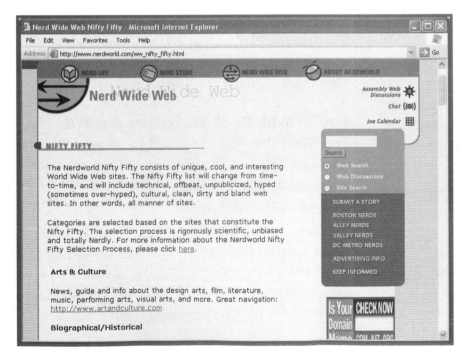

Figure 3.35

The Nifty-Fifty list brings a lot of attention and Web traffic to Web sites that make the list.

The Nifty-Fifty list consists of many different types of Web sites. There is no particular category of Web sites that is preferred. You will find Web sites that are cultural, technology oriented, or downright crazy. Web sites are added and removed from the list at the discretion of NerdWorld's Advisory Board, which usually gets together to make changes on a monthly basis. The Advisory Board's decisions are based on the following criteria.

1. Does the site add something unique, or interesting, or cool to the
   - Web?
   - lives of Web users?
   - nerd community?

2. Does the site use interesting navigation, technology, features, or presentation characteristics? Does the site work as described?

If you think, based on this criteria and what you've seen of the other Web sites on the list, that your Web sites is good enough to be one of the Nifty-Fifty, then you can submit your Web site for consideration by sending an email to **support@nerdworld.com**. Be sure that you include a brief description of your Web site along with its URL.

The World Best Websites Award

The World Best Websites award (**www.worldbestwebsites.com**) is presented to Web sites that implement "best practices" in their design and communications. Particular emphasis is placed on Web sites that are on the leading edge of design and technology. See Figure 3.36.

Sites that are submitted as candidates compete for a number of different awards starting with Merit, and then advancing to Bronze, Silver, and Gold. Once nominated, a Web site is visited repeatedly over a 12-week period. Web sites are judged on a 100-point scoring system based on the following five (equally weighted) major categories.

- Functionality
- Design

- Content

- Originality

- Professionalism and Effectiveness

Winners of the Gold award are eligible to enter an even more strenuous "Level Two" award contest. The criteria used in evaluating Web sites for this award includes:

- Significance

- Exemplary innovation

- Quality standards

- Site performance analysis

- Search engine visibility

- Search engine rankings

- URL clarity

- Differentiation and branding strategy

- Business analysis

- Server security checks

- Hosting efficiency

- Surfer votes and customer endorsements

To submit your Web site as a candidate for the World Best Website award, you can send an email to **webcoms04@worldbest.net** that includes:

- Your name

- Your e-mail address

- Your Web site's title

- Your Web site's URL

- A brief description of your Web site

Alternatively, you can submit your Web site by filling out the form found at **www.worldbest.com/submit.htm**, as shown in Figure 3.37.

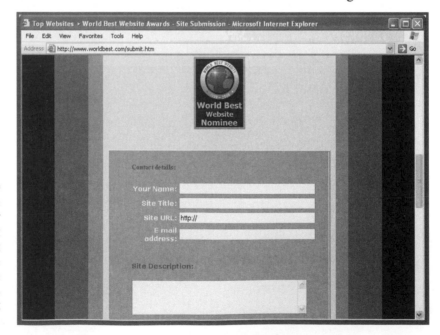

Figure 3.37

If your Web site doesn't garner an award the first time you submit it, take some time to make improvements and then submit it again.

The Webby Awards

Perhaps the most prestigious award any Web site publisher can get is a Webby Award (**www.webbyawards.com**), as shown in Figure 3.38. This award is to be taken very seriously. It is awarded to the best Web site in 60 different categories and operates very much like the Academy Awards, including a once a year gala celebration event.

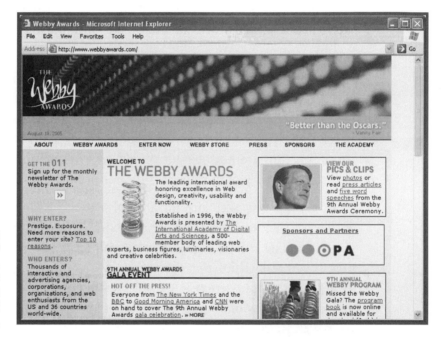

Figure 3.38

Without a doubt, the Webby Awards are among the Web's most prestigious honors.

The Webby Awards are presented by the International Academy of Digital Arts and Sciences in order to honor Web sites that excel in design, functionality, usability, and creativity. Five Web sites are selected for each category judged by the academy. The following six criteria are used in making Web site selections.

- Content
- Structure and navigation
- Visual design
- Functionality

○   Interactivity

○   Overall experience

Candidate Web sites are eligible to win two honors. One is the Webby Award, which is judged by the Academy of Digital Arts and Sciences. The other award is called the People's Award and it is judged by popular vote. In addition, starting in 2005 the Academy will begin designating some Web sites that don't win an award but still show excellence as being Webby Worthy.

The Webby Awards is an annual event. There is a nomination period, followed by an evaluation period. To nominate your Web site for a Webby award or to find out when the nomination period opens up, click on the Enter Your Web Site link at the bottom of the Webby Awards main page. If nominations are not being accepted yet, you will be presented with a form that allows you to sign up for a notification message.

Nominating your Web site for a Webby award is not cheap. As of the writing of the Fourth Edition of this book, the entry fee for a Web site was $195. The entry fee goes down if you want to enter additional Web sites. If you really think that your Web site is good enough to win a Webby Award, you should seriously consider taking a chance and submit your Web site. If you win, or even if you garner a "Webby Worthy" designation, your Web traffic could skyrocket.

Wrapping Up and Looking Ahead

If you offer products, services, or business information at your Web site, you should definitely list your site with business search sites and directories. Business search engines and Yellow Pages offer unique places to get your business and your business-oriented Web site noticed. After submitting your site to these search engines, you should go on to submit your site to search engines and directories that focus on specific industries. These guides can also help your Web site stand out from the crowd, especially when you consider that the major category guides attract millions of visitors, yet have considerably fewer listings than mainstream directories such as Yahoo!.

Finally, don't forget about kids' directories and award sites. Kids represent a significant segment of the Internet community. Thousands of organizations are offering Web awards. Web awards range from daily awards, such as the Cool Site of the Day award, to yearly awards, such as PC Magazine's Top 100.

Now, put this book down and relax a bit. First thing tomorrow morning you'll learn how to submit your site to many search engines and directories simultaneously. As always, the focus will be on using resources that are low-cost or free.

Attracting the Masses

➤ Selling Your Web Site through E-mail

➤ Attracting the Masses with Giveaways, Contests, Sweepstakes, and More

➤ Free Banner Advertising

Many companies offer services that allow you to register with multiple search engines and directories. These so-called registration services are great if you want to quickly spread the word about many different Web page URLs. You'll spend this morning learning about these and other valuable means of promoting your Web site.

Registering with Many Search Engines and Directories Simultaneously

Like search engines and directories, registration services have different submission processes. This session covers registration services: how they operate, what to watch out for, and how to use these services without paying a dime.

Introducing Web Registration Services

Registration services are one of the most innovative types of Web services to come along. The idea is that instead of having to register with search engines and directories one by one, you can use the registration service to register with many different search engines and directories at once. Although one central interface for registering your Web site is wonderful, you still sometimes have to go through a rather lengthy submission process.

While registration services can certainly be helpful, it's best if you go through each search engine or directory site's submission process yourself. When you work hands-on with a search engine or directory site, you get a clear idea of how the site works. When you work with a registration service, you rely on the service to take advantage of how a site works—which doesn't always happen.

Using Registration Services

The registration process usually starts with you entering information into a form. This information may include all the elements you would normally enter into the submission form of a search engine or directory, such as the page title, page description, and personal contact information. Next, you select the search engines and directories to which you want to submit your site. Afterward, you begin the submission process, which often involves having to register each site separately by clicking on individual submission buttons that will send your information to a specific search engine or directory.

Because most search engines and directories use unique categories or require you to fill out other information, you usually enter this additional information during the submission process. For example, before you can submit your page to the Yahoo! Web directory, you need to select a category.

All these intermediate stops along the road mean that the registration process isn't always as easy as the registration services would like for you to believe. Still, the process is an improvement over manual submission if you are in a rush.

Working with Registration Services

Like any service-oriented business, registration services are for-profit enterprises. You can't blame these services for trying to make a buck off their hard work. The cost of registering your site can jump to hundreds of dollars, however, and most registration services base their charges on the number of URLs that you want to register and the number of places to which you submit your URLs. For example, a registration service might charge $30 to submit a single URL to 50 search engines, $60 to submit two URLs to 50 search engines, or $100 to submit one URL to 150 search engines.

Although these rates were much higher in the past, the influx of new registration services is forcing the market to be competitive, resulting in wholesale pricing and better registration engines. But before you shell out your hard-earned cash or corporate money, you should know what you are buying. The first thing you might notice when you examine the resources provided by a registration service is that you've probably never heard of most of these sites. Some of the sites are small and receive very little Web traffic at all. Worse, you might find that some of the sites don't even function.

Additionally, you should note that resource sites are frequently for restricted types of search engines and directories. You will find Yellow Pages directories that take only business listings. You will find directories for Web sites covering specific geographic areas such as Canada, Europe, or Asia. You will also find specialty directories, such as What's New? directories, award sites, and guides to the best of the Web.

In the end, whether you can register with 50 or 500 search engines doesn't really matter. What matters is the number of search engines that you can use out of those available. Fortunately, the best sites are usually those included in the first 50. Because of this you get more bang for you buck if you stick to the basics—and the free services covered in this chapter are the ultimate in getting your money's worth.

The most important thing to consider when you use registration services is the type of site with which you are registering. As you learned in previous chapters, there is a huge difference between a search engine and a Web directory.

Search engines use the URL that you specify to crawl through your entire site and will usually schedule your site for periodic reindexing. Because search engines reindex your site, you only need to register with a search engine once. And because search engines crawl through your entire site, you only need to register the URL to your top-level home page. That said, it is still a good idea to register your Web site with search engines once every six months. This protects your site from being dropped or not being reindexed automatically.

On the other hand, Web directories create a listing only for the page you specify, and they rarely update the listing. Because Web directories focus on pages rather than entire sites, you can register multiple URLs for the same site. The URLs that you submit should be for separate areas that cover different topics.

Because Web directories rarely update listings, you are responsible for updating your listing in the directory if you move the furniture around at your Web site, which doesn't necessarily mean that you should reregister with the directory. Instead, you should check the directory to see whether it has an update or change process. To make life easier on yourself and to avoid having to submit changes for your listings, you can use the redirection techniques discussed in the Sunday Afternoon session under "Gaining Lost Readers from the Error Logs."

NOTE While this chapter focuses on providing you with a list of online registration services, there are also a number of software products that you can purchase and install on your computer in order to set up your own registration process. However, unlike the free services listed in this chapter, these software products will cost you a few dollars. If you are interested in learning more about these software products, check out Appendix A, "Additional Resources on the Web."

In the end, if you use a registration service, don't waste your time reregistering with search engines and directories you've already signed up with. Concentrate on the search engines and directories with which you haven't registered.

1 2 3 Add Masters

Main Page: http://www.123-add-masters.com

Sites: Submits to over 30 search engines for free. A fee-based option is available for submission to over 1,550 search engines, directories, and link sites.

Details: Start by filling out a detailed form describing your Web site and business. After you submit the form, you then submit to each individual search engine. The step-by-step process allows you to select categories and add information needed by each search engine. Unlike some submission services, this site does not include the ability to submit keywords.

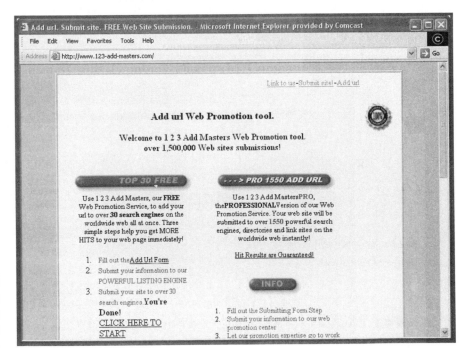

Figure 4.1

1 2 3 Add Masters submits your site to the top 30 search engines for free.

Add Me!

Main Page: http://www.addme.com

Sites: Submits to 14 search engines and directories for free. The submission process takes 5 to 10 minutes. Your information is saved for resubmission.

Details: Before you can submit your site using Add Me! (shown in Figure 4.2), you need to fill out the listing information. Rather than put all the entries on a single page, Add Me! breaks down the submission process into a series of pages that allow you to register with one or more sites. In exchange for using its submission services, Add Me! requests that you add a link to it on your Web site by cutting and pasting a supplied piece of HTML code. Ask Me! also offers a fee-based submission option that will submit your Web site to hundreds of search engines and directories.

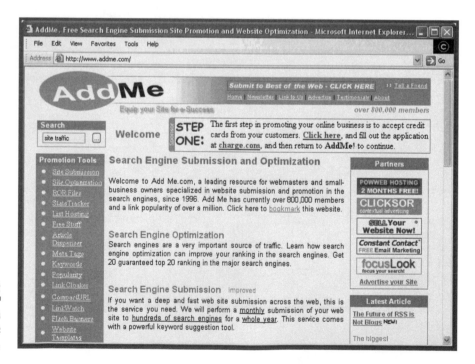

Figure 4.2

Add Me! is a comprehensive registration service.

@Submit!

Main Page: http://www.uswebsites.com/submit

Sites: Submits to 6 search engines and directories.

Details: Enter the main URL for your site and your e-mail address and then submit your information. Within a few minutes, you will receive a confirmation e-mail. Note that other than your URL and e-mail address, you are not asked for any other information, such as a description of your Web site or your Web site's keywords. Make sure your Web site is search-engine friendly before you submit it. In exchange for using this submission service, you are asked to add a link to **www.uswebsites.com** by copying and pasting a supplied piece of HTML code into one of your Web pages.

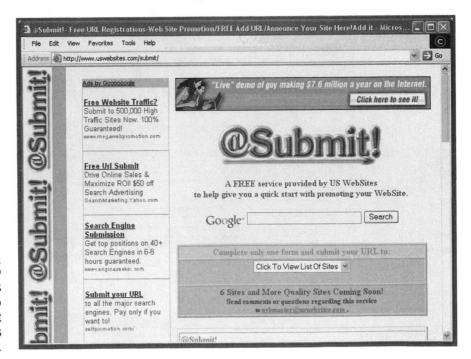

Figure 4.3

@Submit! provides free submission to many different search engines and directories.

Easy Submit

Main Page: http://www.scrubtheweb.com/abs/submit

Sites: Submits to 10 search engines.

Details: The registration process is broken into three steps. Non-members can use Easy Submit to register with 10 preselected search engines. People who sign up for a paid membership can submit to many more search engines.

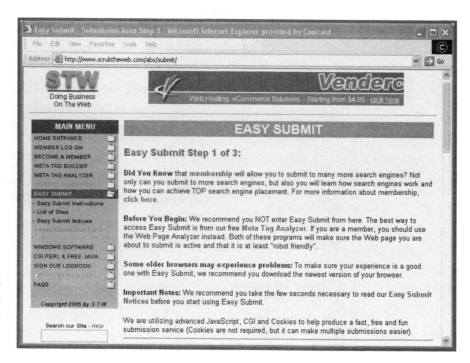

Figure 4.4

Easy Submit provides a simple and straightforward submission process.

Metanet

Main Page: http://metanetpromotions.com

Sites: Submits to over 300 search engines, directories, and What's New? pages.

Details: In order to use this submission service, you must first place either a text or graphic link back to Metanet on your Web site. In exchange, Metanet will register your Web site with over 300 search sites and will resubmit your Web site every month, provided it continues to find its link on your main Web page. Once you have added the required link, you begin by entering your URL and e-mail address. Next, you'll be prompted to supply a whole range of information about your Web site. Once entered, you can go ahead and submit your Web site.

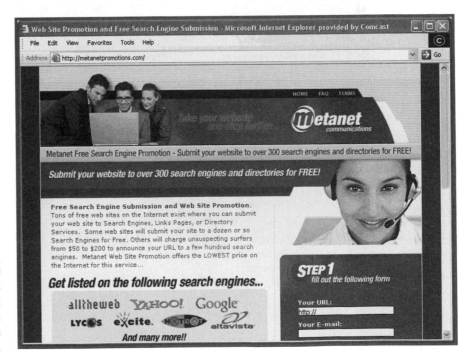

Figure 4.5

Metanet provides automated registration with over 300 search engines.

Submit It

Main Page: http://www.submitit.co.uk

Sites: Submits your Web site to 18 search engines.

Details: You begin by providing the information shown in Figure 4.6. You are then presented with a list of search engines from which you must select and submit to one-by-one after supplying any additional search engine specific information. If you prefer, you can select from numerous fee-based submission options to submit your Web site to hundreds of additional search engines and directories.

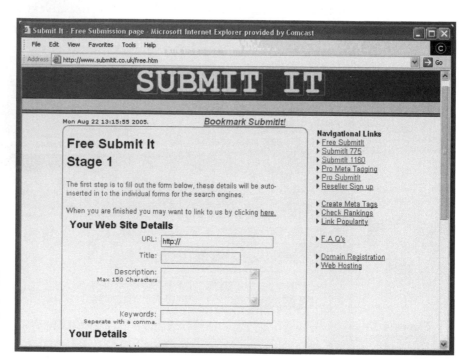

Figure 4.6

Use Submit It to submit to 18 leading search engines.

Submit It! Free

Main Page: http://www.siteowner.com/sifree.cfm

Sites: Submits to Google, Lycos, HotBot, and WebCrawler.

Details: If you are in a hurry and just want to register with a handful of popular search sites quickly, visit Submit It! Free and enter your URL and e-mail address and you are done. This submission service doesn't collect any additional information, so before you use it, make sure that your Web site is search-engine friendly.

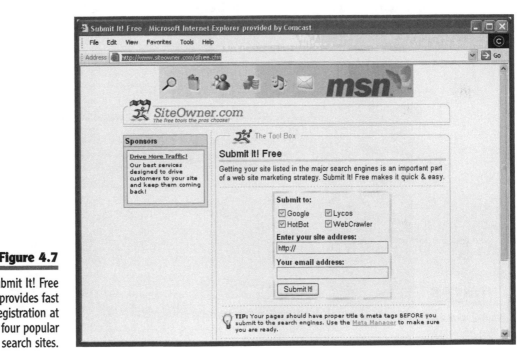

Figure 4.7

Submit It! Free provides fast registration at four popular search sites.

Submit Express

Main Page: http://www.submitexpress.com

Sites: Submits to 40 search engines. The entire submission process only takes 1-2 minutes.

Details: Submit Express provides one of the fastest ways to submit your site to search engines. Enter your URL and e-mail address, then click on Submit. That's all there is to it. A small report is then displayed at the bottom of the submission page showing the results of each submission attempt. In exchange for this free service, you are asked to add a link to Submit Express on your Web site using HTML code that is provided to you.

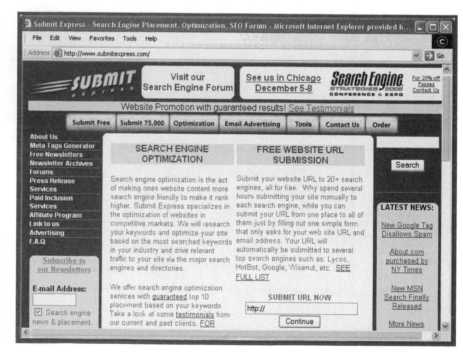

Figure 4.8

Submit Express is fast and easy, but you can't add detailed information about your Web site.

Checking on Your Listings

Once you have finished submitting your Web site to the search engines on your list, you are going to want to keep tabs on how each search engine is managing its links to your Web pages. You'll want to know when your Web site is listed and if anyone is linking to it. This way, if something goes wrong and a particular search engine doesn't add you Web pages to its database within 4-6 weeks you'll know about it and can resubmit your Web site again.

 NOTE If your Web site doesn't get listed in a particular search engine's database, it may be the result of a simple oversight. Or it could be that you mistyped your URL during the submission process and the search engine couldn't find your Web site. However, it could also be that the search engine found something objectionable at your Web site. Before resubmitting, review your Web pages and make sure that you haven't added any content that might be interpreted as spam.

Determining Whether Your Web Site Has Been Listed

There are a number of ways that you can go about checking on the status of your Web pages at various search engines. At a minimum you will want to keep tabs on things at Google and Yahoo!, since they are the two most popular search engines. It might also be worthwhile to check on MSN, since it is growing so quickly every day.

Perhaps the most simple and obvious option is to visit each search engine and enter the URL of your Web site's main page and any other Web pages that you wish to check on. You can also use this option to find out if any of your competitors are listed in a given search engine's database. For example, to see if the MSN search engine has listed any Web pages for **www.tvpress.com**, you would do a search as shown in Figure 4.9.

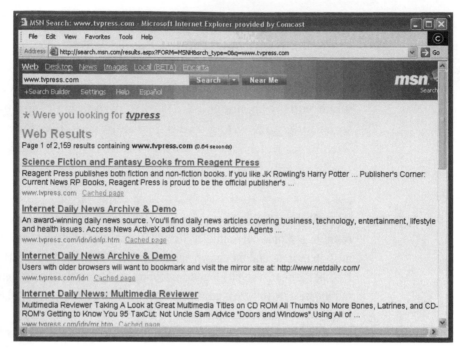

Figure 4.9

Figure 4.9

Checking to see if
the MSN search
engine has added
pages from
www.tvpress.com
to its database.

NOTE If only your URL is listed in the search engine's output results, then the search engine
has most likely added an entry for your Web site to its index, but hasn't crawled your
Web site yet. In this case, be patient but keep checking.

Finding Out Which of Your Web Pages Are Listed

Once you know that your Web site has been added to a search engine's
database, you'll want to check and see which of your pages have been
indexed. You can do this by using your browser to open the search engine's
Web page and entering the `site:` command.

As Figure 4.10 demonstrates, you execute the `site:` command by keying
it into the search engine's search field. Take note that there is no blank
space between the `site:` command and the specified URL.

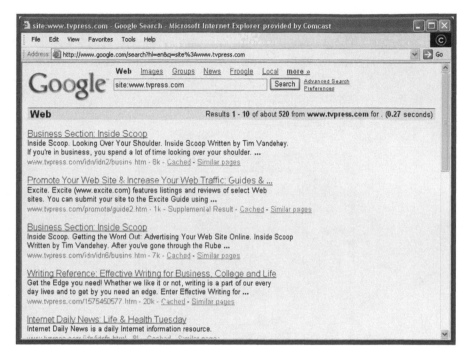

Figure 4.10

Use the `site:` command to determine which of your Web pages have been added to a search engine's index.

Google, Yahoo!, and MSN all support the `site:` command. Other search engines may support this command or provide a different command to produce the same results. You can usually find out specific information regarding the search commands for a given search engine by consulting the search engine's Help area.

After verifying that your Web site is listed in each of the big three search engines, and checking to see which of your Web pages were added to each search engine's database, it is a good idea to check and see if anybody else's Web pages have links to your Web site. After all, the number of good links to your Web pages has a lot to do with how close your Web pages come to making the top 10 search results. Hopefully, you will find that the number of links will grow over time. Otherwise, you may want to investigate different ways of improving the situation such as by singing up with a link exchange service, as discussed later this morning.

To check on links to your Web site using Google and MSN, you can use the `link:` command. For example, to check on the number of links to **www.tvpress.com**, you would enter **link:www.tvpress.com** into either search engine's search field. Yahoo!'s search engine provides access to this same information using the `linkdomain:` command, as demonstrated in Figure 4.11.

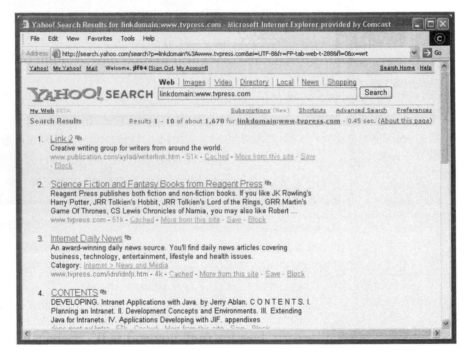

Figure 4.11

Researching the number of links from other Web pages to your Web site.

In addition to directly querying specific searches regarding the link popularity of your Web site, there are a number of Web sites that provide free link checking. For example, at MarketLeap (**www.marketleap.com**) you can submit your URL and the URLs of up to three comparison Web sites (**www.marketleap.com/publinkpop**) and generate a report showing who has links to your Web site. As Figure 4.12 shows, results are retrieved from Google, Yahoo!, and MSN as well as from AOL, HotBot, FAST, and AltaVista.

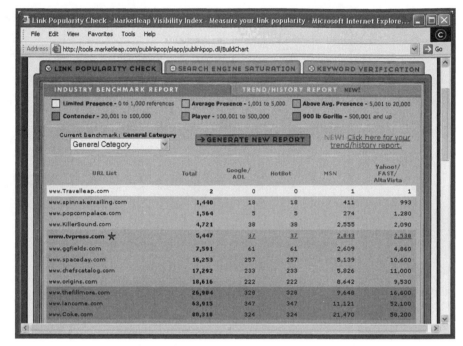

Figure 4.12

Using the Link Popularity Check service at MarketLeap to examine the number and quality of links to your Web site.

Another Web site offering free link checking is LinkPopularityCheck (**www.linkpopularitycheck.com**). As shown in Figure 4.13, all you have to do is supply your Web site's URL, select one or more of the available search engines (MSN, Lycos, AllTheWeb, and AltaVista), and supply your name and e-mail address. Results will be immediately displayed as well as e-mailed to you.

One additional link checking site that your might want to try is Link Popularity.com (**www.linkpopularity.com**). This free link checking service will search Google, AltaVista, and HotBot and immediately display the results. If you want, you can also supply your name and e-mail address in order to sign up to automatically receive a monthly report.

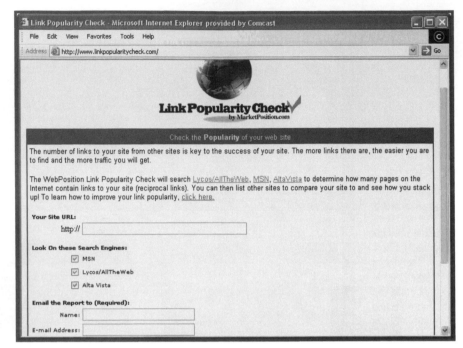

Figure 4.13

LinkPopularityCheck
lets you query up
to four different
search engines.

Selling Your Web Site through E-mail

Plain old e-mail is an extraordinary means of promoting your Web site.
Every day, people send more messages by e-mail than by standard mail,
and why not? Messages sent by e-mail are usually free. The millions of
daily e-mail messages bounce around the globe in one of three forms:
messages sent from person to person, messages posted to a newsgroup,
and messages submitted to a mailing list.

In your promotional efforts, you can use all three ways of distributing
e-mail to promote your Web site. However, nothing will get you into hot
water quicker than sending unsolicited or unwanted e-mail. To help you
steer clear of the pitfalls of e-mail promotion and get the most out of your
efforts, this section shows you the right ways to sell your Web sites
through e-mail.

Web Site Promotion Through Direct E-mail, Newsgroups, and Mailing Lists

E-mail has been around since the earliest days of the Internet, and it is quickly becoming the most widely used electronic communications method. The widespread popularity of e-mail comes from the fact that it is so compulsively usable. Unlike standard mail, you can use e-mail to quickly and easily send the same message to hundreds, thousands, or millions of recipients. Unlike limitations presented by using a telephone, you can send e-mail at any time of the day or night without fear of waking the recipient. Unlike using a fax machine, you can send a message without having to worry whether the recipient has stocked the fax machine with paper or whether the fax line will be busy.

Just as most people don't want to receive calls from telemarketers, unsolicited faxes, or junk mail, most people don't want to receive unsolicited e-mail either. In the world of electronic mail, no four-letter word is more odious than spam. Spamming is the electronic equivalent of junk mail. Any time you send unsolicited or unwanted messages, you are guilty of spamming. Sure, Web advertising agencies will try to sell you on the concept of bulk e-mail by telling you that the word spam applies only to unsolicited messages sent to multiple recipients, multiple discussion groups, or multiple mailing lists. In the end, however, an unsolicited message is an unsolicited message, whether it is sent to one or a thousand recipients.

As anyone who has ever sent unsolicited e-mail will tell you, the consequences can be severe. Your e-mail box might be bombarded with hate mail. Your Internet service provider (ISP) might pull your account. You might even run into legal difficulties. Despite these potential pitfalls, people all over the world continue to spam the electronic byways. The reason is the tremendous value of being able to send messages to anyone, anywhere, at any time.

Although you can certainly take a haphazard approach for Web site promotion through e-mail, there are ways to work within the system and current guidelines for newsgroups and mailing lists without rocking the boat. Working within the guidelines allows you to tap into the wonderful potential of e-mail, newsgroups, and mailing lists while minimizing the risk of backlash.

NOTE You can do your best to work within the system while minimizing the risk, but you won't be able to please all the people all of the time. The simple truth is that some people like to huff and puff. When you encounter someone who cries foul for no apparent reason, you should do one of two things, simply ignore the person or send a brief apology and move on.

The following section offers a look at how you can effectively promote your Web site through direct communications, newsgroups, and mailing lists.

Establishing a Privacy Policy

Before you begin soliciting visitors to your Web site for permission to send them e-mail, you need to earn their trust. After all, very few people are going to give you their name and e-mail address if they think you might abuse their information. In the context of this discussion, abuse refers to spamming visitors with unexpected or unsolicited e-mail or the sharing of personal information with other parties. To alleviate these types of concerns and to make your visitors feel comfortable giving you their contact information, it is essential that you develop a privacy policy and that you display it prominently in a location where visitors can easily find it. For example, most Web sites put a link to their privacy policy right at the bottom of their Web pages.

When you formulate your privacy policy, make sure that you tell your visitors exactly what type of information you are collecting about them and exactly how this information will be used. Also, it is a good idea to mention that you respect each individual's right to privacy and will conform to and respect anti-spam laws.

One way to begin putting together your own privacy policy is to take a look at how somebody else has already done it. For example, Figure 4.14 shows the beginning of amazon.com's privacy notice.

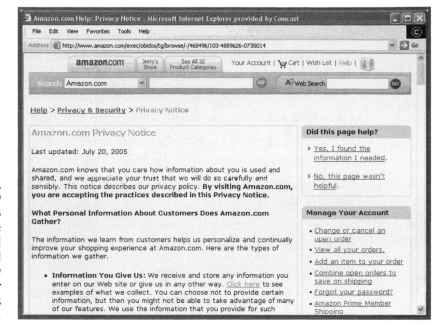

Figure 4.14

Amazon.com's privacy notice is extensive and goes into detail regarding how customer information is handled.

If you want a little help in putting together your own privacy policy, you can get it from **www.privacyaffiliates.com**. All you will have to do is answer a few multiple-choice questions about your customers and your Web site and a custom privacy policy will be created for you. However, this service is not free. At the time the Fourth Edition of this book was written, the fee for creating a privacy policy was $19.95.

Promoting Your Web Site Directly

When you send a message to people using their e-mail address, you are using the most direct method of sending e-mail: person to person. As a rule, you should never send e-mail to anyone who doesn't want it. Instead, you should put together a promotional campaign that is responsive rather than proactive. Don't sent unsolicited e-mail; instead, ask your visitors—and anyone else who contacts you—whether they want to receive promotional material.

Sending Promotional Material

Promotional material that you send to subscribers can take many different forms. For a straightforward marketing approach, you can use advertisements and press releases pertaining to your organization as well as your products and services. You can also use an approach that focuses less on marketing and more on information. With this approach, you send subscribers information on what's new at the Web site, clips from recently published pages, or highlights of interesting places within the Web site.

The best way to invite participation is to add a subscription field to the HTML forms that are already at your Web site. In previous chapters, you saw that many forms used by search sites and directories have subscription fields. These fields ask whether you want to receive information or other promotional material by e-mail.

Subscription fields are often selected by default, which in itself isn't a bad thing, but some search sites go out of their way to ensure that most people who submit their forms join the subscription service. It is a deceptive practice to try and hide the subscription field or to blur the wording so that it isn't clear.

Tips for Direct Mailings

To ensure that you receive subscriptions only from people who are truly interested in what you have to offer, place the subscription field so that it can be clearly seen, use clear wording, and deselect the field by default. Doing so makes subscribing an active process that requires a conscious effort from the reader.

Consider adding a subscription field if you use forms at your Web site that allow visitors to submit comments, sign a guest log, or enter any other type of data. The subscription field can be as simple as the checkbox selection fields shown in Figure 4.15. Here, the subscription field asks visitors whether they want to receive information regarding specified alert levels.

Figure 4.15

Soliciting permission to send e-mail to your visitors.

Some other more general subscription field questions that might be useful include these:

- Can we send you press releases related to our company?

- Would you like to receive advertisements and promotional material from our sponsors?

- Do you want to receive notification when this page is updated?

- Would you like to receive weekly updates on what's new at our Web site?

- Can we send you weekly highlights of interesting areas within our Web site?

The important thing here is to keep things short and sweet. The more information that you ask for, the less likely your visitors will take the time to provide it. Also, you want to make it as easy as possible for your visitors to be able to sign up.

Examine your Web site and look for opportunities to offer this service to your visitors. For example, if you run a regular contest, you might want to offer to send your visitors an e-mail each time the contest deadline approaches. Or you might offer to send an e-mail telling who won the contest or what the next contest prize might be. Likewise, if you give away freebies or downloads, you should consider each of these events as opportunities to remind your visitors of your newsletters and e-mail lists.

Another way to encourage your visitors to sign up for your newsletters and e-mail is to create a *Members Only* area on your Web site where additional content is available. You could provide free access to this area to any visitor that signs up to join your mailing list. Think of these types of opportunities as giving you the chance to build a relationship with your visitors and to encourage repeat traffic and loyalty.

TIP

Always make sure that any e-mail or newsletters you send out include a link back to your Web site and that you give your visitors a reason to visit. For example, you might mention that more information is available back on your Web site about a particular product, service, or topic. In addition, consider encouraging the recipients of your e-mail to pass them on to their friends and colleagues. This will allow you to reach out to new visitors without risking being seen as sending out spam.

Promoting Your Web Site through Newsgroups

Newsgroups are popular places for people with common interests. When you send a message to a newsgroup, you submit the message to a discussion area where everyone who follows the newsgroup can see it. Newsgroups, like Web sites, cover just about every imaginable subject, and whether your Web site discusses cats or conspiracy theories, a newsgroup relating to your topic exists.

Finding Newsgroups You Can Use to Promote Your Web Site

With thousands of newsgroups available, trying to find newsgroups without a little help is very time consuming. Rather than browse newsgroups individually, you should visit a newsgroup archive site such as Google Groups (see Figure 4.16). Google Groups is a new Web service provided by Google.

At Google Groups (**groups.google.com**), you can search through millions of current postings to newsgroups by keyword. You can also browse your way through the hierarchy of existing groups. If you don't see a group that fits your topic, you can create a new newsgroup of your own to get things started.

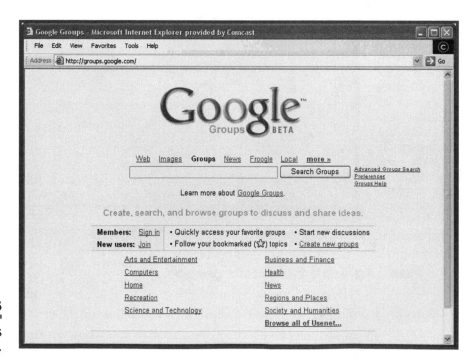

Figure 4.16

Finding newsgroups at Google Groups.

As shown in Figure 4.17, if you did a search on cats, you would find thousands of messages featuring this keyword. By clicking on the message subject line, you could access the most recent messages posted to the specified newsgroup. You'll also find a list of groups related to cats at the top of the page. If you find discussion groups related to topics you want to promote or participate in, write down the name of the discussion group.

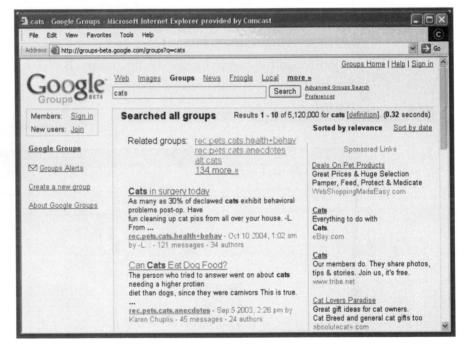

Figure 4.17

Messages using the keyword are shown. If the discussion group is related to a topic you want to promote or use, note the discussion group as one you might want to use.

Posting Tips for Newsgroups

After you have compiled a list of all the newsgroups that might be of interest, you should familiarize yourself with the groups by reading some of the recent postings. Nothing enrages newsgroup participants more than a promotional message that doesn't relate to the topic at hand. Going a step further, some newsgroup participants loathe all advertisements. For this reason, you should

- Spend some time getting to know the group.

- Ensure that your promotional message strongly relates to the subject at hand.

- Use a conversational style without a lot of hype.

- Keep the promotional message short—a few paragraphs at most.

- Post a message to a specific group one time and one time only; if people are interested, they'll respond.

As with direct promotion to individual users, you might want to focus less on marketing and more on information. For example, if a newsgroup participant asks about feline pneumonia and you have a terrific article on this very subject at your Web site, you might want to reply with a message like this one:

> *Feline pneumonia is a serious illness that affects thousands of cats every year. Because my own cat nearly died from pneumonia, I put together an article detailing the symptoms pet owners can look for and the treatments that my veterinarian discussed with me. You can find this article at …*

Promoting Your Web Site through Mailing Lists

Mailing lists are similar to newsgroups but are organized in a different manner. Whereas a message sent to a newsgroup goes to a central discussion area, mailing list messages are sent via e-mail directly to all the people who join the list. Because of the way lists work, you must subscribe to a list before you can participate in the list. After you subscribe, you can read messages posted to the list and post your own messages.

The simple act of posting a message to a mailing list doesn't ensure that it will be sent to list members. Many mailing lists have moderators who review messages before they are actually distributed to the list members. If the message contains anything inappropriate, the moderator might cut out the questionable parts or remove the message entirely.

Finding Mailing Lists You Can Use to Promote Your Web Site

You can find mailing lists by visiting one of the many mailing list archive or index sites. One of the best mailing list directories is available at Tile.net. You can search through the directory using keywords or browse the lists alphabetically (see Figure 4.18).

When you search through the mailing list directory, you will notice that mailing lists aren't organized into hierarchies. In place of hierarchies, mailing lists use a naming system based loosely on the topic of the list or the name of the organization sponsoring the list.

When you find a mailing list in Tile.net, you will see a brief description of the list (see Figure 4.19) as well as the information you need to subscribe to the list.

Mailing lists are one of the most fluid resources on the Internet. Every day, dozens of new mailing lists are born and dozens of old mailing lists fade away into oblivion. Keeping up with this constant change is a chore made possible only with help from the list creators and moderators.

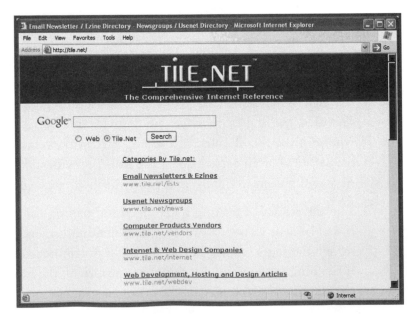

Figure 4.18

You can perform a keyword search in order to locate interesting mailing lists.

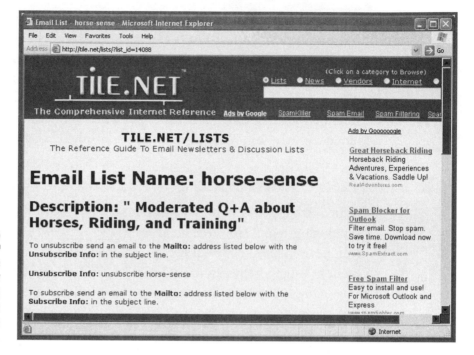

Figure 4.19

All entries include
a brief summary
of the mailing
list along with
instructions on
how to join.

Because of the constant changeover in mailing lists, it is a good idea to check several different mailing list directories before making a decision about which you would like to participate in and possibly use to promote your Web site.

Posting Tips for Mailing Lists

As with newsgroups, you should read some of the postings to a mailing list before you submit anything. With thousands of people on the receiving end of your promotional message, you have to be very careful about the marketing approach you use. Nothing will generate hate mail faster than a blatant advertisement posted to a mailing list.

Rather than post an advertisement, you might want to focus more on information. Ideally, your posting should be helpful and useful to those who read it. For specific tips on creating your posting, refer back to the posting tips for newsgroups.

Almost every mailing list out there has a set of rules. Usually, these rules are outlined in a set of FAQs (Frequently Asked Questions) for the list. Definitely try to find and read the FAQs before you participate in a mailing list. To make it easier to know and follow the rules, most mailing lists send out a confirmation message after you subscribe. In this confirmation message, you will usually find a list of the rules and lots of other good information. Save this message; you might need it later.

"Tell a Friend" Marketing

Direct mail, newsgroups, and mailing lists all provide you with powerful marketing tools. However, *viral marketing* or word-of-mouth marketing can be even more powerful because it leverages the opinions and efforts of your most important resources, your visitors. Let's face it, there are very few marketing techniques that are more powerful than the advice of a friend. By encouraging your visitors to pass on information about your Web site, product, or service, you increase the odds of bringing in new Web traffic.

Whether you realize it or not, you see viral marketing techniques implemented all over the Web. For example, amazon.com implements this referral technique extensively, as demonstrated in Figure 4.20. Somewhere on every page where a book (or product) is displayed at amazon.com is a "Tell a friend about this book" link.

You can implement your own word-of-mouth promotion by placing a link or button next to a product, service description, or on a Web page that you want more people to know about. Make sure your link or button stands out prominently and uses an active voice to encourage visitors to act upon your request. When clicked, you can open up the visitor's e-mail application and fill out the subject title and main body fields with information about your Web site, product, or service. Alternately, you could look to a free service on the Internet to set up and run your referral efforts for you. For example, Bravenet.com (**www.bravenet.com**) provides a free Tell a Friend service at **www.bravenet.com/webtools/index.php**, as shown in Figure 4.21. All you have to do is sign up and add a little customizable

HTML to your Web pages and you'll be ready to go. Multiple templates are available to help you with design and monthly statistics are provided to help you track how things are going.

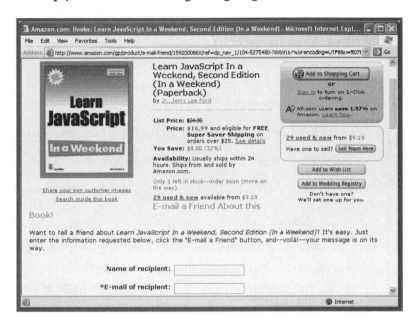

Figure 4.20

Amazon.com takes viral marketing to a whole new level.

Figure 4.21

Bravenet.com can assist you in setting up and administering your Tell a Friend marketing efforts.

Announcing Your Web Site, Products, and Services by E-mail

Promoting your Web site through topical discussions is a terrific way to build traffic over the long term. Another way to build traffic is to announce your Web site, products, and services through e-mail. Although you can certainly announce your Web site in newsgroups that discuss topics similar to those at your Web site, you can use several additional avenues for making announcements. These avenues include

- Using newsgroups specifically for announcements.

- Using business-oriented newsgroups.

- Using marketplace, commerce, and for-sale newsgroups.

You can browse current postings to any of the newsgroups discussed in this section by visiting Google Groups (**groups.google.com**). After you read some of the postings and are sure that the list is right for you, you can post your announcement. The key is to style your message in a manner that is appropriate for the discussion group.

When you make an announcement, you might want to organize your message like a press release that covers your Web site or the products and services that you discuss at your Web site. Ideally, your message will only be a few paragraphs long and fewer than 500 words. Brevity is important because most readers won't spend more than a few seconds glancing at your message.

In the body of the message, you should include the URL to your Web site or the particular area within your Web site that you are promoting. It's a good idea to repeat a URL at the top and bottom of the message, or to direct readers to different URLs within the Web site. This way, anyone scanning the message can zero in on the all-important URLs.

Announcement Newsgroups

Just as you can list your Web site in a What's New? directory, you can also list your Web site in discussion groups that are devoted to Web announcements. Although most announcement groups focus on announcements for new Web sites, some discussion groups focus on products and services.

Newsgroups that you can use to announce your Web site include

alt.biz.misc

biz.marketplace

comp.infosystems.www.announce

comp.internet.net-happenings

misc.news.internet.announce

Business Newsgroups for Making Announcements

If you have ever wondered whether a place exists where blatant advertising and capitalism rule the day, look no further than the biz.* newsgroup hierarchy. In the biz.* newsgroup hierarchy, you will find dozens of newsgroups devoted to announcements for products and services. Although many of the announcements in biz.* newsgroups are filled with hype, the most successful announcements are the ones that focus less on marketing and more on information.

The primary newsgroups in the biz.* hierarchy that might be of interest in your promotion efforts include

alt.biz

alt.biz.misc

biz.books.technical

biz.general

biz.digital.announce

biz.marketplace.computers.discussion

bis.marketplace.discussion

More Newsgroups for Announcements

With thousands of discussion groups available, the listings in this chapter are only the tip of the iceberg. If you know what to look for, you can find dozens of other places to post announcements.

With newsgroups, searching the hierarchy listings for keywords is usually the best way to find what you are looking for. You can do this at **groups.google.com**.

To find business-related newsgroups that might accept your announcements, try using some of these keywords in your search:

announce

biz

business

commerce

forsale

marketplace

www

Creative Signature Files

An e-mail signature is an extra you can add to the end of all your e-mail messages. This trailer can help you promote your Web site as well as your products and services each time you send an e-mail message. Your signature can be styled as a mini-promotion for your Web site or anything else that you want to highlight.

Although you might see e-mail signatures that run 10-20 lines, most signatures are fewer than 5 lines. As a rule of thumb, 3-5 lines are usually a good length for an e-mail signature. Because your e-mail signature will go out with all your mail unless you delete the signature, it's a good idea to limit the hype.

Listing 4.1 demonstrates how you might want to format your own e-mail signatures. This should give you an idea of how you can create a signature that is effective yet doesn't look like an advertisement. If your e-mail application allows you to create a signature using fancy fonts or special formatting, keep in mind that this formatting is created with HTML and may not be displayed with any special formatting in another e-mail application. Additionally, you can improve readability in compliant e-mail applications by using simple font types and readable font sizes.

Listing 4.1   Sample E-mail Signatures

```
William R. Stanek

Editor-in-Chief, Internet Daily News—http://www.netdaily.com/

Author of several tech books—http://www/tvpress.com/writing/

-

Jerry Lee Ford, Jr.

Information Security Professional and author of computer books

Looking for something new? Visit the Thomson Course Technology
Web site at http://www.courseptr.com
```

TIP When you add URLs to your signature (or anywhere within an e-mail message, for that matter), be sure to include the "http://" as part of the URL. If you do, most e-mail programs will make this a hypertext link that users can click on to immediately visit the URL.

Most e-mail applications allow you to create a signature file. In some cases you do so using an ordinary text file. After you create and save the signature file, you can use the standard features of your favorite e-mail applications to add the e-mail signature to all your outgoing messages. Most modern e-mail applications also provide you with a built-in editor to assist you in creating your own custom signature. For example, if you used an online e-mail service such as Yahoo! mail, you would set up your signature as outlined here:

1. Open you browser and log in to **mail.yahoo.com**.

2. Click on the Mail Options link located in the upper right-hand corner of the screen.

3. Next, click on the Signature option located in the Personalization section.

4. Type in the text for your signature file in the space provided.

5. Select the Add signature to all outgoing messages option.

6. Click on Save, and you are finished.

If you use a desktop e-mail application, such as Microsoft Outlook Express, the process is pretty much the same. Outlook Express also allows you to create a custom signature without ever leaving Outlook Express. The steps you need to follow to create a signature are as follows:

1. Go to Tools and choose Options.

2. Click on the Signatures property sheet.

3. Click on the New button located in the Signatures section.

4. Enter your signature in the text window.

5. Click on the checkbox for the Add signatures to all outgoing messages option.

6. Click on OK, and you're finished.

Take a Break

Congratulations! You are halfway through the Sunday Morning session. It is time to take a break. Crank up the radio. Grab a drink and get something to eat. When you return you will learn about a number of different and exciting ways to bring more traffic to your Web site.

Advertising on eBay

There is no doubt that eBay has become a major force on the Web. It provides a Web service that facilitates the buying and selling of products all over the world. For individuals and companies with something to sell, eBay provides a service known as an eBay store, as shown in Figure 4.22.

If your Web site has something to sell or if you plan on starting to sell something, eBay may be your ticket to success. At the time that the Fourth Edition of this book was written, you could set up a new eBay store starting at just $15.50 a month. This automatically puts you in front of millions of eBay shoppers. You'll have total control over how your online store looks. You decide on the content, graphics, and colors. Your store will get its own URL and your customers will even be able to pay online via credit card.

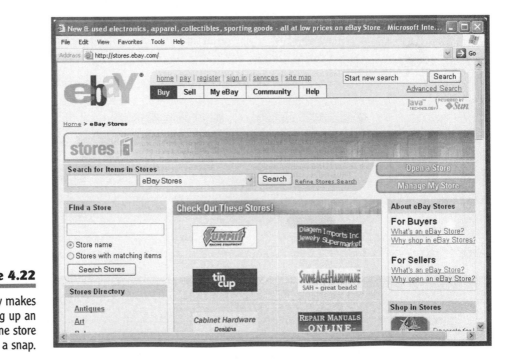

Figure 4.22

eBay makes setting up an online store a snap.

In order to open a store, you must open an eBay account and place your credit card on file. You can the open up a new store by logging in to eBay, going to **stores.ebay.com**, and clicking on the Open a Store button. Once opened, you can set up your store as demonstrated in Figure 4.23. As you can see, the store shown belongs to TennisExpress (**www.tennis express.com**).

As you can see in the figure, TennisExpress has a considerable inventory of tennis products for sale. You can click on any of the items shown in the store to learn more information, purchase it, or place a bid on it, as demonstrated in Figure 4.24.

Take note of the bottom half of Figure 4.24. As you can see, the owners of this eBay store are giving the customer more information about their business, including the graphic showing the store owners' real Web site (**www.tennisexpress.com**). This will encourage customers to visit them on the Web (see Figure 4.25) and potentially make purchases directly from this Web site, thus bypassing eBay completely.

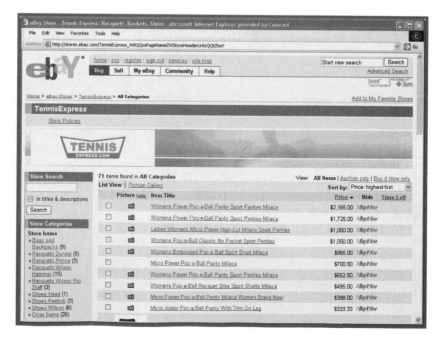

Figure 4.23

TennisExpress is an online Tennis store.

Figure 4.24

Examining a tennis racket being sold at TennisExpress's eBay store.

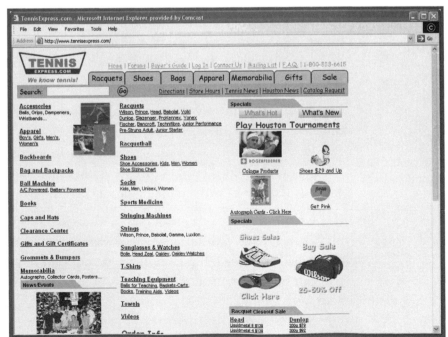

Figure 4.25

By setting up an eBay store, online businesses can drive even more traffic to their Web site.

Attracting the Masses with Giveaways, Contests, Sweepstakes, and More

Traditional marketers have used giveaways, contests, and sweepstakes for years to make their sponsors stand out from the crowd. The simple truth is that we all love the chance to win something for nothing, and whenever we have the opportunity to enter a contest or giveaway, we usually go for the gusto. Web advertisers have pushed traditional giveaways and contests onto the World Wide Web, where the quest for freebies can truly bring the masses to the sponsor's Web site.

Can't Get 'em Any Other Way? Give It Away!

Giving things away is a great way to build traffic to your Web site. Whether you want to pass out bumper stickers or trips to Europe, people will want to enter your giveaway. Beyond outright giveaways are contests and sweepstakes that ask the participants to answer questions or enter a creative work, such as a poem or a jingle for a commercial.

Giveaways, contests, and sweepstakes promoted on the Web are often direct tie-ins to similar promotions running in print media. If your organization is already planning a giveaway or contest, advertising it on the Web can bring your message to an eager audience of millions.

Universal Studios (**www.universalstudios.com**) is a company that understands the promotional power of giveaways. Universal Studios (whose sweepstakes have been referenced in four editions of this book) follows the pointers offered in this book and understands how to promote contests that tie-in with company products (see Figure 4.26).

If you have the clout of a major corporation behind you, promotional tie-ins between your Web site and a giveaway or contest running in the print media will work well. But even if you are not part of a major corporation, you can benefit tremendously from running a contest or sweepstakes at your Web site.

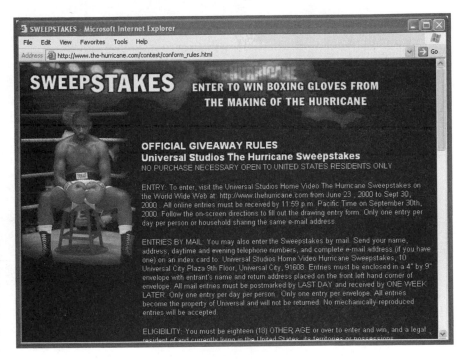

Figure 4.26

Universal Studios
understands the
promotional power
of giveaways.
They sponsor
new giveaways
all the time.

Although many traditional promotional campaigns center around giveaways, contests, and sweepstakes, savvy marketers know that the interactive and dynamic nature of the Web opens doors and removes the traditional boundaries and restrictions of print media. On the Web, your giveaway can become part of an interactive trivia quiz with questions that change dynamically each time the page is visited. You can even create an interactive treasure hunt with clues scattered throughout your Web site.

The Web allows you to conduct other types of promotions as well, such as online games that give something away to participants with the best scores. With an online game, contestants get to have fun while trying to win prizes. Online games can range from simple puzzles and teasers to actual video games programmed in Java or another programming language.

Figure 4.27 shows the online games available at Headbone Zone. Kids can not only play the games at Headbone Zone (**www.headbone.com**), they can also sign up to get a new game delivered each day via e-mail.

Figure 4.27

Headbone Zone
provides interactive
games for kids
of all ages.

Using a giveaway, contest, or sweepstakes to increase traffic at your We
site is a good idea, but it's definitely not the only reason to give things
away. By using a giveaway, contest, or sweepstakes you can also

- Build awareness for your products and services.

- Familiarize readers with other areas of your Web site.

- Build a profile of your readers based on a survey or questionnaire
  that is part of the submission form.

Later in this session, you'll learn about different types of giveaways and contests that you might want to use in your promotional efforts. These include

- Free-for-all giveaways and sweepstakes

- Contests for artists, writers, and other creative people

- Trivia quizzes, games, puzzles, and teasers

Although giveaways and contests are great for increasing your traffic, the actual amount of traffic increase you see at your Web site will depend on what you are giving away and how well you promote the giveaway. Keep in mind that the key to success isn't so much *what* you give away, but *how* you give it away. If your hook is great, your giveaway or contest will attract the masses. To help you promote your giveaway or contest, this book will introduce you to Web sites that specialize in freebies, giveaways, and contests. After all, people need to find your giveaway or contest in order to participate.

What to Watch Out For: The Legalities

Although nothing builds traffic like a good giveaway or contest, there are many things you should consider before you get started. Your primary concern should be the legal ramifications of publishing your giveaway or contest on the Web.

By putting your contest on the Web, you make it available to participants throughout the world, which might make your contest subject to certain laws. Every country has its own laws, and these laws often vary by region within the country as well. For example, each state in the U.S. has its own rules regarding giveaways and contests.

Before you publish your contest or distribute any information related to your contest, you should check applicable federal, state, and local laws regarding contests and giveaways. The best places to research global laws are the Law Library of Congress (**www.loc.gov/law/public/law.html**) and the Guide to Law Online (**www.loc.gov/law/public/law-guide.html**).

Disclaimers for Age and Residency

Because of the extreme diversity of international laws, most organizations that run contests and giveaways restrict their promotions to specific countries. When you restrict your contest to a specific country or countries, you should post a clear disclaimer along with any contest information. The purpose of the disclaimer is to protect your interests and ensure that you don't accidentally violate the laws of another country.

If you've browsed Web sites that run contests or giveaways, you have probably seen a disclaimer that says "U.S. and Canadian residents only" or "U.S. residents only." By restricting a contest to the U.S. and Canada, or the U.S. only, you limit your liability—which is always a good idea.

Another thing to consider is the age of the participants. Because many U.S. states require that participants in contests be at least 18 years old, you should place an age restriction on the contest. You can blend the age restriction right into your original disclaimer, such as "U.S. and Canadian residents 18 and older only" or "U.S. residents 18 and older only." Granted, verifying a person's age over the Internet is difficult; however, clearly marking the age restriction can only serve your best interest.

Other Disclaimers

Generally, within the U.S. and Canada, your sweepstakes or giveaway should be free, meaning that you shouldn't require entrants to purchase something in order to enter and win. In this way, your sweepstakes or giveaway is truly giving something away for nothing. You should post a clear disclaimer at the contest site that notifies readers that no purchase is necessary to enter the contest. An exception is a creative contest, such as an art contest or writing contest that charges an entry fee.

You should also publish a statement to ensure that participants know that local laws apply to the contest and that the contest is void where prohibited. Voiding the contest where prohibited protects you from inadvertently violating the local laws.

Putting the Rules Together

Now that you have made a start on the rules for your contest or giveaway, you should put these rules together in an official form that you can publish on your Web site. In the official rules, you should spell out exactly what you will be giving away and the value of the prizes. If you will be giving away one Sony 19-inch TV valued at $399, specify this exactly.

After you've decided on the rules for your contest or giveaway, you should publish them for the entire world to see. Ideally, you will place a summary of the rules on all the contest pages and make the detailed rules available with a hypertext link.

The following is an example set of rules for a fictitious contest called the Happy Peacock Sweepstakes. As you read it, keep in mind that this is a made-up example that serves only to illustrate some of the points made in this section.

Rules for the Happy Peacock Sweepstakes:

1. No purchase necessary to enter.

2. To enter the sweepstakes, fill out the official entry form at the Happy Peacock Web site. We accept only fully completed entry forms. Only one entry per person is allowed.

3. Sweepstakes begins January 1, 2006, and ends on December 31, 2006. Your entry must be received no later than midnight on December 31, 2006. Winners will be selected in a random drawing.

4. Sweepstakes is open to residents of the United States who are 18 years of age or older. All submissions become the property of Happy Peacock. All federal, state, and local laws and regulations apply. Any taxes due are the responsibility of the winner. Void where prohibited or restricted by law.

5. One first-place prize: Happy Peacock gift set, valued at $299. Ten second-place prizes: Happy Peacock T-shirt, valued at $25 each. Twenty third-place prizes: Happy Peacock coffee mug, valued at $9 each.

6. A list of prize winners will be published at the Happy Peacock Web site within 15 days of the end of the sweepstakes. Happy Peacock reserves the right to substitute a prize of equal or greater value.

TIP

If you need help creating forms, or putting a process in place to collect form results, check out Response-O-Matic at **www.response-o-matic.com**. Response-O-Matic will help you create your forms, collect the data your visitors enter, and send you the results via e-mail. All for free.

Boosting Traffic with Giveaways and Sweepstakes

Giveaways and sweepstakes are great for boosting traffic at your Web site. Every day, thousands of people search the Web looking for the latest giveaways and sweepstakes—and why not? They can win hats, T-shirts, books, jewelry, trips, and much more simply by filling out a form. Although there is not much difference between a giveaway and a sweepstakes, the term sweepstakes is often used when sponsors and advertisers donate prizes.

Creating a Giveaway or Sweepstakes

When you put together a giveaway or sweepstakes, remember that the prizes themselves are not what attract readers as much as your execution. As a matter of fact, you could give away T-shirts and get more visitors than a site giving away trips to Europe.

Although the organization giving away trips to Europe would argue their case heatedly, the reality is that a well-designed and well-promoted giveaway will be successful regardless of the prizes. Well-designed giveaways and sweepstakes have a professional polish that makes them fun, easy to enter, and visually appealing. Well-promoted giveaways and sweepstakes are announced in all the right places, which includes key pages at your Web site and Web guides that promote freebies.

NOTE

You'll learn all about guides that promote freebies shortly, under the heading "Sites That Promote Your Freebies."

The best giveaways and sweepstakes have a theme that helps sell people on the idea of the giveaway or sweepstakes. If you are giving away trips, it is not just a "trip," but a "passport to adventure." If you are giving away cruises, it is not just a cruise, but "barefoot strolls along windswept beaches, romantic dinners for two, and quiet, moonlit evenings topside."

After you decide on the type of giveaway or sweepstakes to run, consider the prizes that you will award. As stated earlier, the prizes don't have to be extravagant, but they should be worth the time and effort it takes to enter the contest. Additionally, entering the giveaway or sweepstakes should be as easy as filling out an entry form that asks for contact information, such as name, address, and phone number.

You might also want to add a questionnaire or survey to the entry form. Questionnaires can help you learn more about the type of people who visit your Web site. You can find out whether they use your products and services. You can also learn about visitor preferences, such as their favorite area within your Web site, or their interests.

Looking at an Actual Sweepstakes

A good case study for a well-designed and well-promoted sweepstakes is Frommer's monthly sweepstakes. The sweepstakes ties in with Frommer's travel magazine and books, and is a featured part of Arthur Frommer's Budget Travel Online Web site (see Figure 4.28). The sweepstakes has sponsors who advertise on the contest pages and on the Web site. The sweepstakes serves several purposes.

- The sweepstakes builds traffic to the Web site by inviting visitors to return to the site regularly. Prizes are given away regularly and visitors must return to register each month.

- The sweepstakes highlights sponsors by providing direct links to the Web sites of the sponsors.

○ The sweepstakes entry form asks visitors to provide contact information and to answer a questionnaire, which provides valuable geographic and demographic information that the publishers might not be able to otherwise obtain.

○ Information entered by visitors is often sold to companies that are interested in reaching this target audience. This sale can provide secondary income for the company.

Figure 4.28

Prizes are what bring visitors, but you might be surprised to learn that a simple T-shirt contest can bring in as many visitors as a $50,000 giveaway. The secret is in the presentation and promotion.

 NOTE Never sell information without prior notification. If you plan to sell information gathered through the sweepstakes, you should state this explicitly in the contest rules and in your site's privacy policy.

Frommer's enhances the main sweepstakes entry form by adding input fields that allow visitors to provide the e-mail addresses of up to 10 other people who may be interested in the contest. Visitors are invited to provide this information based on the promise that it will increase their chances of winning. The entry form also provides subscription fields that allow visitors to sign up for a number of newsletters. All in all, it's a well-rounded effort to invite visitor participation, collect visitor information, and increase Web traffic.

Gaining Readers with Contests

Contests reward people for their talents or creativity. Because contests often require judging and extensive work on the part of the producer, some contests charge a nominal fee, such as $5, to enter. Charging an entry fee for something like a writing contest that offers prestige, publication, and cash rewards to the winners makes sense. Charging an entry fee for a contest that is meant more for fun than to be a career builder doesn't make sense.

Running a Contest

Contests can be just as much fun for you as they are for the participants. Your goal should be to use the contest to build traffic to your Web site. Ideally, your contest will tie in to and promote your business, products, and services. For example, developers of word processing applications might want to sponsor a write-off for the most creative or bizarre advertising gimmick for their product.

The type of contest that you run will depend largely on your interests. If you are interested in comedy, you might want to have a contest that rewards the funniest submissions. If you are interested in graphic design, you might want to have a design contest. If you love poetry, you might want to have a poetry contest.

To keep your contest as hassle-free as possible, you will want to decide on the specific formats that are acceptable for submissions. For a writing or poetry contest, you might want to specify in the rules that all submissions must be saved as standard ASCII text files with a .txt file extension. Similarly, for a design or art contest, you might want to specify that all submissions must be saved in either GIF or JPEG format.

Additionally, any time you ask for creative submission, you should set limits on the size or length of entries. For a writing contest, you might want to limit entries to 5,000 words. For a design contest, you might want to limit the size of artwork to 1280 × 1024, with a file size of less than 2MB.

After you decide on the type of contest you want to run, you need to think about how you will judge the contest. Most small contests are judged exclusively by the contest developer. Creative contests, such as writing, art, or design contests, are usually voted on by a panel of judges. Alternatively, you can remove yourself from the judging process entirely by letting visitors to your Web site vote for the best submission. The bottom line is that your judging process should be fair yet manageable using your current resources.

As with giveaways, you can use an entry form to accept submission for the contest, and you might want to add a questionnaire to the entry form as well. Keep in mind that if you run a creative contest, many participants will have their entry in separate text or graphic files. Currently, the easiest way to submit files is as an attachment to an e-mail message. For this reason, you might simply want to supply an e-mail address for submission rather than use an entry form.

TIP   You should state explicitly how many times visitors can enter and how many times they can win. Put this information in the official rules. For example, if visitors can enter only once and win only one prize, state this as a contest rule.

With creative works, you must consider one more thing: U.S. and international copyright law. Creative works are the property of the creator unless the rights are granted or sold. Thus, if you plan to publish the winning works at your Web site, you need permission, and you should ask for this permission right in the entry form. The minimum rights that you will want to retain are one-time world-electronic rights to the winning entries. Furthermore, you should state that winning entries will be published at your Web site.

Looking at an Actual Contest

An example of a Web site that uses contests to promote itself and its products is iWon (**www.iwon.com**), shown in Figure 4.29. The Words "I" and "Won" have a wonderful ring that describes the site's theme. The idea behind the site is to attract visitors with the promise of a chance to win great sums of cash. The entire theme of the Web site is built around the contests being offered rather than the products being advertised.

iWon takes the contest site concept to a new level, making it possible for visitors to win huge amounts of money just by visiting the site. The site offers daily prizes for $10,000 each weekday, $1,000 each weekend, and an annual prize of $25,000,000.

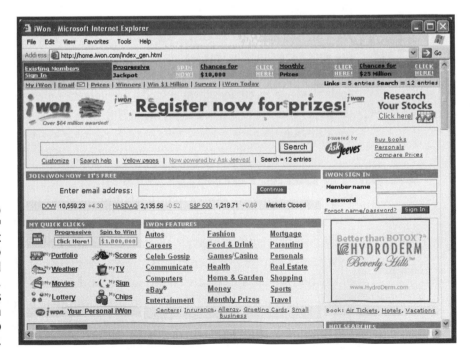

Figure 4.29

A great contest theme can help build traffic and sell your products. Nothing gets visitor's attention like a chance to win money.

Everywhere you look there are graphical and text links trying to lead you to other areas of the Web site. These links and graphics are reminders that the site has more to offer and that the real goal is to sell you something.

Using Games, Puzzles, and Teasers to Attract Visitors

Games, puzzles, and teasers can bring in the masses simply because they are entertaining. People of all ages love to play games that are challenging, fun, or stimulating. Games, puzzles, and teasers are good ways to keep visitors coming back to your Web site again and again. Many game sites take game playing to another level by offering additional incentives such as prizes. In this way, the game sites make a good thing better by rewarding people for playing. When rewards are involved, you can bet that visitors will come back again and again. Keep in mind that your prize doesn't have to be anything of value. You could simply publish the winner's name prominently on your home page, grant the winner a free home page, or something else that doesn't really cost you anything.

TIP   Use your games, puzzles, and teasers as an opportunity to encourage "Tell a Friend" viral marketing by prominently displaying a button or link that opens the visitor's e-mail application and encourages them to send a pre-formatted message about your product, service, or Web site to a friend or colleague.

Creating a Game, Puzzle, or Teaser

When you think of games, you probably imagine the zippy video games you see in the arcades. You could certainly spend months programming a truly awesome game for your Web site, like the folks at Cartoon Network (**www.cartoonnetwork.com**), as shown in Figure 4.30. However, some of the best games are those that are simple and compulsively playable. Most card games, such as poker or solitaire, aren't popular because of rip-roaring action; they are popular because they are easy to learn yet challenging to play.

Figure 4.30

Cartoon Network provides free access to professional quality online computer games.

One game to consider is a treasure hunt. Treasure hunts are really popular during the holidays, especially at Easter. In a treasure hunt, you hide clues or treasures throughout your Web site and sometimes at participating Web sites. You can display clues or treasures directly on your Web pages using text and graphics. You can also link standardized treasure icons to secret pages at your Web site that describe an item in the treasure hunt.

With a treasure hunt, you need a submission page that lets participants submit a list of all clues or treasures they've collected. Usually, prizes in a treasure hunt are awarded to the participants who find all the treasures first. To ensure fair play, you might want to periodically change the clues and treasures during the hunt.

A trivia quiz is another game that is a lot of fun and easy to produce. Although trivia quizzes cover any topic, you might want to link the quiz to the theme or topic of your Web site. The best trivia quizzes have at least five challenging questions to which participants can get answers immediately. To keep visitors coming back, you might want to make the trivia quiz a weekly or monthly feature.

If you are giving away prizes on a trivia quiz, you can post answers with a list of winners at a later date. Because many people might know the answers to your trivia questions, you really don't want to award prizes to everyone who submits the right answers. Instead, you might want to award prizes randomly from the list of participants who submitted the right answers.

Another type of game to consider is a puzzle. The best puzzles are word-based brainteasers, such as a crossword puzzle or a word association game. With a puzzle, you will probably want to reward participants simply for playing and submitting their answers.

A great way to build steady traffic with a puzzle is to change the puzzle often and award prizes randomly to the participants who answer a certain number of puzzles correctly in a given period of time. For example, you can publish a different puzzle every week and award prizes randomly to anyone who gets the answer to four different puzzles in a particular month.

Finding Free Online Games to Add to Your Web Pages

There are a number of Web sites where you can go to find free games that you can add to your Web site. For example, you'll find a free version of a JavaScript-based hangman game at **hangman.bappy.com**. Figure 4.31 shows how the game will look when a visitor starts it from your Web site.

Another site where you can find an assortment of free JavaScript games is **javascript.internet.com**. All that you have to do is add the free JavaScript code to your Web pages to get these games up and running.

Looking at an Actual Treasure Hunt

Museum Mania (**www.musuemmania.com**) features a number of online treasure hunts (see Figure 4.32). The goal of the treasure hunt is to follow a set of clues located at the links embedded in your questions. Once you find the items referenced in the clues, you can submit an entry to see how well you did.

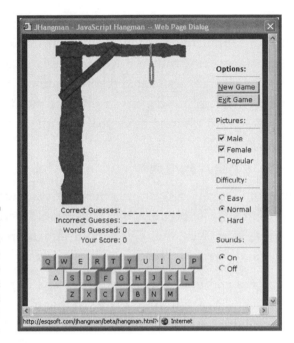

Figure 4.31

All you have to do is copy and paste the free code into one of your Web pages and you are ready to host a free game of hangman on your Web site.

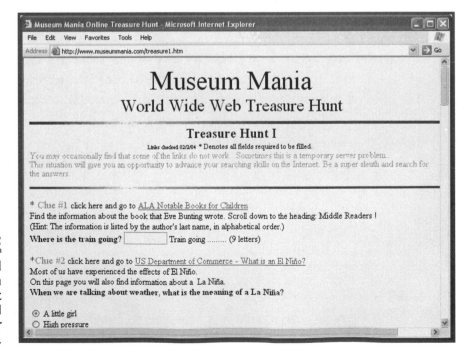

Figure 4.32

A well-designed treasure hunt can be a terrific promotional vehicle for your Web site.

Before visitors submit their answers to any of the many treasure hunts, they are asked to submit information about themselves, including their name, age, school, and city. Museum Mania is able to use this information to track detailed statistics related to the contest participants. These statistics are used to determine the effectiveness of the Web site's effort to interest young people in learning more about history.

Sites that Promote Your Freebies

You need to promote your giveaway, contest, or sweepstakes to make it successful. Although your promotion efforts should definitely begin at key areas within your Web site, you should also promote the contest through guides and directories that specialize in freebies.

In this section, you will find a brief review of some of the most popular contest directories. When you submit your freebie to a contest directory, be sure to provide the URL to the main contest page and a brief description of the contest. The contest description should specify when the contest ends as well as any age and residency requirements.

Promoting Your Freebie at FreeStuff2000 and Playhere

FreeStuff2000 (**www.freestuff2000.com**) is a terrific guide to fun and free things on the Web. The site is organized into areas that cover broad, entertainment-related topics (see Figure 4.33).

Notable attractions are the sections for Canadian freebies and baby freebies. Because FreeStuff2000 appeals to a very diverse audience, it is a good place to submit a contest listing. To submit your contest, giveaway, or sweepstakes to FreeStuff2000, click on the Contact Us link on the main page and fill in the form that is provided. Be sure to provide a description of your contest.

NOTE FreeStuff2000 is based on the original Playhere Web site, which has been featured in previous editions of this book. At the time the Fourth Edition of this book was published, Playhere was still available at **www.playhere.com**.

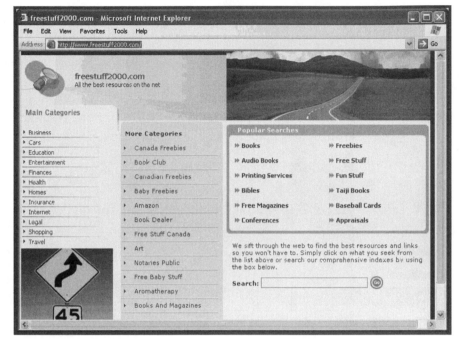

Figure 4.33

In addition to a great contest directory, FreeStuff2000 provides lots of other fun resources.

Promoting Your Freebie at TheFreeSite.com

TheFreeSite.com (**www.thefreesite.com**) is an extensive guide to just about everything that is free on the Web. Features in the catalog include free games, services, samples, screen savers, newsletters, and so on (see Figure 4.34).

Before you submit a listing to TheFreeSite.com, you should wander through the site to familiarize yourself with the various listing categories. Listings are displayed with a title and a detailed description that includes any relevant information about a particular freebie.

To submit your freebie, visit the Web site and click on the Submit a Freebie link. You'll be required to add a link to TheFreeSite.com. Be sure to include the URL to your freebie page, a description for the contest, the contest's start and stop dates, and any other requirements.

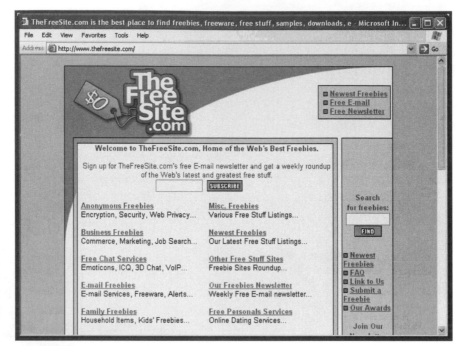

Figure 4.34

TheFreeSite.com is a growing resource to contests, giveaways, and sweepstakes.

Promoting Your Freebie at Virtual FreeStuff

Virtual FreeStuff is a guide to freebies that you can find anywhere, regardless of whether they are available on the Web (see Figure 4.35). You can find the home page for the directory at **www.dreamscape.com/frankvad/free.html**.

Rather than organize the guide by contest, the developers chose to organize the site according to the type of freebies offered. Because of this unique approach to showcasing freebies, the directory is divided into dozens of categories. Categories exist for games, e-books, financial aid, and even music and video.

Listings at Virtual FreeStuff are fairly extensive and include requirements as well as a description of each contest. Keep in mind that many of the listings in Virtual FreeStuff appear in more than one category.

You can submit your listing to Virtual FreeStuff by sending an e-mail to **frankvad@dreamscape.com**. To ensure that you get the most out of your listing, take the time to explain the types of prizes you give away, as well as how often prizes are awarded.

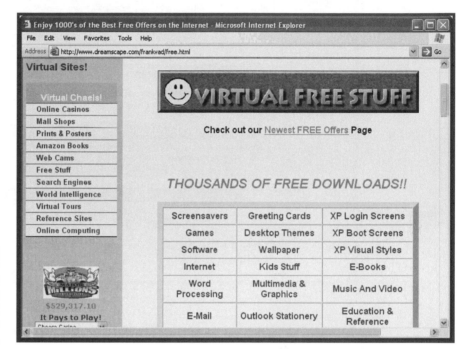

Figure 4.35

Organization by freebie type makes it easy to find what you are looking for at Virtual FreeStuff.

Other Places to Promote Your Freebies

With thousands of organizations giving away freebies, it's no surprise there are dozens of Web guides to free stuff. Other freebie guides that you might want to submit a listing to include Free-n-Cool, ContestGuide, FreebieList, and 1FreeStuffSite.

Free-n-Cool (**www.free-n-cool.com**) is a guide to everything on the Web that is free and—per the judgment of the site's creators—cool. The guide is divided into several key sections, including New Totally Free Stuff, New Almost-Free Stuff, New Contests and Giveaways, and New Cool Sites (see Figure 4.36). To promote your contest or giveaway, check out the New Totally Free Stuff and New Almost-Free Stuff sections. The distinction here is between outright giveaways and contests that award prizes to participants.

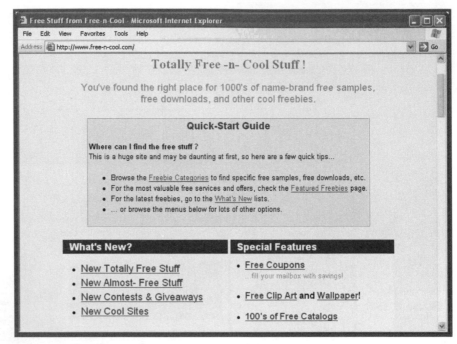

Figure 4.36

Free-n-Cool is a guide to what's free and cool on the Web.

You can submit your freebie to Free-n-Cool by sending e-mail to **link request @free-n-cool.com**. If you want to increase your chances of getting listed or being more prominently listed, add a link on your page to Free-n-Cool.

ContestGuide.com (**www.contestguide.com**) is a fairly comprehensive guide to contests. This site has a unique focus in that it organizes listings according to how often you can enter a contest (see Figure 4.37). It has listings for contests that let you enter one time only, daily, weekly, and monthly. You can submit a listing to ContestGuide by filling out the submission form at **www.contestguide.com/webmasters.html**.

Another great contest guide is FreebieList (**www.freebielist.com**), shown in Figure 4.38. You can browse by category to find where your freebie best fits. To submit a listing to the directory, use the submission form found at **www.freebielist.com/add.htm**.

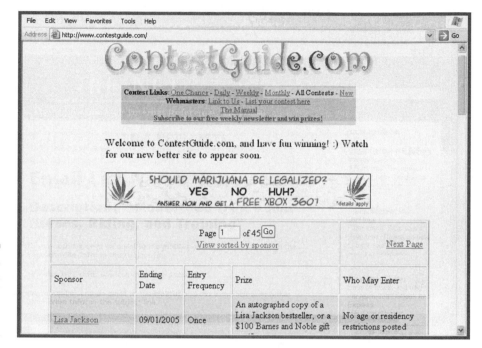

Figure 4.37

Most of the listings in ContestGuide are organized according to how often you can enter the contest.

Figure 4.38

FreebieList offers a wide variety for Web surfers and is a good source to promote your giveaways.

One last freebie Web site for you to check out is 1 Free Stuff Site (**www.1freestuffsite.com**). This directory, shown in Figure 4.39, includes free stuff and samples. To add your freebie, you need to first add a link to the 1 Free Stuff Site and then drill down into the category where you want your freebie listed and then click on Add Link.

Figure 4.39

1 Free Stuff Site makes it easy for you to get your freebie listed in its directory.

Other Ideas for Attracting the Masses

Just in case you don't feel that you have enough ideas on your list that you'd like to follow up on to help your Web site attract more attention, here are a few more good ideas. These ideas are targeted at adding more content to your Web pages in order to encourage repeat traffic.

Providing a Tip of the Day

One idea that you can use to keep your visitors coming back over and over again is to create a Tip of the Day (or week). If your tips offer really useful information, your visitors will return to learn more. In addition, by offering tips, you position yourself as a subject matter expert on whatever topic you are covering. For example, the folks at WUGNET (**www.wugnet.com**) encourage repeat traffic by providing a computing tip of the day, as shown in Figure 4.40.

Of course, you'll need to set aside enough time and effort to really make your Tip of the Day worth coming back to. If you are willing to put forth the effort, your tips may help you build up a steady following.

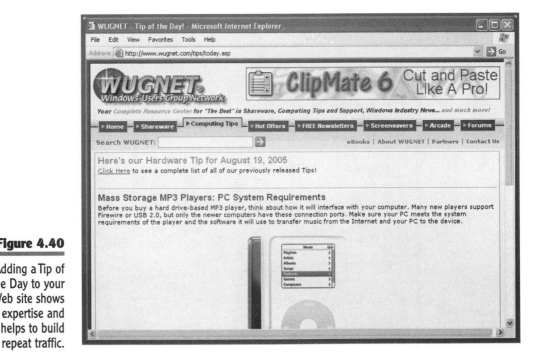

Figure 4.40

Adding a Tip of the Day to your Web site shows expertise and helps to build repeat traffic.

Adding External Content to Your Web Pages

For whatever reason, people like to participate in short surveys or polls that cover topics that are of interest to them. For example, at **www.vote.com**, you will find a new political poll each day. People that are interested in politics and current events enjoy going to Vote.com just to express their opinions on a given survey question and to see how their opinions stack up with other people's opinions.

Your poll doesn't have to be very long. A single well-formed true/false or multiple choice question will do just fine. For example, take a look at Figure 4.41, which shows a typical poll posted each day at the Greta Wire area on **www.foxnews.com**.

If you want help in the formation and presentation of your polls, check out Free Online Surveys (**www.freeonlinesurveys.com**), as shown in Figure 4.42. Here you'll find everything you need to put a poll (for up to 50 respondents) on your Web site and to provide instant results. If the popularity of your poll rises, you'll be able to pay a fee and accommodate larger audiences.

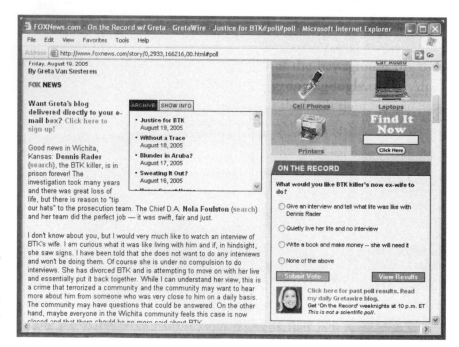

Figure 4.41

A good poll consists of one well-formed question that is of interest to your target audience.

Setting Up a Survey

Coming up with fresh content every day may represent more of an effort than you have time to commit to. If this is the case then you should investigate opportunities for posting other people's content on your Web site.

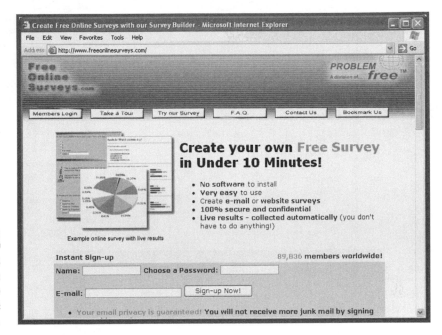

Figure 4.42

Free Online Surveys provide a service that you can use to set up and manage small polls.

Newspapers have been doing this for years, with columns like Dear Abby and comics like the Family Circle. You can travel to any major city in the U.S. and pick up a newspaper and expect to find both of these resources.

Well, you can do the same thing on your Web site. For example, let's say that you want to add a little lighthearted humor to your Web site. You could certainly sit down once a day and draw your own funny cartoon. But what do you do when you don't have the time or cannot come up with a funny new idea? The answer might be to sign up at Bravenet (**www.bravenet.com**) for the free daily cartoon service, as shown in Figure 4.43.

All you have to do to get up and running is to set up a free account at Bravenet and then click on the FREE Daily Cartoon Service link at **www. bravenet.com/webtools/index.php**. You'll be given a little HTML to add to one of your Web pages and you'll be ready to go. As part of this service, you'll also get access to monthly statistics, the ability to select from multiple templates in order to specify the presentation of the cartoon, and an "E-mail to a Friend" viral link.

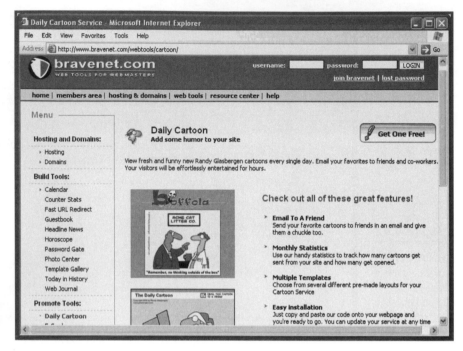

Figure 4.43

Spice up your Web
site by adding
content that
changes every day.

Setting Up Your Own Affiliate Program

One way to increase your Web traffic is to solicit others to help bring
traffic to your Web site. You can do this by setting up your own affiliate
program. Affiliate programs have been around on the Web since 1996
when amazon.com started offering a commission-based sales program
(see Figure 4.44).

In addition to helping you sell your products or services, an affiliate
program can help to strengthen your search engine ranking because of the
links that each of your affiliates will place on their Web pages back to
your site. There are many different types of affiliate programs out there.
Some, like amazon.com's, are commission based. Others, such as eBay,
pay a flat fee whenever an affiliate brings in a new customer or a returning customer that makes a bid or purchase (see Figure 4.45).

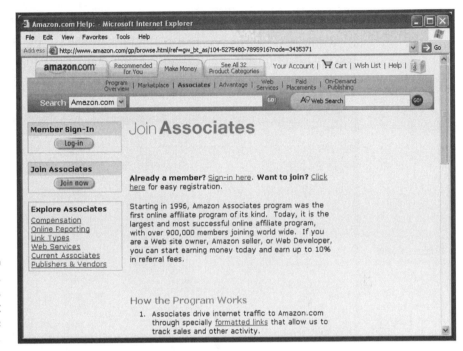

Figure 4.44

Amazon.com runs one of the Web's oldest and most successful affiliate programs.

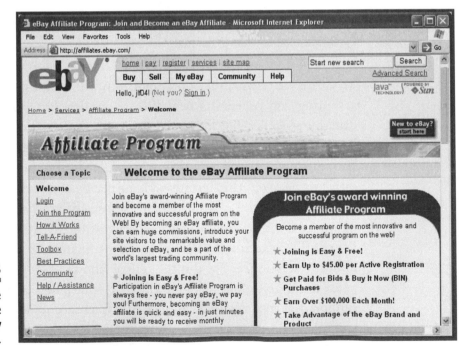

Figure 4.45

Some affiliate programs like eBay's pay flat fees.

Other affiliate programs are click-through based, like Google's AdSense program (see Figure 4.46). In this program, Google displays text- and graphic-based content on affiliate Web pages that is deliberately matched up to provide complementary content to the subject covered on affiliate Web pages.

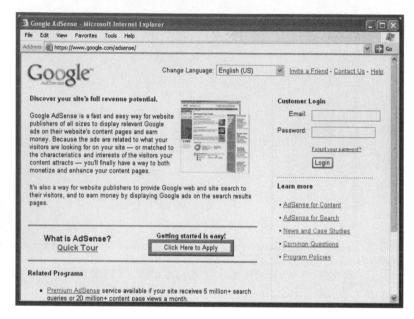

Figure 4.46

Google's AdSense program pays affiliates whenever a visitor clicks on the text or graphic advertisement placed on the affiliate's Web pages.

To create your own affiliate program, you will need to create a process for accepting and processing new affiliate applications, come up with eye-catching graphics and links, and develop a system for making payments based on results. To set something like this up from scratch can be a daunting task. Fortunately, there are a number of online affiliate program services that you can sign up with to get your affiliate program going. One such Web site is AffiliateShop (**www.affiliateshop.com**), shown in Figure 4.47. This service won't be free though. At the time that the Fourth Edition of this book was written, AffiliateShop was charging a $45 monthly service fee. For this fee you get the HTML you need to add to your Web page, along with all kinds of other goodies, like ad tracking, support for an unlimited number of affiliates, and support for a tiered commission system.

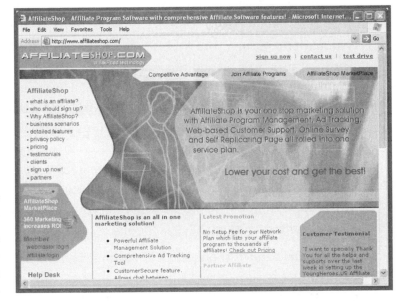

Figure 4.47

AffiliateShop provides a complete set of services to get your affiliate program up and running.

Another affiliate program to consider is the Affiliate Tracking Network (**www.affiliatezone.com**), shown in Figure 4.48. As of the time that the Fourth Edition of this book was written, there was a $149 set up charge and a $34.95 monthly fee for the Affiliate Tracking Network's basic service.

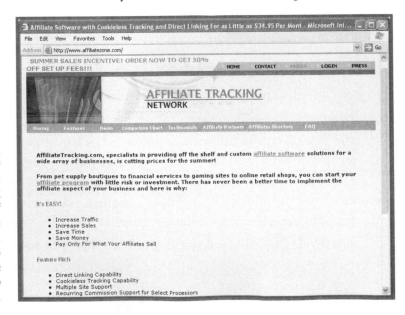

Figure 4.48

The Affiliate Tracking Network offers a number of different affiliate program packages, allowing you to grow your affiliate program to any size.

Sponsoring a Virtual Web Site Launch

No matter how long your Web site has been around, it's never too late to spruce it up a little bit and re-launch it again. There's no better way to get the ball rolling than to host your own virtual Web site launch. To make your virtual launch successful, you need to spread the word. Not only this, but you need to coordinate your various virtual Web site invitations/announcements so that they all take effect in plenty of time to notify everyone. This means getting your information posted on What's New? sites, updating your banners, sending out your newsletters, posting your invitations in newsgroups, and getting your direct mail campaign all going at the same time.

Your virtual launch shouldn't be too different from the types of launches that you see businesses and stores do all the time. For example, you might want to set up a contest or give something away to the first 10 people that register.

Once you've got everything all set up, don't rush through the experience. There is no reason why your virtual grand opening can't last more than a day or two. In fact, you might want to run the event for a week or even a month.

Free Banner Advertising: No Joke

If you have browsed the Web, you have probably seen hundreds of banners. The banner is the most frequently used advertising method on the Web. A typical banner ad is placed at the top or bottom of a Web page so that it can catch the viewer's eye and possibly prompt the viewer to click on it. Most advertisers pay thousands of dollars to display a banner ad. Why pay thousands of dollars, though, when you can advertise for free? By becoming a member of a banner exchange, you can advertise at thousands of member Web sites without spending a dime—no joke.

What the Heck Is a Banner Exchange?

Ever since the first one sprang onto the scene in 1996, banner exchanges have spread like wildfire. Most banner exchanges have a broad focus that allows just about any type of banner advertising. There are also specialty banner exchanges that focus on specific communities of interest, such as travel Web sites.

You can think of a banner exchange as a cooperative advertising program in which participants work together to advertise each other's Web sites, products, or services using banner advertising. The amount of free advertising you receive is directly related to the amount of advertising you give to other participants.

Although cooperative advertising isn't exactly a new concept, it is definitely a breakthrough for anyone who wants to get his or her Web site noticed. Because most banner exchanges have a network of thousands of participants, you can use the exchange to promote your Web site, products, and services to a massive and extremely diverse audience.

How Do Banner Exchanges Work?

The wonderful thing about banner exchanges is that the exchange is responsible for managing the network. To accomplish this, most exchanges have a banner management system that tracks when and where banners are displayed throughout the network. Every time you display the banner of another member, you receive a credit. Based on these credits, the management system ensures that your banner is displayed at other sites in the network.

If you had to manually edit your Web pages to change banners, the banner exchange wouldn't be of much use. Fortunately, the banner management system is responsible for rotating the banners as well. To enable automatic banner rotation, exchange members are given a section of HTML code that allows the management system to dynamically update banners when the page is loaded. The code snippet also includes an account number that allows the management system to track where and when a banner is displayed and to give credit appropriately.

An added benefit of the banner exchange is the ability to track and view the performance statistics for your banner. Depending on the banner exchange, your performance statistics can range from up-to-the-minute accounting to weekly account summaries. Either way, the stats usually tell you how many times your banner was displayed as well as how many times someone clicked on your banner. Generally, you will need to visit the banner exchange to view the stats.

In Web lingo, the word *impression* describes the instances in which your banner is displayed. The number of times that someone clicks on your banner is called the *click through*. When you divide the total click through by the total impressions, you come up with a *click-through ratio*. Some banner exchanges use the click-through ratio to determine the effectiveness of your banner advertising.

To get a better understanding of click-through ratios, consider the following examples:

- Joe's home page displays a banner ad at the top of the page. Last week 5,000 people visited Joe's home page and 150 clicked on the banner ad. Joe's click-through ratio was 3% (150 / 5000 = .03).

- Ziggy's White Pages display banner ads at the top and bottom of every page. Last week 25,000 people visited the site and there were a total of 100,000 page views (with 200,000 total impressions). Banners were clicked on 5,000 times. Ziggy's click-through rate for all ads was 2.5% (5,000 / 200,000 = .25).

Exchanging Your Banner

Before you can participate in a banner exchange, you must become a member, which usually involves filling out detailed contact information on yourself, your Web site, and your business. You are also asked questions about the type of material you publish at your Web site and the types of sites that can be promoted at your site. Although most banner exchanges unanimously prohibit promoting explicit or offensive Web sites, a rating system usually is in place that covers everything from kids-only sites to sites for mature audiences.

The purpose of the rating system is to protect the interests of the exchange members. After all, if your Web site is for kids, you don't want someone to display a banner that is directed at adults. By the same token, you might not want to display advertising for kids at your adult-oriented Web site.

After you complete the membership process, you will be given a section of HTML code that you can add to any pages at your Web site. The purpose of this code is to display the banner advertising of other exchange members. Your unique account number for the exchange is a part of the HTML code. For this reason, you should copy the code that the exchange gives you and paste it directly into your Web pages without making any changes.

Because you receive a credit each time someone views a banner advertisement at your Web site, your first instinct might be to add the banner code to every page at your Web site. Instead, consider limiting your banner placement in well-visited areas of your Web site and primarily on top-level pages. You shouldn't inundate visitors with advertising or make them wait for banners to load on every page.

NOTE Banner exchanges have many checks and balances in place to ensure that the exchange system is fair. For example, exchanges typically prohibit the use of more than one banner from a single exchange on a single page. In most cases, however, nothing stops your from putting banners from other exchanges on a single page.

After you receive the banner code, the next step is to submit your banner to the exchange. Most exchanges have a form that you can use to submit your banner. Otherwise, you might have to send your banner to the exchange as an e-mail attachment.

Creating a Banner Advertisement

The banner exchange process starts with creating a banner to be displayed at other Web sites. You banner doesn't have to be designed by a professional but should entice people to read it and click on it. Although you will see banners with high-powered graphics, it is not the catchy graphics that attract the viewer's eye as much as the information.

Information is the key to a successful banner, especially when the file size of your banner is severely limited by the banner exchange. Most banner exchanges restrict your banner to a file size of less than 8KB—a tiny amount in the world of high-powered graphics. When you develop your banner, the file size limit should be one of your overriding concerns.

Banner exchanges also specify the exact dimensions of the banner. A typical banner size is 678 pixels wide by 60 pixels high. To enforce these dimensions, the HTML code from the exchange usually sets the height and width of the banner to these dimensions. Still, you should create your banner with these dimensions in mind. Web browsers will use the dimensions to resize a nonstandard banner, which might distort your image and make it unreadable.

The last restriction most banner exchanges enforce is that your banner must be a noninterlaced GIF image. Furthermore, you usually cannot use transparent or animated GIFs. If you don't know what noninterlaced, transparent GIFs mean, don't worry. Simply save your banner as a standard (noninterlaced) GIF. Most graphics programs will use this standard format unless you specifically change the settings, so don't change the save options.

TIP If you want to work with multiple banner exchanges, you should note the limits of file and image sizes for each. Then you should design your banner with these limits in mind. By resizing your banner to fit the requirements of each exchange, you can use the same banner repeatedly.

Selecting a Banner Exchange

No two banner exchanges are the same. When you select a banner exchange, you need to look past the gilded doorways that say you can promote your Web site for free. Instead, look into the heart of the exchange's management system.

Banner exchanges use what is called an exchange ratio to indicate the display-to-credit ratio offered by the exchange. The most common exchange ratio is 2 to 1. If an exchange has a 2 to 1 ratio, this means that for every two times that someone views a banner on your Web site, your banner will be displayed at a member site one time.

A quick check of the math tells you that, at an exchange ratio of 2 to 1, half of the impressions are going somewhere other than to banner exchange members. Here is where sponsorship comes into the picture. To make up for the costs of running the exchange, most banner exchanges sell the additional space to sponsors. With the average banner exchange racking up millions of impressions every day, a 2 to 1 exchange radio has a pretty hefty profit margin.

Beyond the exchange ratio, you should look at the features of the exchange's banner management system. Everything that you do at an exchange should be handled through a password-protected account. Standard features of the account should be to view your current statistics, modify your account profile, and submit a banner. What's more, you should be able to access any of these features directly at the exchange's Web site, and the management system should handle updates automatically.

Some exchanges offer additional features, such as *targeting*. With targeting you can select the specific categories of Web sites that will display your banner and, often, the categories of banners displayed at your own Web site. In this way, your banner is seen only by audiences that you select, which includes audiences that are interested in products, services, or information similar to what you offer at your Web site.

Finally, you should look at the total membership of the exchange and the throughput of the exchange's Web connection. *Throughput* refers to the transfer rate between the server and the client computers. Together, the number of members and the throughput can suggest an average throughput, which in turn tells you how long your visitors will wait for banner ads to display. For example, a banner exchange with 25,000 member sites and a T1 connection to the Web is probably overloaded. As a result, visitors to your Web site might experience longer-than-normal delays while the banner loads.

Without getting into specific measurement criteria, one way to check the performance of a banner exchange is simply to visit pages of current members and see how long banners take to load. To get a solid assessment, you should check on several different days and at different times of day. Keep in mind that peak usage times are typically during the week and specifically at midday.

Banner Exchanges for the Masses

Now that you know the ins and outs of banner swapping, you are ready to take the next step and join the exchanges of your choice. To help you on your way, this section lists some of the most popular banner exchanges.

Exchanging Banners with LinkBuddies

LinkBuddies (**www.linkbuddies.com**) manages an exchange service consisting of more than 50,000 member sites (see Figure 4.49). It supports targeted advertising with over 150 categories. Although targeted advertising is one of the key reasons for the success of LinkBuddies, the exchange has many other features that make it a winner.

LinkBuddies offers a 2 to 1 exchange ratio to its members. When other member banners are not displayed, the exchange displays its own banner as well as the banners of paid sponsors. LinkBuddies provides detailed reporting, including hourly, daily, and monthly data.

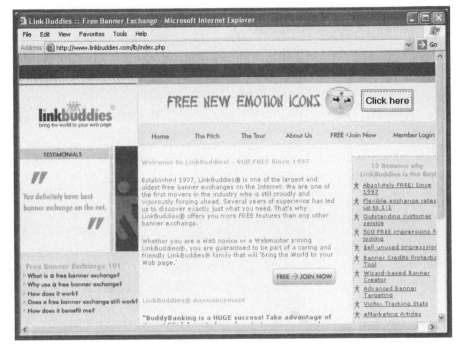

Figure 4.49

LinkBuddies allows you to target ads to specific audiences.

Exchanging Banners with Exchange-it!

Exchange-it! (**www.exchange-it.com**) provides an effective banner exchange service with a 2 to 1 exchange ratio (see Figure 4.50). Exchange-it! let's you target your advertising by choosing from more than 300 different categories and provides daily and weekly banner advertisement statistics.

Using CyberLink Exchange

Another exchange to consider is CyberLink Exchange (**www.cyberlink exchange.comwww.cyberlinkexchange.com**). Although this exchange doesn't have the polished appearance of most other exchanges, it offers many extras, including a fairly advanced system for targeting specific audiences (see Figure 4.51).

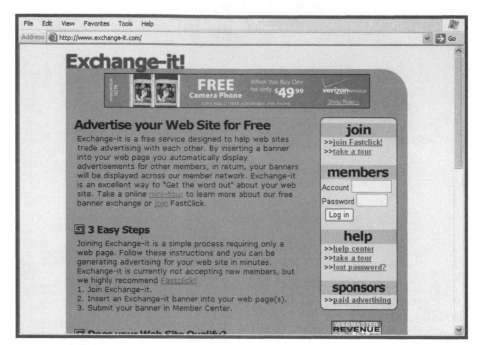

Figure 4.50

Exchange-it! provides an easy-to-use banner exchange service.

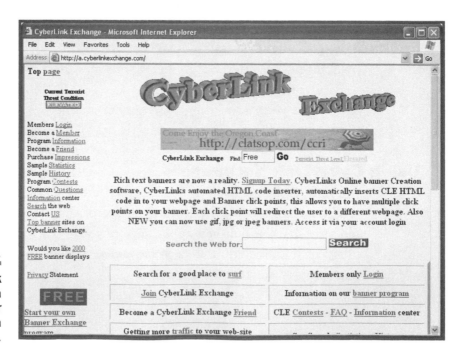

Figure 4.51

CyberLink Exchange is a small banner service with a lot of attitude.

CyberLink offers a variable exchange ratio that ranges from 2 to 1 to 3 to 2. A bonus is offered when visitors to your site click on a banner ad. To submit your banner to the CyberLink Exchange, you must make your banner 400 × 40.

Other Banner Exchanges

LinkBuddies, Exchange-it!, and CyberLink are just a few of a growing number of banner exchange Web sites. A few other free banner exchange services that you might want to look into include:

- **Express Marketing—www.express-marketing.com/ bannersignup.html**

- **e-bannerx.com—www.e-bannerx.com**

- **Click4Click—www.click4click.com**

- **BannerZero—www.bannerzero.com**

Analyzing Off-Page Factors

The major search engines have had plenty of time to figure out various ways of dealing with spamming techniques employed by less than scrupulous Web site publishers. Part of the arsenal employed by search engines is *off-page* ranking analysis.

What makes off-page factors attractive to search engines is that Web site publishers have very little ability to manipulate them. One of the major off-page factors is *link analysis*. Using link analysis, search engines gauge a Web page's relevance by examining both the number of links to the Web page and the quality of those links. Quality, in this context, refers to the ranking of the Web pages that provide the links. The higher ranked a Web page is, the higher the quality of its link.

Another off-page analysis tool employed by search engines is *click-through analysis*. In click-through analysis, the search engine counts the number of times that Web surfers click on a link when presented with it (compared to links for competing Web sites).

Building a Strong Ranking Through Links

Increasing the ranking of your Web page should be a major goal of your Web site promotion plans. One way to do this is to contact other Web sites and ask them to trade links with your Web site. To come up with a list of sites to contact, open up your Web browser, visit one of your preferred search engines, and then do a search using your keywords and keyword phrases. Make a list of the top Web sites that appear in the results.

Getting links from quality Web sites is one of the keys to improving your own Web site's ranking. So rather than trying to get every Tom, Dick, and Harry to trade links with you, focus on the top sites that show up in your search engine results. Since many of the sites that will appear in your search results may be direct competitors, they may not take you up on your offer to exchange links. However, if you are lucky, some Web sites will agree in order to try and increase their own ranking.

Of course, just because you find other Web site owners who say that they will exchange links with you, that doesn't mean that they will hold up their end of the bargain. So, from time to time you will want to check on these Web sites and send an e-mail to their owners if you don't see a link to your Web site. Alternatively, you might want to check out LinkCheckPro (**www.link-check.net**). LinkCheckPro is a software program that you can download and install and then configure to automate the process of checking on the status of all your reciprocal links. You can even set up LinkCheckPro to send a e-mail to your link partners when necessary.

Avoiding Link Farms

Be careful to make sure that in your enthusiasm to improve your Web page's rankings you don't get caught up in a *link farm* scam. A link farm is a large group of Web pages created for the sole purpose of trying to trick search engines into increasing the Web page's ranking. While it is perfectly legitimate to exchange links with other Web sites (which is one of the basic principles that makes the Web work), it is not at all proper to set up Web pages just so you can establish links with them to your real Web site.

Increasing Your Traffic with Web Rings

One of the problems with looking for information on the Web by performing keyword searches using search engines is that the results usually include superfluous and unrelated links. You must sift through any superfluous results to get to the Web sites that actually contain the type of information that is being looked for.

Directories offer an alternative to search engines. One particular and popular type of directory that more and more Web surfers are turning to is *Web rings*. A Web ring is a free service that organizes related Web sites into groups based on common subject matter.

What makes Web rings popular is that once a site in the ring is found that contains the type of information a Web surfer likes, there is a really good chance that the rest of the Web sites in the ring will also be exactly what the Web surfer is looking for.

How Do Web Rings Work?

Web rings are organized into major categories, each of which contains any number of subcategories. Drill down far enough, and you will find individual Web rings. Each Web ring is started by an individual owner. It is up to the owner to accept or reject requests by Web site owners to join the Web ring. Each Web site in the Web ring contains navigational controls for moving around in the ring, as demonstrated in Figure 4.52.

A central Web ring server controls Web ring navigation. This server prevents dead ends from breaking the ring by automatically forwarding a Web surfer on to the next available Web site in a ring.

Working with the Major Web Rings

There are currently two major Web rings.

✪ WebRing—dir.webring.com/rw

✪ RingSurf—www.ringsurf.com

Figure 4.52

Each Web site has navigational controls for moving forward and backward in the ring and for randomly accessing Web sites in the ring.

As of the writing of the Fourth Edition of this book, WebRing was hosting almost 50,000 rings in its directory. RingSurf was not far behind with just over 40,000 rings. Both Web ring services are 100% free. To join a ring, you just sign up with the hosting Web ring service and fill out a request form. If the Web ring owner approves, you will be sent a little HTML along with instructions on what to do with it. If you don't see a ring that covers your topic, you can start up your own ring. However, you'll have to find four other Web sites to join your ring before the hosting Web ring services will add your Web ring to its directory listings.

Short on Time? Try Paid Inclusion

If you are in a hurry to get your Web site noticed and don't have 4-6 weeks to wait for the major search engines and directories to get you listed, you can always spend a few dollars and go with paid inclusion services.

Every major search engine accepts some sort of paid listings. This means that within 1-2 days, your Web site could start appearing in the top results for searching that use your specified keywords. As a start, you might set up an account with Google's AdWords program or Yahoo!'s Search Marketing program (formerly known as Overture). For example, if one of your keyword phrases was "cuckoo clock," you might agree to pay 20 cents per click. If nobody else has agreed to this much, your link would be displayed in the top spot. If somebody later came along and agreed to pay 25 cents, you'd slip down one position in the rankings, unless you increased your price.

Both Google and Yahoo! require that you set up a starting account balance and that you pay a minimum price per click. However, if you are careful in your selection of keyword terms, you should be able to get started for $50 and stretch this startup cost into 1-2 months of advertising. Hopefully, your free search engine and directory listings will start appearing before you exhaust your funds, at which time you can stop paying to advertise your site. Of course, if you are happy with the results, you could always elect to keep your paid advertising efforts going.

Locating Sponsored Links

Both Google and Yahoo! display paid links at the top of the screen and along the right-hand side of their search results, as demonstrated in Figure 4.53. To identify them even further, paid results appearing at the top of the screen are displayed with a different background color, whereas paid results on the right-hand side of the screen are separated from the rest of the results by a vertical bar. In addition, both areas display a "Sponsored Links" or "Sponsor Results" label.

Google AdWords

Google administers its paid listings through its AdWords program (**adwords.google.com**). This program charges customers a per-click fee, meaning that you only have to pay when somebody actually clicks on

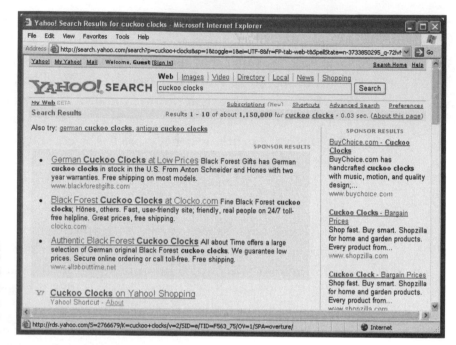

Figure 4.53

Search engines use various techniques to help make their paid listings stand out.

your paid link (as opposed to simply seeing it). As of the time that the Fourth Edition of the book was written, there is a one time $5 activation fee and you are required to pay a minimum 5 cents per click fee. For $50, you ought to be able to get a good 4-6 weeks' worth of advertising.

 NOTE By the end of this 4-6 week period, your free search engine and directory listings should start to appear and you might then want to stop paying for this service.

Yahoo! Search Marketing

Yahoo! refers to a paid inclusion as a sponsored search. You can sign up for Yahoo!'s program at **searchmarketing.yahoo.com/srch** by clicking on the Sign Up button. Yahoo! requires a $30 initial deposit. In addition, you are also required to spend a minimum of $20 per month. The minimum bid requirement for each click is 10 cents.

Again, just as is the case with Google's AdWords program, you only pay when someone actually clicks on your paid links. And, you can count on your listing appearing in the search results of other search engines. For example, in the case of Yahoo!, you could expect to see your listing appear in AltaVista.

Other Paid Inclusion Programs

While Google and Yahoo! may be the two most popular paid inclusion programs, there are plenty of other good programs out there that you can sign up for to reach an even larger audience. These search engines include:

- MSN—search.msn.com

- FindWhat—www.findwhat.com

- LookSmart—search.looksmart.com

You will find plenty of other paid advertising opportunities with other search engines. In addition, the major metasearch engines also accept paid listings. For example, Mamma (**www.mamma.com**) calls its paid listings Mamma Classifieds.

Keep 'em Coming Back

Have you ever visited a Web site that contained some incredibly useful or entertaining content only to realize a few days later that you have no idea how to get back? Perhaps you can't remember the full URL or the Web site's name. Surely, this is something that has happened to everybody a time or two.

Given that every major Web browser has a bookmarking capability, there is no reason why anyone should ever lose track of an important Web site. Still, it happens all the time, and it is not always the Web surfer's fault. Much of the time this predicament could be averted if only the Web site owner would place a friendly reminder on his or her Web page. This reminder need not be complex; it could be something as simple as a well placed piece of text that says "Bookmark this page." Figure 4.54 demonstrates the application of this simple strategy at Health & Fitness Tips (**www.health-fitness-tips.com/ health-fitness-tip**).

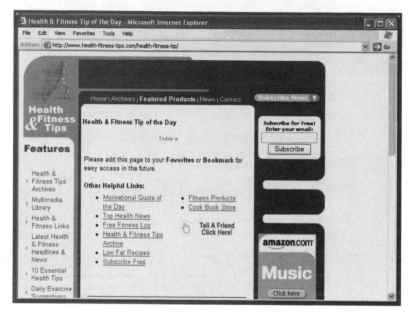

Figure 4.54

Don't just hope your visitors will bookmark your Web pages—ask them to do it.

Wrapping Up and Looking Ahead

Now that you know how to attract the masses to your Web site, it is time to take a look at who's visiting your Web site and how you can improve it, which is exactly what you'll learn in the next session. The first step to understanding your site's visitors is to examine your Web site's statistics. Web site statistics provide just about everything you need to determine who is visiting your site and why. Once you know who's visiting and why they're visiting, don't forget to keep the pages and links at your site up to date. Every visitor counts, especially when you are trying to increase traffic to your Web site. You need to do everything within your power to build a steady readership. To attract and maintain an audience over the long haul, you need to maintain your site and provide visitors with lifelines when you move or delete files.

Discovering Who's Visiting Your Web Site and Why

➤ Capturing and Analyzing Web Site Statistics

➤ Locating Problems with Your Web Site

➤ Using Web Site Statistics to Improve Your Web Site

➤ Reviewing Your Progress

Your Web site's statistics are the single most important means for discovering what people really think about your Web site, and you might be surprised when you discover which of your resources are bringing in visitors, and which resources aren't. If you're tempted to pay only cursory attention to this section, ask yourself this: What do I really know about the flow of traffic to my Web site? How do I know which pages are drawing visitors and which ones are being skipped? If you make assumptions about your visitors that the stats don't support, then your lack of awareness could cost you dearly.

So settle in with a good cup of coffee or some juice to get you alert—it's Sunday afternoon and time to roll. By the end of the afternoon, you'll know how to find out who is visiting your site and why. You'll also know how to make use of your Web site's statistics to begin increasing your Web traffic.

Using Web Stats to Understand Your Site's Visitors

Web site stats tell you much more than which Web pages at your Web site interest visitors. By tracking stats, you also learn many things about the people who visit your Web site, such as how long they visit, whether they really read the pages that you present or just skip on by, what days of the week are the most popular, what time of day is the best time to make updates, and a whole lot of other things. For example, Web site statistics typically reveal:

- How many people are visiting your Web site each day, week, and month.

- The type and versions of browsers being used by your visitors so that you can determine which types of technologies are best deployed.

- The IP address of each visitor, allowing you to discover where they come from.

- The time and date of each visit, allowing you to determine the best time for making changing to your Web pages.

- The keywords that your visitors are using to locate your Web site so that you can fine-tune your keywords and keyword phrases.

You need to know who is being drawn to your Web site so that you can keep them coming back for more and attract others like them. You need to know about errors and other circumstances that could make your site an obstacle course, which could prevent visitors from coming or staying. You need to get your hands on some useful information so that you can make informed decisions.

Traditional retailers have been tracking information about their customers for a long time, using the information they gather to customize their marketing and advertising plans. Likewise, online retailers and Web sites do their best to track customer habits and to learn as much as possible about the likes and dislikes of the Web surfers who visit their Web sites. Take amazon.com for example. Amazon.com places a great deal of emphasis on learning everything that it can about each customer's likes and dislikes. By tracking individual habits, amazon.com is able to create customized Web pages that it thinks each customer will find helpful. Amazon.com displays these custom pages as demonstrated in Figure 5.1.

Jerry's Store

Figure 5.1

Amazon.com puts a lot of work into tracking customer activities in order to fine-tune its Web site and marketing plans.

As Figure 5.1 shows, amazon.com has created a customized page called Jerry's Store in which merchandise is presented that amazon.com thinks may be of interest to Jerry based on the information that has been collected on him. By tracking visitor activity, amazon.com is able to fine-tune the way it runs its Web site in order to make it more successful. Similarly, you can begin collecting and tracking user activity on your Web site. One way to do this is by asking your visitors to tell you something about themselves when they fill out forms or send you e-mails in order to sign up for your contests, newsletters, sweepstakes, and so on. Web site statistics can be just as valuable to you when it comes to learning more about your visitors. Best of all, Web site statistics allow you to collect data without depending on your visitors to take the time to provide it to you. By taking the time to collect and analyze Web site stats, you empower yourself with information that you can use to make your Web site a better place to visit. This effort will remove your site from the ranks of hit-or-miss Web sites and give it the stamp of professionalism.

Options for Collecting Web Site Statistics

When it comes to collecting and analyzing Web site statistics, you have two options: software-based and on-demand. With the software-based option, you install an application on your Web server and use it to process the contents of your Web server log files. With the on-demand option, you sign-up with a Web-based service, which collects and presents your Web traffic data. Which of these two options you decide to go with will depend on a number of different factors.

NOTE Of course, depending on the service provider you are using, your options when it comes to installing custom software may be limited. If your service provider is too restrictive, the on-demand option is probably going to work best for you.

The software-based option works best when you want total control over your Web site's data. This option is viable when you have a talented IT staff capable of running the software. This option requires that you purchase a copy of the software, which involves a one-time cost. With this option, you will also have to make sure that your Web server is capable of accommodating the overhead of running the additional software. Otherwise, you may need to upgrade or replace your Web server.

TIP If you are paying an ISP to host your Web site, you may find that the ISP has already purchased and installed Web site analysis software on the Web server, in which case you may be able to use it for a small additional fee.

On the other hand, if you are comfortable with allowing a third party to collect and process your Web statistics, you may want to go with a on-demand service, especially if you don't already have available in-house IT staff to do the job. While this option avoids a potentially hefty one-time cost, it does require a monthly service fee. This option also allows you to get up and running almost immediately. As you will see in the sections that follow, there are plenty of software programs that you can use to analyze your Web server's log files. In addition, there is no shortage of on-demand Web services either. In addition to software and on-demand services that perform specialized tasks, there are also companies that have developed versions of their Web site analysis tool that you can either purchase as a stand-alone software program or sign up and use as an on-demand Web service. Two of the best are WebTrends (**www.webtrends.com**), as shown in Figure 5.2, and NetTracker (**www.sane.com**), as shown in Figure 5.3.

Figure 5.2

WebTrends provides advanced log analysis features that you can use to get a detailed picture of who is visiting your Web site.

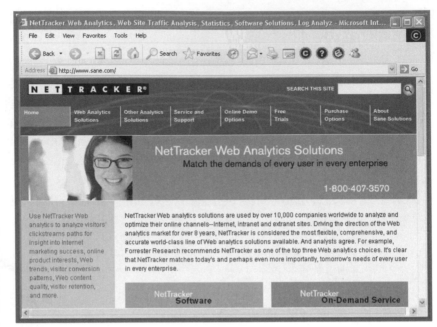

Figure 5.3

NetTracker is a world class application capable of providing any required level of log analysis.

Selecting Your Web Traffic Analysis Tool

Before continuing, you should install a Web traffic analyzer and locate your server log files. Alternately, you should find and register with an on-demand Web service that will collect and present your Web statistics to you.

If you choose to install Web site traffic analysis software on your Web server, you will need to start by getting your hands on the software. In addition to the Web site traffic analysis applications just discussed, you may want to review the list of software presented in the book's appendix, "Additional Resources on the Web." Here you will find information about a number of other Web site traffic analysis applications. If any of these applications suit your fancy, pick one and then download and install a free trial copy. Then, if after taking a test run you find you like it, purchase a licensed copy. The list of Web site traffic analysis applications that you will find in the appendix includes:

- **FastStats**
- **MozillaTracker**

- ✿   **NetTracker**

- ✿   **PageStats/HitCount**

- ✿   **Surfstats**

If you choose to sign up with an on-demand Web service that will collect your Web stats for you, you will have to sign up with one and follow the instructions that will be provided to set up your pages so that the service can begin collecting your data. In addition to the on-demand Web services just discussed, you may want to also check out the following additional online services:

- ✿   **Web Stats Gold—www.webstatsgold.com**

- ✿   **Web-Stat—www.web-stat.com**

The sections that follow provide essential details for making sense of the reports that you'll be able to generate and also provide high-level instruction on how to use the information found in these reports to understand and improve your Web site.

Web Site Stats Are a Necessary Evil

Yes, Web stats truly are a necessary evil. Everyone hates the thought of statistics. However, if you don't track the status at your Web site you will never truly understand who is visiting your Web site and, more importantly, why. The following list shows a few more reasons why you should take the time to track your Web site's stats:

- ✿   To discover popular and unpopular resources.

- ✿   To learn more about the people who visit your site.

- ✿   To learn more about the effectiveness of your banner advertising.

- ✿   To obtain information on search engine usage and referring sites.

- ✿   To determine which browsers and platforms people use when visiting your site.

Before you start having flashbacks of high-school algebra class, you should know that tracking and analyzing Web site stats isn't rocket science. As a mater of fact, tracking and analyzing stats is fairly easy as long as you follow the advice presented in this afternoon's session.

NOTE If you decide to go with the option of processing the log files located on your Web server, you'll need to know where the Web server's log files are stored. The location of the Web server log files is defined when a server is installed. The best way to find the Web server log files is to ask your service provider or the Web master for your server where these files are stored.

Keep in mind that if you have your own domain, such as **www.yourname.com**, you should have separate log files regardless of whether you actually have your own server or you use someone else's server. If the same server handles multiple domains, the logs probably have a prefix that indicates the domain. Otherwise you—like anyone using a service provider—will share server logs with everyone else using the server.

Regardless of whether you analyze your own Web site's log files or use an on-demand Web service to collect and process your stats, you can expect to get the same basic information. The following sections provide you with an overview of the types of data and reports that you can expect and provides you with insight on how to analyze this data in order to make improvements to your Web site.

Discovering Popular and Unpopular Resources

By tracking and analyzing stats, you can discover which of the pages at your Web site are visited most often. Although you might think that your top-level home page is the most popular, this isn't always the case. In fact, your analysis might reveal that most people visit some other page at your Web site. This is because the Web allows anyone to visit any Web page at your Web site, and visitors don't have to start at your home page.

One report that you will want to generate is one that tracks popular Web pages. Depending on which Web traffic analysis tool you use, the name of this report will be different. You should look for a report named something like Most Requested Pages or Most Popular Pages.

Another report that you might want to look for is one that depicts how much traffic each major area of your Web site receives, as shown in Figure 5.4. Using a report like this, you can determine which area of your Web site needs additional attention versus which pages you may wish to further exploit by using viral and permission marketing techniques.

Figure 5.4 is a picture of a sample NetTracker report made available on **www.sane.com/products/NetTracker/web_content.html**.

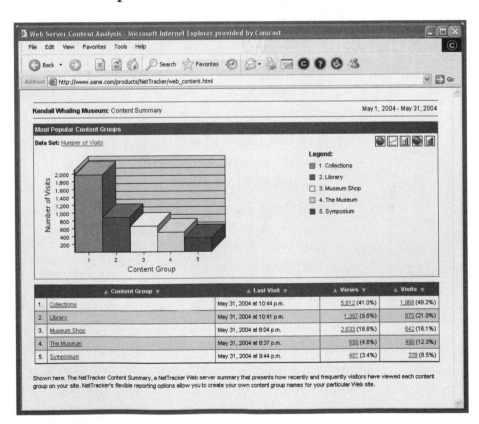

Figure 5.4

Examining a Content Summary report to see which areas within a Web site are being visited most often.

You might also be interested in looking to see if you can generate reports that show which Web pages are visited most often and which Web pages receive the least attention. These reports might be called something like the Most Requested Pages and Least Requested Pages reports.

Other types of reports that can tell you about the popularity of your Web pages include

- **Most Accessed Directories**. Identifies which directories were most frequently accessed. This report is useful when you want to identify popular areas of your Web site.

- **Most Downloaded File Types**. Identifies the most popular type of downloaded file.

- **Most Downloaded Files**. Identifies the executable or document files that are most frequently downloaded.

- **Top Entry Pages**. Identifies which pages were most frequently the first page requested at the site. You can use this report to better understand why people visit your site.

- **Top Exit Pages**. Identifies which pages were most frequently the last page requested at the site. You can use this report to help understand why users leave your site.

- **Top Paths Through the Site**. Identifies paths users most frequently take through the site. You can use this report to better understand how users navigate pages at your site.

The main purpose of generating all of these different types of reports is to gain an insight as to how people are visiting your Web site. Using the information presented in these reports, you can determine what content your visitors appreciate most and try to provide more of it. You can also find out which pages your visitors are just skimming through and try to improve them in order to give your visitors a reason to slow down and look around. Finally, by looking for common exit points in your Web site, you can focus your efforts on trying to find ways to redirect your visitors back to other parts of your Web site and increase your overall level of stickiness.

Learn More About the People Who Visit Your Site

By tracking your Web site's stats, you also can learn more about the people who visit, such as where they live, where they work, and how they access your Web site. One of the best ways to learn more about your Web site is to track visitor demographics. For example, you can expect to find reports that identify which countries your visitors are coming from.

Depending on which Web traffic analysis tool you use, you may also find that there are also other types of demographic information you might be able to track, such as

- User profiles by region

- The U.S. state or Canadian province from which users most frequently visit

- The organizations your visitors are most frequently from, such as whether they are from government, military, education, or commercial organizations

- Whether a particular user is a new user or is returning for a subsequent visit

- Session information for top users

- The number of visits per user

Find Out When People Visit

Finding out when people visit your Web site is extremely useful, especially if you use this information to plan updates for your Web pages. As Figure 5.5 shows, you can use stats to determine the activity level at your Web site throughout the week. For example, you might discover that Friday is your busiest day of the week in terms of the number of times your pages receive hits or the amount of data that is transferred. At the same time, you might determine that Sunday is the slowest day of the week.

Figure 5.5 is a picture of a sample NetTracker report made available on **www.sane.com/products/NetTracker/web_traffic.html**.

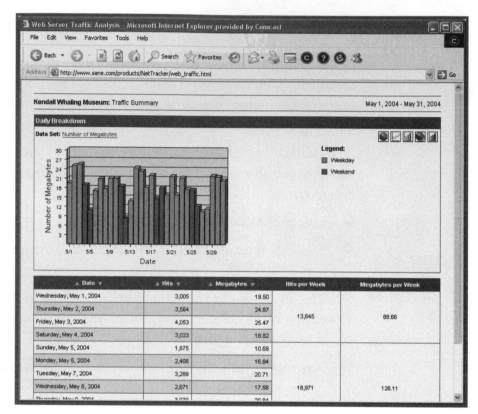

Figure 5.5

Traffic summary
reports can be used
to determine which
days of the week
are the busiest
and which are
the slowest.

Using this information, you could better determine when to post updates to
your Web site and when not to post updates. For example, assuming that
Friday was your busiest day, you might want to post updates on Sunday in
order to provide your biggest audience with the most up-to-date information.

Other types of activity reports that you might want to look for include

○ **Bandwidth Usage**. Shows the volume of activity according to the
amount of data transferred.

○ **Activity Level By Hour of Day**. Shows the busiest hours of the
day.

○ **Activity Level By Time Interval**. Summarizes activity by week or
month.

Learn More About Banner Advertising

These days most Web sites have banner ads, and your site is probably no exception. Yet do you know if the banner exchange you are using is telling you the truth about click-through rates? Well, your Web site stats can tell you exactly how many people are viewing banner ads on your site and how many people are clicking on those ads.

Normally, you'll need to tell your analysis software about the specific campaigns you are running. For example, you might have the following three ongoing ad campaigns running

○ IBM Laptop Giveaway Ad

○ Dell Laptop Giveaway Ad

○ Compaq Desktop Giveaway Ad

Assuming that these ad campaigns are linked to specific banners, each time a particular banner ad is displayed or clicked on, information would be recorded. Again, depending on which Web traffic analysis tool you are working with, reports will be named differently. Regardless, you should be able to find reports based on banner ads viewed and banner ads clicked. You should also be able to analyze data showing the ratio of Ad Views to Ad Clicks (e.g. the Click-Through Rate).

The value of this kind of information is that you can use it to determine which of your advertising efforts is the most successful and which efforts are not working out. This information can then be used to help you make the best use of your limited time, effort, and dollars. As an example, check out Figure 5.6, which shows an example of a NetTracker Campaign Summary report made available on **www.sane.com/products/NetTracker/web_roi.html**.

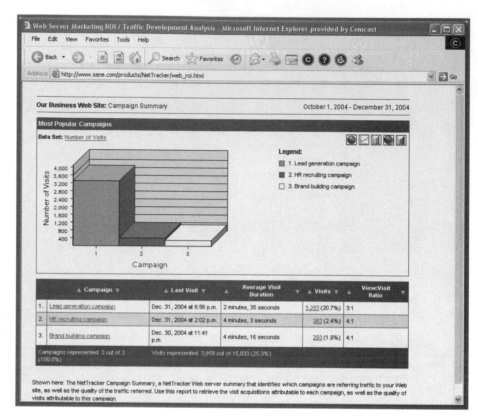

Figure 5.6

By tracking your sales campaigns, you can learn how to best spend your time, effort, and money.

Obtain Information About Referring Sites, Search Engines, and More

The analysis of your Web site statistics can tell you exactly how users got to your Web site. A key report you'll want to obtain is a Referrer report (or Referring Site report). The report tells you how visitors find their way to your site. This report will show you the search engines and directories from which most of your visitors are coming. In addition, you may see an entry for No Referrer, which means identifying the number of your visitors who enter your Web site by directly entering the URL of one of your Web pages into their browser.

The referrer information can also be used to obtain information on which search engines are used to find your Web site. This information will provide you with a list of the top search engines being used as well as the keywords or keyword phrases entered as search parameters.

Determining the Browsers and Platforms Being Used

Often, Web sites are designed with specific types of users in mind. These users probably fit a specific demographic or geographic target and you've probably made some assumptions as to how tech-savvy these users are as well. For example, in your design guidelines, you might have stipulated that the Web site is designed for users with the newest generation of browsers. You might have even taken this a step further by saying that the Web site was designed for users with the most modern browsers and Windows-based operating systems. To validate the technology assumptions that you've made, or to help establish future guidelines, you'll want to track browser and platform usage.

Most Web site tracking software provides reports for tracking browsers by type and version. A Browser By Type report will tell you the types of browsers being used but doesn't necessarily tell you the browser versions being used. This information is typically provided in a Browser By Version report.

Zeroing In on Visits

Perhaps the *visit* is the most meaningful Web site statistic. A visit is a collection of hits and page views that pertain to a specific person who requested files from your Web site. When you count visits, you are counting the number of people who stopped by your Web site.

NOTE A *hit* is a term that represents a file access. If a Web page contains five graphics, then six hits would be registered. That's one hit for each graphic that is loaded and one hit for the Web page itself. A *page view* is a representation of a Web page that is accessed. By tracking page views you can determine which pages are visited most and which receive the least amount of visits.

Putting Visits Together

Just as there's a big difference between someone shopping at your store 1 time and 50 times, so there is a big difference between someone visiting a Web site 1 time and 50 times. You need to limit the scope of visits to a specific time period, such as all consecutive file requests that are separated by no more than 30 minutes. Following this, you would say that if a person browsed your site for 5 minutes one day and 15 minutes the next day, you'd have two visits. On the other hand, if a person browsed your site for 10 minutes, went away, and then came back 15 minutes later, you'd have a single visit.

Tracking Visits

Tracking software counts visits by limiting the scope of visits to specific time frames. When you track individual visits, you are mostly interested in the summary information, such as

- How long did the person visit?

- What page did the person start on?

- What areas did the person visit?

- How long did the person stay in each area?

- What was the total number of hits for this visitor?

- What was the total number of page views for this visitor?

For example, let's look at a scenario in which a Web site has had three visits. A summary of the first visit is outlined below.

> Minimum length of visit:
>> 12 minutes, 4 seconds
> Start page:
>> /
> Main pages visited and duration:
>> / - 2 minutes 10 seconds
>> vpjic.html - 1 minute, 36 seconds

vpepc.html - 5 minutes, 28 seconds

joboppframes.html - 2 minutes, 50 seconds

Total hits:

97

Total page views:

27

The summary for the second visit is outlined below.

Minimum length of visit:

5 minutes, 40 seconds

Start page:

/idn/cissue/resmul.htm

Main pages visited and duration:

/idn/cissue/resmul.htm - 37 seconds

idnfp.htm - 5 minutes 3 seconds

/idn/bio/biorev.html - unknown duration

Total hits:

13

Total page views:

3

The summary for the third visit is outlined below.

Minimum length of visit:

5 minutes, 25 seconds

Start page:

/idn/cissue/resmul.htm

Main pages visited and duration:

/idn/cissue/resmul.htm - 5 minutes 25 seconds

idnfp.htm - unknown duration

Total hits:

5

Total page views:

2

Getting the Big Picture

The big picture takes into account all visits to the Web site during a specific period of time, such as the 15-minute time slice. When you put together the big picture, you must ask yourself many important questions. The answers to these questions will help you understand who is visiting your Web site and why. The main questions that you will want to ask include:

✿ What was the total number of visitors for this time period?

✿ What was the length of the average visit?

✿ What was the average duration of a page view?

✿ What was the average number of page views per visitor?

✿ What was the average number of hits per visitor?

✿ What domain classes and geographic areas are represented?

When you examine your Web site over a period of days or weeks, you will want to ask these additional questions:

✿ What are the busiest hours of the day?

✿ What are the busiest days of the week?

✿ What are the most requested pages?

✿ What are the most common last pages requested?

To put this in perspective, let's go back to the three visits you just looked at and create the big picture. When you answer the main questions, you come up with stats that look like this:

Visitor count:

3

Duration of analysis:

15 minutes

Length of the average visit:
  7 minutes, 3 seconds
Average duration of page views per visitor:
  10.67
Average number of hits per visitor:
  38.3
Domain classes and geographic areas:
  50% Net
  50% Com

With these stats in hand, you can now answer the all-important questions concerning who is visiting and why. The list that follows provides descriptions that can help you make sense out of the stats discussed so far. Keep in mind that these are generalities meant to get you started thinking about how you can use these stats to promote your Web site and to make your Web site a better place to visit.

- **Visitor count.** Tells you how many people are visiting. You can use this to gauge the true popularity of your Web site. Whereas a new or low-traffic Web site might get 5 to 100 visitors a day, a popular Web site might get 5,000 to 10,000 visitors a day.

- **Length of the average visit.** This is an indicator of whether people are really reading pages at your Web site or just browsing. It can also be an indicator of whether people like what they see. The longer the average visit, the more information the visitor is finding and reading.

- **Average duration of page view.** This can be an indicator of whether people are reading or just browsing. When you examine this statistic, you also need to keep in mind the length and style of pages that you have at your Web site. Are they highly textual, highly graphical, or both?

○ **Average number of views per visitor**. Generally, the more pages people view, the happier they are; and if people are viewing many pages at your Web site, they are finding information that interests them. When you count page views, you need to keep in mind the setup of your pages. Do you use frame sets that result in multiple page views? Do you use client pull to create slide shows?

○ **Average number of hits per visitor**. Over time, you can use this information to estimate the number of visitors.

○ **Domain classes and geographic areas**. This can tell you where people visiting your Web site live and work, which is great information to have if you want to attract advertisers.

○ **Busiest hours of the day**. Tells you the time of day when most people visit your Web site. This statistic can help you plan daily updates, promotional campaigns, and advertising.

○ **Busiest days of the week**. Tells you the day of the week when most people visit your Web site. This statistic can also help you plan weekly updates, promotional campaigns, and advertising.

○ **Most requested pages**. Tells you the pages that visitors find the most interesting and/or useful. Can be used to tailor your Web site to visitors' need and to help you determine which pages should receive most of your attention.

○ **Most commonly requested last pages**. Can help you spot trends and bad pages. If the last page requested has lots of links to external Web sites, this statistic tells you that this is the point from which most visitors are leaving. If the last page requested doesn't have links to external Web sites, you might want to examine the page in question.

You'll find that Web site traffic analyzers can put together all the reports you'll need for the big picture. One such report is the NetTracker Visitor Profile report (see Figure 5.7), which focuses on showing which areas of a Web site are visited, the average length of a visit, the number of visits, and the number of repeat visits.

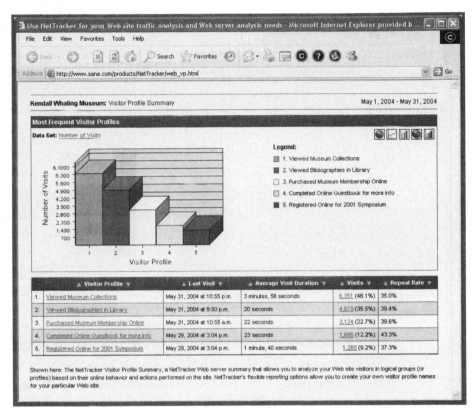

Figure 5.7

Examining a summary profile of visitor activity.

Figure 5.7 is a picture of a sample NetTracker report made available on **www.sane.com/products/NetTracker/web_vp.html**.

Taking a Break

If you haven't created traffic reports for your Web site, you should do so now. Once you generate the reports, ask yourself the questions previously pointed out. The next part of this session covers how to gain visitors who otherwise would have been lost because of bad links at your site or bad references from other sites. But before you dive in, take a break! You deserve it. Grab yourself a cup of coffee or tea.

Gaining Lost Readers from Error Analysis

After pouring your time and resources into your Web site, do you really want to risk losing people who visit your Web site but don't get to where they expected? Not really, especially when every visitor is someone who could help spread the news about your terrific Web site. Don't lose visitors once they've found a doorway into your slice of cyberspace. Nothing stops would-be visitors dead in their tracks like an error. They see errors as brick walls and often race off as quickly as they can click on the mouse. How many times have you seen the dreaded 404 - - File Not Found error message? Did you hang around the Web site that you tried to access, or did you just click on your browser's Back button and head off in some other direction?

Errors are often the result of bad links in your Web pages or bad references to your pages from other Web sites. When it comes to finding and fixing bad links in your Web pages, you have total control and can easily track down the problems—if you know how. When it comes to bad references to the pages at your Web site, you might think that finding and fixing these problems is beyond your control. However, nothing could be further from the truth. You can fix errors regardless of their source, and you're about to find out how.

Errors: We All Hate Them

We all hate errors, yet we've grown so accustomed to them that they seem like an everyday part of the quest to browse the Web. Stop and think for a moment about your reaction when you encounter a File Not Found error. Your reaction, be it restrained contempt or outright indignation, is mirrored thousands of times every day around the world.

After your initial outrage passes, what is your next reaction? You probably click on your browser's Back button to return to the site that sent you to the wrong address. Or perhaps you enter a new URL into your browser and head off into another direction. Web surfers are seldom persistent enough to puzzle through the error to figure out another way to get at the information using the bad URL. As a result, just about every time your server displays an error, you lose a visitor—maybe forever.

When you are trying to increase traffic at your Web site, the last thing you want to do is lose visitors. Thus, one of the keys to increasing and maintaining traffic to your Web site is to reduce errors and help visitors find their way, which is exactly what you're about to learn.

There are three major trouble spots that can cause you to lose potential visitors forever. They are

- Missing files
- Lost connections
- Server time-outs

All of these trouble spots can be identified and tracked by your Web site traffic analysis tool.

Missing Files

The most common errors are those that relate to files the server can't find. Contrary to what you might think, the Web publisher is to blame for this error more than the Web surfer is. Bad links are a key reason for the File Not Found error. When you create a Web page, you add hypertext links that relate to pages at your Web site as well as other Web sites. Although all your links might work perfectly when you first create your Web site, things change over time. You update your Web pages. You move your Web pages to different locations. You combine some Web pages. You delete other Web pages.

Unfortunately, every time that you move or delete Web pages, you might unwittingly start an avalanche of errors. A visitor who bookmarked one of the Web pages that you moved or deleted can't get to the Web page anymore. Another visitor who created a page showing links to her favorite

Web sites, now has an invalid link pointing to your Web site. Worse, the search engines with which you registered haven't reindexed your Web site; now, hundreds of people who look for resources like yours can't find your pages anymore.

How Can You Fix the Problems?

Use your Web site analysis tool to generate a Page Not Found report. You can then use the report to help you find trouble spots at your Web site. Start by printing the report. Next, compare the file names in the report to the actual files on your Web site. If you find a file that is in the report and available on your Web site, use your browser to retrieve the file from your Web server. Be sure to use the same URL that the user entered. If the file loads without problems, cross the file off the list and move on to the next one. Here, there was probably an intermittent problem with the user's Internet connection, which doesn't necessarily mean that anything is wrong on your Web site.

If the file doesn't load in your browser, check the file name. Does the file name on the server exactly match the URL you entered? Most servers are case-sensitive, meaning that the mixture of uppercase and lowercase letters must match exactly. When you find a naming problem, you have a bad reference in one of your Web pages that you need to fix. The easiest way to find the problem page—and possibly other pages that contain the bad reference—is to search your Web directories for the bad reference.

For example, a bad reference to a Web page called welcome.htm that should have been referenced as welcome.html could be fixed as follows:

- ✪ Change to the directory containing your Web pages. If you have multiple document directories, examine each in turn.
- ✪ Search for references to the file name welcome.htm.
- ✪ Record the list of file names containing the bad reference.
- ✪ Edit the files and correct the bad references.

Some Web page editors allow you to find and replace links in multiple pages using a single command. For example, with HomeSite by Macromedia (**www.macromedia.com/ software/homesite/**), you can tell the editor the name of a link you want to replace and the pages in which you want to replace it.

If you don't have a naming problem, you might have a permission problem. On most Web servers, the directory and the file must have specific permission before visitors can access your files. Generally, the directory needs to be executable and the file needs to have read access. If you don't know how to check or set file permissions, ask your Internet service provider.

Next, highlight all the files that don't relate to Web pages of other document files, such as references to image files. Most likely, the highlighted list of files points to broken references in your Web pages. Fix these references either by updating the related page or by moving the file to where it is supposed to be.

Now that you've narrowed the list a bit, look for URLs that belong to files that you've moved or deleted. When you find a reference to a file that you moved, jot down the new name of the file. When you find a reference to a file that you deleted, make a note to yourself that the file was deleted.

Because users are looking for these files and you want to build—rather than lose—readership, you will want to redirect these lost visitors to the new location of the resource. Alternatively, you can create a placeholder document with the old URL, telling visitors that the resource is no longer available and then redirecting them to another area of your Web site. The job of the placeholder page would be to direct lost visitors to the resource for which there were looking. This redirection could be done as simply as providing instructions explaining that things have changed and providing the visitor with the correct URL. Alternatively, although it involves some pitfalls, you could consider automating the redirection process. For details on how to redirect users to new locations, see the upcoming section titled "Redirecting Lost Readers".

Although the remaining files on your list should pertain to true errors on the part of the user or someone else, you don't want to discard the list just yet. Take a look at the list one more time and ask yourself whether any patterns exist. For example, you might find that a number of visitors are consistently mistyping the name of one of your Web pages. If you think there is a chance that the spelling of your page's name is confusing to some of your visitors, change it.

Lost Connections

Lost connections are often the result of impatient visitors not wanting to wait for your page, its graphics, and other multimedia files to finish loading. Consequently, if you find a page that has lots of lost connections related to it, you might want to examine the page and change it so that it either loads quicker or follows sound design techniques that allow the visitor to use or peruse the page before it finishes loading.

If you have pages with lots of text, graphics, or multimedia, you might want to periodically check for lost connections. To do this, create a Lost Connection report using your Web site traffic analysis tool. For example, Figure 5.8 shows a NetTracker Page Delivery Summary report, which lists, among other things, information about the number of aborted requests for various Web pages.

The NetTracker report is made available on **www.sane.com/products/ NetTracker/web_technical.html**.

Unfortunately, sometimes the connection is lost after the server completely transfers the file but before the client completely processes the data. In this case, you might not be able to determine the cause of the error and should just move on to the next item on the list.

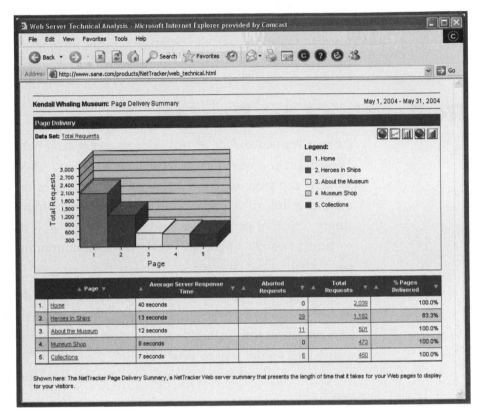

Figure 5.8

Keep an eye on the number of aborted requests. They may indicate technical problems at your Web site.

Time-Outs

Although time-outs are rather rare on Web servers, this coverage would be incomplete without at least mentioning how to spot them. A time-out is sort of like the server getting impatient with the client and wanting to move on. You probably won't see time-outs unless you have large multimedia or compressed files that are retrieved using the standard Web file transfer protocol, HTTP.

The first step in dealing with time-outs is to generate a Client Error report. If you see time-outs frequently for the same file, you might want to tell your Internet Service Provider about the problem. Although the service provider should be able to set the time-out ratio higher, the service provider might also tell you that the byte site for the offending files is unreasonably large. In the latter case, you might want to break the large file down into several smaller parts.

Redirecting Lost Readers

As you learned earlier in this section, every time you move or delete a Web page, you can start an avalanche of errors. Anyone who has bookmarked the page that you changed will get an error. Anyone who has created a link to the page from his or her own Web site will be unwittingly directing people to a dead end. Anyone who uses a search engine to find resources might also get a retrieval containing references to the pages that you've changed.

The result is that lots of people who otherwise would have visited your wonderful niche of cyberspace get lost. They hit the proverbial brick wall and run off in some other direction. And they might never return. When a user gets all the way to your Web site through the maze of cyberspace, do you really want to risk losing that user because of something that you can fix?

To remedy this situation, you should create a placeholder document. The key to the placeholder document is that it takes the place of a Web page or other document that you moved or deleted, and then redirects the user to a different location at your Web site. If you have a list of documents that you've moved or deleted, why not create a few placeholder documents right now? Every visitor counts.

TIP   The way to avoid brick walls and placeholder documents altogether is to plan out your Web site before your build it. The simplest planning rule is to give each area of your Web site its own directory to start with, and to make the default document for this directory the home page for the area. Unfortunately, in the real world, most Web publishers don't like to plan things out before they dive in, which means they should use placeholder documents to help direct traffic whenever necessary.

Redirection Basics

The technique you use to redirect visitors can be as simple as the one shown in Figure 5.9. Here, you tell visitors that the resource has been moved or deleted. Next, you provide them with the URL of the new resource or an escape route to another location at your Web site. The source for the redirection page is shown in Listing 5.1.

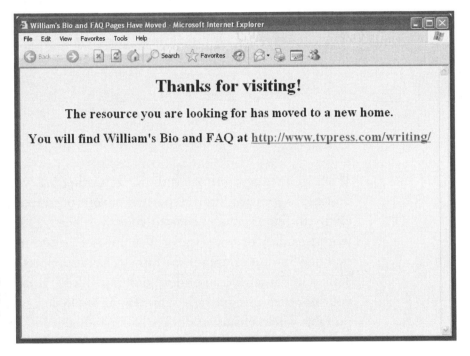

Figure 5.9

A simple but highly effective redirection technique.

Listing 5.1 Redirecting the User

```
<HTML>


  <HEAD>
    <TITLE>William's Bio and FAQ Pages Have Moved</TITLE>
  </HEAD>
```

```
<BODY BGCOLOR="#ffffff">

  <DIV ALIGN=CENTER>

    <H1>Thanks for visiting!</H1>

    <H2>The resource you are looking for has moved to a
new home.</H2>

    <H2>You will find William's Bio and FAQ at

      <A HREF="http://www.tvpress.com/writing/">

        http://www.tvpress.com/writing/

      </A>

    </H2>

  </DIV>

</BODY>

</HTML>
```

When you redirect visitors as shown in Listing 5.1, you come as close as possible to ensuring that 100 percent of your misdirected visitors have the ability to find their way back to your Web page. This technique should work regardless of what type of Web browser visitors may use, be it an old or a new version or even if the browser only supports a text-only display. This is important because more and more often, visitors may show up at your doorstep using a variety of new technologies, such as WebTV and portable wireless handless devices like cell phones and BlackBerry devices.

More Redirection Techniques

One problem with the previous redirection solution is that it requires visitors to click on an extra link on their way to your Web pages. For some visitors, this extra effort is enough to drive them away. Another option available to you for redirecting lost visitors is to automate the redirection process using client pull technologies. With client pull, you insert an instruction in the Web page that tells the visitor's browser to retrieve a different Web page. This way, the visitors can get to your Web page without having to make an extra click.

When it comes to client pull technologies, your choices are somewhat limited. Your primary options are the META Refresh tag or a client-side scripting language such as JavaScript. Unfortunately, as you are about to learn, both of these options have their issues.

The META Refresh Tag

Previous editions on this book used to teach readers about the use of the META Refresh tag as an effective means of redirecting lost visitors. However, a lot has changed on the Web in recent years, making this option a questionable choice.

The META Refresh tag is placed in the HEAD section of an HTML page. You use the HTTP-EQUIV attribute of the <META> tag to tell the browser that you want to refresh the browser window. You use the CONTENT attribute of the <META> tag to tell the browser two things: how long to wait and what document to load.

An example of the <META> tag is

```
<META HTTP-EQUIV="Refresh" CONTENT="10 URL=http://www.tvpress.com/
writing/">
```

Here, the HTTP-EQUIV attribute is assigned the keyword Refresh, which tells the browser that you want to prepare to refresh the current window. The CONTENT attribute has two parts separated by a semicolon and a space. The 10 tells the browser to wait ten seconds before refreshing the browser window. The next part of the CONTENT attribute tells the browser the URL of the page that you want to load into the refreshed window. The URL must have the full path specified, including http://.

Figure 5.10 shows and example of a page that redirects the visitor to a new location at a Web site. As you can see, the page displays an information message explaining what will happen. Just in case the user's browser doesn't support the technology, the appropriate links are placed on the page as well. The markup for the sample page is shown in Listing 5.2.

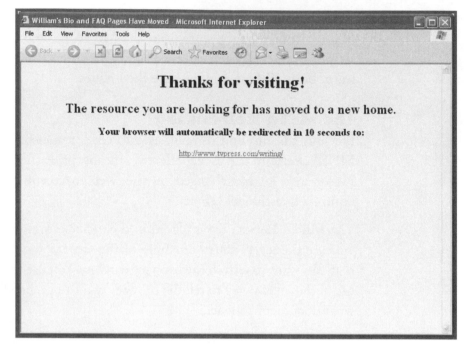

Thanks for visiting!

The resource you are looking for has moved to a new home.

Your browser will automatically be redirected in 10 seconds to:

http://www.tvpress.com/writing/

Figure 5.10

Although this looks similar to the previous redirection technique, the auto-redirect will take the visitor to the new location automatically.

Listing 5.2   Automating the Redirection Process

```
<HTML>

  <HEAD>

    <TITLE>William's Bio and FAQ Pages Have Moved</TITLE>

    <META HTTP-EQUIV="Refresh" CONTENT="10;
URL=http://www.tvpress.com/writing/">

  </HEAD>


  <BODY BGCOLOR="#ffffff">

    <DIV ALIGN=CENTER>

      <H1>Thanks for visiting!</H1>

      <H2>The resource you are looking for has moved to a
new home.</H2>
```

```
     <H3>Your browser will automatically be redirected in 10
seconds to:</H3>

        <A HREF="http://www.tvpress.com/writing/">

          http://www.tvpress.com/writing/

        </A>

      </H2>

    </DIV>

  </BODY>


</HTML>
```

Unfortunately, this seemingly innocent use of the META Refresh tag can end up getting you into trouble. The reason for this is that some less than scrupulous Web site publishers have used a variation of this redirection technique, referred to as doorway pages, to try and spam search engines. They do this by creating a number of simple Web pages that are exact copies of one another, except that each Web page is overloaded with a specific keyword phrase and designed to achieve a high keyword relevance for a specific search engine.

In many cases, the keyword phrase for which each page has been optimized may have little if anything to do with the content of the Web sites the these Web pages are redirecting visitors to. For example, one of these Web pages may be designed to attract Web servers doing a search on rock music while another is designed to match up against a search for science-fiction. Spamming occurs when all these Web pages redirect the Web surfer to a Web site that has nothing to do with these keyword phrases, as might be the case if the Web site where surfers are being sent was an online discount shop.

Because of misuses like the one shown above, many search engines now consider any use of the META Refresh tag as spam. As a result, if you employ this redirection technique in your Web pages, you now run the risk of your pages being lowered in rank or even being removed from the search engine's database.

NOTE There are a number of legitimate uses of the META Refresh tag. For example, some Web sites use it to create slide shows on their Web sites. Other Web sites use the META Refresh tag to generate a splash screen. Each of these uses of the META Refresh tag is perfectly legitimate and you might want to use them on Web pages that you don't plan on submitting to search engines.

Scripted Client-Side Redirection

A safer option for automatically redirecting Web pages is to use a Web scripting language, such as JavaScript. Currently, none of the major search engines open or inspect the content of externally referenced files. To avoid any possible misinterpretation of your code as being spam, you can place your JavaScript code in an external file and call the external JavaScript from within your Web page. For example, Listing 5.3 shows an example of how to set up a Web page to use an external JavaScript to control Web page redirection.

Listing 5.3   A JavaScript Redirection Example

```
<HTML>

  <HEAD>
    <TITLE>William's Bio and FAQ Pages Have Moved</TITLE>
    <script language="JavaScript" src="TestRedirect.js"></script>
  </HEAD>


  <BODY BGCOLOR="#ffffff">
    <DIV ALIGN=CENTER>
      <H1>Thanks for visiting!</H1>
      <H2>The resource you are looking for has moved to a
new home.</H2>
```

```
<H2>You will find William's Bio and FAQ at
  <A HREF="http://www.tvpress.com/writing/">
    http://www.tvpress.com/writing/
  </A>
  </H2>
 </DIV>
</BODY>

</HTML>
```

Highlighted in bold is a JavaScript statement that tells the browsers to open and execute an external JavaScript file named `TestRedirect.js`, that is located in the same directory as was the Web page. The code that resides in this external JavaScript file consists of a single statement as shown below.

```
location.href("http://www.tvpress.com/writing/")
```

This statement loads the specified Web page into the browser, while still leaving an entry for the original URL listed in the browser's history file. The net effect is that the Web surfer should automatically be redirected to the appropriate Web page. However, in the event that the Web surfer's browser does not support JavaScript or has its JavaScript support disabled, the Web surfer will still be able to find his or her way to your Web pages by clicking on the URL link that will be displayed.

NOTE Despite being supported by every major Web browser, JavaScript is not universally supported. For example, some visitors may disable JavaScript support in an effort to defend against computer viruses. Handicapped visitors may use text-only browsers in conjunction with text-to-speech software and not be able to support JavaScript. In addition, many small hand-held portable Web connection appliances don't support JavaScript either. However, despite these exceptions, JavaScript redirection should be effective 99 percent of the time.

Redirection Using Your Web Server

Although these client-side redirection techniques work well, more and more Web servers are starting to support automatic redirection. With automatic server-side redirection, the Web server takes over and maps the old URL to the new one, which makes the redirection completely transparent to the visitor. For example, you could tell the Web server to map all requests for **www.tvpress.com/fun/** to **www.tvpress.com/summer/**.

Most commercial Web servers support URL redirection. You'll find, for example, that Microsoft IIS and Netscape Enterprise make this task fairly easy to accomplish. However, you'll need access to the Web server's administrative tools, which you might not have if you use a service provider.

No More 404 - - File Not Found

The typical errors that servers report are meaningless to most people, and even the people who know what the status codes mean probably would much rather have a helpful pointer than an error that says 404 - - File Not Found. Fortunately, there are ways to fix it so that the nondescriptive and meaningless errors reported by servers go the way of the dinosaur.

When the Web server software was installed, the technician who set up the server defined specific parameters that told the server how to report errors and which error documents to display. Because the default error documents are rarely replaced, chances are good that visitors to your Web site see the standard nondescript error messages. You can confirm this by entering an invalid URL that refers to your Web site, such as

http://www.your-server.com/nothingatall.html

For example, take a look at Figure 5.11, which shows how the 404 - - File Note Found error is typically displayed. As you can see, it's not particularly friendly or helpful to lost Web surfers.

If your server reports a vague error message, don't worry; this can be changed by defining new error documents. On most servers, regardless of

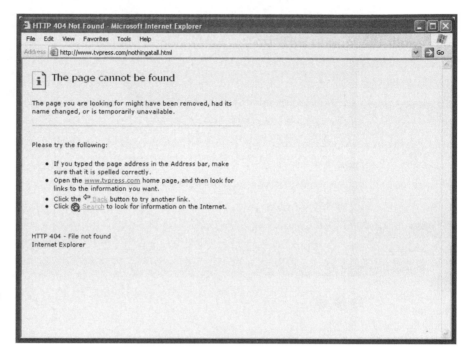

Figure 5.11

A generic 404 - -
File Not Found
error message.

operating system, you can define the documents to retrieve when an error occurs. For example, with Microsoft IIS, you can tell the server the name and location of the page you want to load when a certain error occurs.

With the thought of eliminating the dreaded 404 - - File Not Found error forever, take a chance and talk to the head technician or Web master who works for your Internet service provider. The question to ask is, "Can you help me set up unique error documents for my domain, or, at the very least, is it possible to create some informative error messages for everyone who uses the Web server?" For example, take a look at Figure 5.12, which shows how the folks at **www.sun.com** have enhanced their 404 - - File Not Found error message. The new message not only apologizes to visitors but also provides navigation links at the top and bottom of the pages in order to give their would-be visitors alternative paths into the Web site.

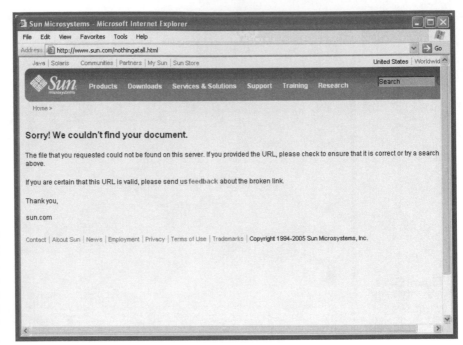

Figure 5.12

The Sun Microsoft Systems Web site provides its visitors with alternative navigation links as well as the ability to report errors.

Taking Advantage of Free URL Analyzers

Of course, the best possible way to handle a 404 - - File Not Found error is to correct it. To do this you must know where the errors are occurring. One way to make this determination is to visit each of your Web pages and to test the validity of each link by clicking on it. If your Web site is fairly small, this shouldn't be a problem. But if your Web site has grown to more than a handful of Web pages, this exercise can quickly become tiresome.

So the question is, "are there free tools available on the Internet to help automate this task?" The answer, as you no doubt now expect, is yes. For starters, check out Link Checker (**www.siteowner.com/badlinks.cfm**), as shown in Figure 5.13.

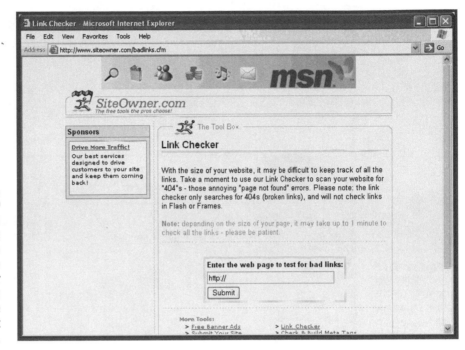

Figure 5.13

Link Checker is a free online service that you can use to spider your Web site looking for Web pages with links that generate 404 - - File Not Found errors.

To use Link Checker all you have to do is enter the main URL for your Web site and click on Submit. Link Checker will then spider your Web site and report on any 404 - - File Not Found errors that it discovers.

Another free online Link checking service is Link Valet (**www.htmlhelp. com/tools/valet**), as shown in Figure 5.14. Link Valet begins by spidering your Web site. Once it is done, it can present its findings in either a summary or a full report. In addition to reporting on your 404 - - File Not Found errors, it will also point out any links that are being redirected.

One last link validation option that you may want to consider trying out is REL Link Checker Lite, which is available as a freeware application that you can download from **www.relsoftware.com** and install on your computer, as shown in Figure 5.15.

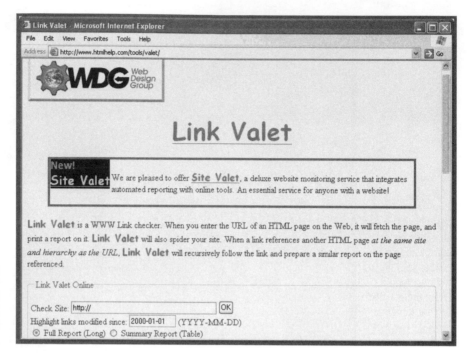

Figure 5.14

Link Valet reports on link errors and will also identify any redirect links.

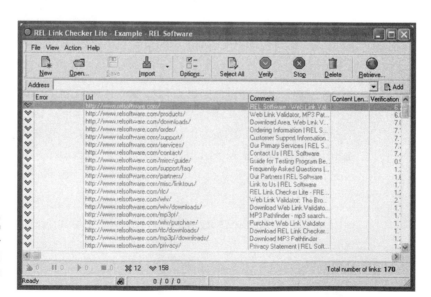

Figure 5.15

REL Link Checker Lite is distributed as a freeware application.

REL Link Checker Lite is designed to spider Web sites that contain 1,000 or fewer links. If your Web site contains more thinks than this, you might want to look into trying a free trial of Web Link Validator (also available at **www.relsoftware.com**).

A Few Last Word on Errors

Errors are showstoppers. Don't let your visitors think that your Web site is gone. Every visitor counts, especially when you are trying to increase traffic to your Web site. But the reason for fixing trouble spots goes well beyond preventing the loss of wayward visitors. To attract and maintain an audience over the long haul, you need to maintain your site and provide visitors with lifelines when you move or delete files.

Finally, You Know What to Do—So What's Next?

Right about now, you are probably wondering why this book keeps saying that you can use the Web site reports to make your Web site a better place to visit as well as to increase your Web traffic. After all, the title of the book is *Increase Your Web Traffic In a Weekend* not *Make Your Web Site a Better Place to Visit*.

The simple truth is that the long-term success of your Web site is based upon understanding your Web site's good points and bad points. By understanding your site's good points, you learn how to market your Web site to the world. By understanding your Web site's bad points, you learn what you need to do to fix the problems. If you don't fix the problems at your Web site, you might lose visitors just as fast as you find new ones.

The following steps will make your Web site a better place to visit:

- Direct users to popular areas
- Clean up unused pages
- Avoid dead-ends
- Fix errors

After you take a close look at your Web site, you can move on to the next step, which is to find your niche in cyberspace and formulate a plan that uses your niche to market your Web site to the world.

Web Site Analyzers

Now, given that you have most likely made all sorts of modifications to your Web pages, this might also be a good time to take a few minutes to get a third party's opinion on the overall construction of your Web pages. There are any number of Web sites that provide Web page analysis. For example, there is the Manvish e-Services Website Analyser (**www.manvish. com/eservices/seo/analyser.htm**), shown in Figure 5.16.

Figure 5.16

The Manvish e-Services Website Analyser provides an extensive analysis of your Web pages.

The Manvish e-Services Website Analyser will analyze your Web page's META tags, keyword density, load time, overall size, and much more. To use this free service, enter your URL and e-mail address and click on the Analyze button.

You also might want to investigate the Web site analyzers provided at Site Solutions (**www.sitesolutions.com**) and WebSiteOptimization.com (**www.websiteoptimization.com/services/analyze**). The Web site analyzer provided by Site Solutions provides the ability to perform a keyword or keyword phrase analysis. The Web site analyzer provided by WebSite Optimization.com focuses on analyzing the size of your Web pages and offering up advice on how to improve Web page load time.

Directing Users to Popular Areas

Every road sign you can add to the Web makes cyberspace just a little bit more enjoyable, so why not create a few road signs that direct visitors to popular areas at your Web site? Your road signs don't need to be extravagant. You can use plain-old text to create links to other pages at your Web site.

Obviously, you don't want to tell visitors about every single Web page you've published. Instead, you want to direct visitors to the popular areas of your Web site by creating links to the top-level page within the specific areas you want to promote. The idea here is that people visiting your sports information page, for example, might also be interested in your sports equipment page. However, they can't get to the sports equipment page if you don't tell them it exists.

Say that your Web site's statistics show that seven pages at the Web site get the most traffic. The URLs for the hypothetical pages are

- **http://www.verycooldays.com/**—your main home page.

- **http://www.verycooldays.com/summer/**—a page that promotes summertime activities.

- **http://www.verycooldays.com/summer/water-skiing.html**—a page within the summertime activities area that covers water-skiing.

- **http://www.verycooldays.com/surfing.html**—a page within the summertime activities area that covers surfing.

- **http://www.verycooldays.com/equipment/**—a page that discusses where you can look on the Web to get the best bargains in sports equipment.

- http://www.verycooldays.com/equipment/forsale.html—a page that lets people post ads to sell their sports equipment.

- http://www.verycooldays.com/equipment/tips.html—a page that provides tips for getting the best value for your money when you buy sports equipment.

When you examine the seven most visited pages, you might see that three specific areas of the Web site are getting the most traffic.

- The main home page

- The summertime activities area

- The sports-equipment area

The home page is the place to toot your horn about the main areas at your Web site, but you also need to do so on the top-level pages within the Web site. Although you might think that most visitors start on the site's home page, this isn't always true. In fact, most people probably start their visit on some other page. For this reason, you should tell anyone visiting the summertime activities area that you have this wonderful sports-equipment area, and vice versa.

By promoting both areas, you increase page views at your site and let visitors know that your site really does have a lot to offer. On the Web page at **http://www.verycooldays.com/summer/**, you could add a clear road sign that directs visitors to the sports equipment area, such as

```
Sports Equipment
    *   Find the best bargains on the Web
    *   Get money-saving tips
    *   Post your own for sale ad
```

Then, on the Web page at **http://www.verycooldays.com/equipment/**, you add another road sign that directs visitors to the summertime activities area. The markup for the road sign is as follows.

```
Fun in the Sun

Interested in summer-time sports like scuba diving,

water skiing, and surfing? Why not stop by

our Fun in the Sun headquarters?
```

Cleaning Up Unused Pages

After studying your Web site to see how you can direct traffic to popular areas, you should take a hard look at pages that rarely get visitors. Although your first impulse might be to delete these pages or stop updating these pages, this might not be the right solution. Rather than remove or neglect these pages, you should ensure that other pages at your Web site have clear road signs that tell people what these pages are all about. You might also want to consider combining the information on this page with information on another page.

Say that your site's stats show that two pages at the Web site rarely receive visitors. The URLs for these pages are

- **http://www.verycooldays.com/summer/background.html**—a background page for the summertime activities area.

- **http://www.verycooldays.com/summer/scuba/deepwater.html**— a page that promotes deep-water scuba driving.

After examining the background page, you might discover that you can summarize the information and place it on the top-level Web page for the summertime activity area. In this way, visitors to this area of the Web site get a quick summary without having to visit the background page. By adding the information to the top-level Web page, you make the area a better place to visit.

Next, you look at the page that promotes deep-water scuba diving. Your scuba diving pages are divided into three categories: fresh water, salt water, and deep water. Although the fresh water and salt-water scuba pages attract lots of visitors, the deep-water page is rarely visited. The problem here might be organization; perhaps your top-level page needs to explain that deep water refers to deep-sea scuba diving with submersibles and that you also feature video from a Galapagos undersea expedition.

Avoiding Dead Ends

Dead ends are showstoppers. All your Web pages should end with links that lead back to a main page, the previous page, or the next page in a series of pages. Links at the bottom of a Web page are subtle reminders that the Web site has more to offer. By adding links to the bottom of your Web pages, you make navigating your Web site easier, thereby helping to retain your Web traffic. Remember, if Web surfers visit your sports-related Web site, they are interested in sports; why not help them find the information they are looking for?

Links at the bottom of a Web page can be as basic as

```
Back to Fun in the Sun
```

Or you can use mini-menus that tell visitors about other areas of your Web site, such as

```
Our Home Page  |  Fun in the Sun  |  Sports Equipment
```

Another form of a dead end is a page that causes the visitor to lose interest in your Web site. For example, a page full of errors or inconsistencies might make the visitors think the rest of your Web site isn't worth visiting. For this reason, you might want to look for pages that are often the last page people visit and see if they need updating.

Understanding Your Niche

After you use a Web site analyzer to track your site's stats, you should have a better understanding of what attracts visitors to your Web site. Understanding your niche and using it to your advantage are the keys to success when you try to promote your Web site to the world. By taking the time to learn exactly why people visit your Web site, you save yourself a barrel full of heartaches.

Before they started tracking their stats, the creators of **www.verycooldays. com** thought that the underwater video sequences they published online were the main events at their Web site. As it turned out, the Web pages covering deep-sea scuba diving were the least visited. Although you could say that the problem was poor organization, it turns out that the Web site had lots of other things to offer visitors.

Although the creators of the Web site started out building a resource for scuba divers, they ended up with a Web site that covered many different water sports, including water skiing and surfing. They also created a wonderful guide to buying sports equipment online. Looking back, they saw their niche covered two different areas:

○ Resources for anyone who loved water sports

○ Resources for buying and selling sports equipment online

Unfortunately, the site's banners and logos promoted the site as "A great place for anyone who loves scuba diving." Worse, the developers of the site used this same slogan whenever they had an opportunity to promote the Web site. When they registered with search engines, they hyped their great scuba-diving center and forgot the other areas. When they traded links with other sites, they asked the other Web site publishers to be sure to tell people about the site's scuba-diving resources. Even though they did indeed attract visitors who were interested in scuba diving, they missed out on many other opportunities to increase the traffic to their Web site.

As you can see, the creators of **www.verycooldays.com** should have taken the time to put together a better picture of their Web site before they started promoting their site as a great place for anyone who loves scuba diving. A better description of their Web site would have been this:

A terrific site for anyone who loves water sports! We have tons of resources covering scuba diving, water skiing, surfing, and many other water sports. We also have a terrific guide to sites that sell sports equipment. Our buying tips might save you a bundle.

The creators of **www.verycooldays.com** could also create separate descriptions for each popular area at the Web site. This would allow them to promote the Web site as a whole and each area separately. For example, the next time they register with a search engine, they could use the combined description and then register each area separately as well.

Before you continue, create descriptive blurbs for your Web site. Start by identifying the most popular areas at your Web site; then use the subjects that these cover to come up with a brief description that identifies your Web site's niche. Afterward, create separate descriptions for each popular area at your Web site.

Reviewing Your Progress and Planning More for Next Weekend

Wow, the weekend is over already! Hopefully, after reading the sessions and following along, you have a great start on the long-term improvement of your Web site's traffic.

What Have You Done This Weekend?

The first step of putting the motion in promotion is to register your Web site in all the right places. Because search engines are the primary means of getting your site noticed, this book offered you an extensive look at how search engines work and how you can optimize your Web pages for indexing. Although there are hundreds of search engines, it is not practical or worthwhile to submit your Web site to every single one of them. Instead, make the most of your time and resources by registering with the major search engines.

But registering with the major search engines is only the beginning of the promotion process. Next you need to look at Web directories. Just as there are hundreds of search engines, there are hundreds of Web directories as well. As with search engines, you should focus your efforts on the major Web directories. Afterward, you should look to business search engines and

Yellow Pages directories. These business-oriented search and directory sites are great places to tout your products, services, and commercial Web site.

Because you also want your Web site to be accessible to people for specific types of information, the next step is to register with industry- and category-specific directories. Beyond these directories, you'll find specialty directories. Whether your site covers home decorating or famous poets, there are specialty directories that will want your listing.

Awards can make all the difference in the world when it comes to increasing traffic to your Web site. Not just any old award will do, though. The best awards are those that are long lasting and meaningful. Still, when all is said and done, the popularity of the award site is the most important factor in determining whether the award will help increase the level of traffic at your Web site. The busier the award site, the better the chances that the site's award will increase traffic to your Web site.

One way to spread the word quickly about your Web site is through a registration service that allows you to register with multiple search engines and directories. Although registration services are useful for registering multiple URLs with directories, you get the most out of your Web site's listing by registering your site with individual search engines and directories.

In the final parts of the book, you saw many additional ways to increase your Web traffic, such as e-mail and freebies. Believe it or not, e-mail is a terrific way to promote your Web site. When you promote your Web site through e-mail, you can use the direct, person-to-person method as well as newsgroups and mailing lists. Beyond e-mail, you can steal the thunder of traditional marketers by using giveaways, contests, and sweepstakes. Because everyone loves the chance to win something for nothing, freebies can truly bring the masses to your Web site.

You also learned different ways to compete in the big leagues with banner advertising. The banner is the most heavily used advertising method on the Web. Although most advertisers pay thousands of dollars to display a banner ad, you can advertise through a banner exchange network without spending a dime.

You want visitors to remain at your site, and you want them to return. These are two of the biggest reasons not only to promote your Web site, but also to work to improve it. After people have found the doorway into your slice of cyberspace, you want to give them every reason to stay. Nothing stops visitors dead in their tracks like an error. Errors are often the result of bad links in your Web pages or bad references to your Web pages from other Web sites. Using Web traffic analyzers you can fix errors regardless of their source.

After you gather stats for your Web site and know who is visiting your site and why, the next step is to put the stats to work. Not only can you use the stats to make your Web site a better place to visit, you can use them to find your niche in the wonderful world of cyberspace. Enhancing your Web site based on what the stats tell you and using your Web site's niche to your advantage are key ingredients that will help you attract the masses.

A Final Note

Just because you've reached the end of this book doesn't mean that your promotion efforts should end. Next weekend, if you have some time, go back and revisit any sessions or topics in the book that you might not have explored as much as you'd like.

After you take another look at the session, use the main topics in this book to outline a long-term promotion plan. Your plan should focus on the items that you will need to periodically address, such as

- Tracking Web site stats (weekly or monthly)

- Looking for problem areas at your Web site (weekly or monthly)

- Updating your listings in directories if you move the furniture around (only as necessary)

- Resubmitting your site for awards (wait two or three months between submissions)

- Participating in mailing lists and newsgroups (daily or weekly)
- Updating your banner (monthly)

That's it. Have some fun this evening. On the other hand, if you're enjoying this creative brainstorming, you might want to keep at it for a while.

APPENDIX

Additional Resources on the Web

Throughout the weekend, as you worked your way through this book, you have been introduced to online services and software products that you can use to help increase the traffic coming to your Web site. In this appendix, the book provides you with additional information regarding a number of other software applications that you might want to check out. To help organize this material, the information presented is broken down into the following categories:

- **Site Management Programs.** Applications that can help you manage your Web site more effectively.

- **Site Submission.** Applications that can assist you in getting your Web sites registered with the major search engines and directories.

- **Web Authoring.** Applications that can help you develop your Web pages in a search engine friendly manner.

- **Connectivity.** Applications that can help you make sure you don't lose Web traffic due to problems with slow downloads or poor communications.

For each software application that is covered, you will find information regarding its functionality. You'll also find a description of its purpose, information on whether you can download and try the application as shareware or freeware, and a high-level overview of specific product features.

Site Management Programs

In this section, you are introduced to a number of software applications that you can use to help you manage your Web site effectively.

AccuTagger

Developer Site: http://www.cyberspacehq.com

Product Page: http://www.cyberspacehq.com/products/Accutagger/ home.shtm

Product Description: AccuTagger is designed to assist you with the creation and management of your Web page's <META> tags. It helps in the generation of numerous <META> tags, including the Description and Keywords tags.

Distribution: Free trial available.

Major features include:

❂ Automated Web page analysis

❂ Built-in spell checking

❂ Best guess <META> tag generation

❂ Automated report generation

FastStats

Developer Site: http://www.mach5.com

Product Page: http://www.mach5.com/products/analyzer/index.php

Product Description: Use FastStats to collect Web site management information from your Web server log files, such as the number of hits your Web site gets each day, the search engines your visitors are using, and the keywords that visitors used to find your Web site. Data can be presented in table or graphic formats. FastStats can also be used to track down bad links and to check on Web server performance.

Distribution: Free 30-day trial.

Major features include:

- Detailed reporting to assist Web site publishers in analyzing the cost effectiveness of their advertising

- A graphic hyperlink tree depiction of how visitors move through your Web site

- Over a dozen reports that measure site sickiness

LinkProver

Developer Site: http://www.tafwebsoftware.co.uk/index.html

Product Page: http://www.tafwebsoftware.co.uk/index.html

Product Description: LinkProver assists you in keeping your Web site up-to-date by providing you with the ability to check on the graphics embedded in your Web pages. LinkProver can also check on all your links and will warn you if any of your links point to non-existent Web pages.

Distribution: Freeware.

Major features include:

- The ability to check your Web pages locally or online

- The ability to specify whether to check external links in addition to links internal to your Web site

- The ability to view results instantly, as they are collected

- The ability to generate HTML reports

MozillaTracker

Developer Site: http://www.stefan-pettersson.nu

Product Page: http://www.stefan-pettersson.nu/site/mozillatracker/

Product Description: MozillaTracker is a log analyzer that can be used to report Web site statistics, including the type of browser or operating system your visitors are using. Data can be presented as text or HTML and printed as reports.

Distribution: Freeware.

Major features include:

- The ability to view data by visitor operating system or browser

- The ability to sort data alphabetically or by the number of hits

- The ability to filter data based on browser version or browser titles

NetTracker

Developer Site: http://www.sane.com

Product Page: http://www.sane.com/products/NetTracker/ softwareoption.html

Product Description: NetTracker is a log analysis application that provides you with the ability to track usage of one or more Web sites. It includes a wide collection of built-in reports as well as the ability to generate custom and ad hoc reports. You can use it to track the success of your banner advertisements, examine which keywords visitors are using to find your Web site, and find out which of your pages are being visited the most.

Distribution: Free 15-day trial.

Major features include:

- Built-in and custom reporting with filtering options

- Trend reports that help you examine traffic over time

- The ability to examine data collected from logs or from embedded Web page tags

PageStats/HitCount

Developer Site: http://www.tomahawktech.com

Product Page: http://www.tomahawktech.com/pagestats.aro

Product Page: http://www.tomahawktech.com/pagecount.aro

Product Description: PageStats provides you with the ability to track visitors to your Web site, allowing you to find out how they got there, their browser type, and arrival times. HitCount provides the ability to count the number of visits made to any page on your Web site and to graphically display this information on your pages or to keep track of it behind the scenes.

Distribution: Free 30-day trials.

Major features include:

○ Use PageStats to collect detailed data about each visitor

○ Use PageStats to track the popularity of particular Web pages and examine how visitors traverse your Web site

○ Use HitCount to track the number of visitors for each of your Web pages

○ Use HitCount to determine the effectiveness of your banner advertising

PowerMapper

Developer Site: http://www.electrum.co.uk

Product Page: http://www.electrum.co.uk/products/mapper.htm

Product Description: PowerMapper provides Web site publishers with a tool for creating interactive site maps, which in turn provide simple site navigation and visualization. PowerMapper crawls through a Web site, producing a site map containing thumbnail images of each page, and automatically creates a site map in HTML or GIF format. It also verifies links and detects broken HTML tags.

Distribution: Free 30-day trial.

Major features include:

- The ability to generate site maps for any Web site
- The ability to visually examine your Web site's structure
- The ability to print out your site maps
- The ability to report on broken links and invalid HTML

Search Engine Commando

Developer Site: http://www.searchenginecommando.com/

Product Page: http://www.searchenginecommando.com/

Product Description: Search Engine Commando provides you with a tool for measuring the progress of your Web site promotion campaign. You can also use it to submit your Web pages to search engines and create ranking reports.

Distribution: Free trial.

Major features include:

- Supports all the major search engines
- Works with multiple Web pages and URLs
- Provides automated scheduling
- Generates reports showing how well your Web pages rank against your competition

SERanker

Developer Site: http://www.monocle-solutions.com

Product Page: http://www.monocle-solutions.com/seranker/home.shtml

Product Description: SERanker provides you with the ability to analyze your Web site's search engine ranking. Use it to study your Web site's rankings over time to see how changes that you make help or hurt your ranking. SERanker also provides you with the ability to generate keywords based on an analysis of the top ten Web site listings that you specify.

Distribution: Free trial available.

Major features include:

- The ability to generate a ranking analysis for your Web pages
- Works with the most popular search engines
- The ability to automatically generate keyword lists

SEPopular

Developer Site: http://www.monocle-solutions.com

Product Page: http://www.monocle-solutions.com/sepopular/home.shtml

Product Description: SEPopular provides you with the ability to increase the chances of appearing in the top ten search results by calculating your Web page's relevance in order to increase your understanding of your Web site's ranking.

Distribution: Freeware.

Major features include:

- The ability to query top search engines for data to analyze
- The ability to reach back up to 3 years for data from competitor Web sites
- The ability to compare your Web site to other Web sites

Surfstats Log Analyzer

Developer Site: http://www.surfstats.com

Product Page: http://www.surfstats.com/./ssl_prod.asp

Product Description: Surfstats Log Analyzer provides you with dozens of reports regarding various statistics for your Web site and its visitors. It uses Web server log files to retrieve information that you can use to determine how your Web site promotion campaign is doing over time and to find any errors that may be occurring.

Distribution: Free 30-day trial.

Major features include:

- The ability to view Web site hits and page views
- The ability to watch specific pages
- The ability to determine which Web pages visitors are using as entry points to your Web sites and which pages are being used as exit points
- The ability to track your banners, determine search engines' referrers, and to tell when visitors are bookmarking your Web pages

TopDog Pro

Developer Site: http://www.topdogsoftware.biz/

Product Page: http://www.topdogsoftware.biz/

Product Description: TopDog is a Web site positioning and ranking application. It queries the top search engines for your Web site and keywords, showing where you and your competitors are positioned. TopDog eliminates the chore of visiting each search engine, typing in your keywords, and analyzing the results. TopDog produces reports on your Web site and on your competitors and alerts users to changes in rank.

Distribution: Free trail available.

Major features include:

- ✪ The ability to determine ranking for any specified keywords
- ✪ Support for unlimited number of Web sites
- ✪ Customizable reporting
- ✪ Built-in scheduling

WebSpeed

Developer Site: http://www.tafwebsoftware.co.uk/index.html

Product Page: http://www.tafwebsoftware.co.uk/index.html

Product Description: WebSpeed helps you keep from losing visitors when your Web pages are too graphic intensive and take too long to load. It helps you to make sure that your Web site is a better place to visit by measuring how long it takes for visitors to download your Web pages at various modem speeds.

Distribution: Freeware.

Major features include:

- ✪ The ability to visually simulate download time with a progress bar
- ✪ The ability to take into account periodic Internet congestion
- ✪ The ability to test more than one Web page at a time

Site Submission

This section presents a collection of software applications that you can use to help you in your efforts to register your Web site with the major search engines and directories and ultimately get your Web sites noticed by as many people as possible.

AddWeb Website Promoter

Developer Site: http://www.cyberspacehq.com/

Product Page: http://www.cyberspacehq.com/products/addweb/

Product Description: AddWeb Website Promoter is designed to increase your Web site traffic by automatically submitting your site to hundreds of Internet search engines and directories. Use its built-in Web site analysis capabilities to make sure that your Web site is as search engine friendly as possible.

Distribution: Free trial available.

Major features include:

- Web page-ranking analysis
- Tools for working with `<META>`, `<ALT>`, `<TITLE>` tags, and other HTML specific tags
- Submission of multiple sites in one run
- Keyword analysis
- Link checking

Dynamic Submission

Developer Site: http://www.submission2000.com/

Product Page: http://www.submission2000.com/product.html

Product Description: Dynamic Submission is a Web site search engine submission tool that will help you to register your Web pages with hundreds of search engines. In addition, this product also includes a collection of search engine optimization tools that you can use to analyze and improve the search engine friendliness of your Web pages.

Distribution: Free trial available.

Major features include:

- A keyword library and keyword builder tool
- Link popularity checking
- A <META> tag generator
- URL verification
- Web site rank analysis and reporting

Exploit's Submission Wizard

Developer Site: http://www.exploit.net/

Product Page: http://www.exploit.net/wizard/index.html

Product Description: Submission Wizard is a search engine submission application that helps you to automate the submission of your Web pages to all the major search engines. It also includes filters that help you to weed out search engines that are not relevant to your Web site.

Distribution: Free trail available.

Major features include:

- Built-in filtering based on Web site content
- Support for all major search engines
- Report generation
- Assistance in manually submitting to search engines that are not directly supported
- Automated submission scheduling

SubmitWolf Pro

Developer Site: http://www.trellian.com/

Product Page: http://www.trellian.com/swolf/index.html

Product Description: SubmitWolf Pro is designed to help you promote your Web site. It maintains a database that includes information about all the major search engines and directories and hundreds of automated submission scripts. Just select a search engine and SubmitWolf Pro will download and fill in its submission form and submit it for you.

Distribution: Free trail available.

Major features include:

- Works with all major search engines

- Built-in submission guard protection prevents spamming search engines and directories

- Provides the ability to work with paid submission services

WebPosition

Developer Site: http://www.webposition.com

Product Page: http://www.webposition.com

Product Description: WebPosition is a collection of tools that can assist you in improving your Web site's ranking with the major search engines. It specializes in analyzing competition, Web page optimization and submission, keyword analysis, and rank reporting.

Distribution: Free 30-day trial.

Major features include:

- The ability to establish a baseline for keyword analysis

- The ability to perform keyword research and analysis

- The ability to analyze and make recommendations for improving your Web pages

- The ability to automate the submission of your Web pages to selected search engines

Web Authoring

In this section you will find software applications that will help you to build effective and more search engine friendly Web sites.

HTML Power Tools

Developer Site: http://www.tali.com

Product Page: http://www.tali.com/tools.html

Product Description: HTML Power Tools consists of eight separate tools that you can use to develop your Web site. Use these tools to make sure that your Web pages are as search engine friendly as possible.

Distribution: Free 30-day trial.

Major features include:

❍ HTML syntax checking and link validation

❍ Built-in HTML spell-checking

❍ <META> tag creation and management

❍ Search and replace edit features

MetaWizard

Developer Site: http://www.tafwebsoftware.co.uk/index.html

Product Page: http://www.tafwebsoftware.co.uk/index.html

Product Description: MetaWizard helps facilitate the process of creating <META> tags for your Web pages by guiding you, step-by-step through the <META> tag creation process. MetaWizard makes <META> tag creation easy by making sure that your Description and Keywords <META> tags are properly formatted.

Distribution: Freeware.

Major features include:

- ○ The ability to generate Keyword <META> tags
- ○ The ability to generate Description <META> tags
- ○ The ability to create other types of <META> tags

SiteXpert

Developer Site: http://www.xtreeme.com

Product Page: http://www.xtreeme.com/sitexpert/

Product Description: SiteXpert provides you with the ability to automatically generate your own site maps. No coding is required. Just run SiteXpert and point it to your Web site's main Web page and it will crawl its way through your Web site and generate a site map. Numerous formats are available.

Distribution: Free trial available.

Major features include:

- ○ Automatic Web site crawling
- ○ Built-in link validation
- ○ Cross-browser compatibility
- ○ 11 different site map formats from which to select

TagCheck

Developer Site: http://www.tafwebsoftware.co.uk/index.html

Product Page: http://www.tafwebsoftware.co.uk/index.html

Product Description: TagCheck helps you to find errors in your Web pages by analyzing your HTML code and reporting on common errors, including missing or poorly nested HTML tags.

Distribution: Freeware.

Major features include:

- ✿ The ability to find misspelled tags
- ✿ The ability to verify that correct tag attributes are used
- ✿ The ability to check for mismatched quotation marks
- ✿ The ability to check for matching opening and closing tags

Connectivity

This section presents software applications that assist Web site owners by providing tools for checking and verifying Web site connectivity.

Connection Keeper

Developer Site: http://www.gammadyne.com/

Product Page: http://www.gammadyne.com/conkeep.htm

Product Description: Connection Keeper is a software application that you can use to prevent your Internet connection from going inactive. Web site publishers can use it to monitor their Web sites and verify that Web pages are downloading correctly.

Distribution: Freeware.

Major features include:

- ✿ Minimal use of system resources or bandwidth
- ✿ The ability to control the time interval used to ensure an active Internet connection
- ✿ The ability to monitor Web site availability
- ✿ Instant popup or e-mail notification messages when problems are detected

Magic NetTrace

Developer Site: http://www.tialsoft.com

Product Page: http://www.tialsoft.com/mnettrace

Product Description: Magic NetTrace is an IP tracer tool that you can use to track down and identify the source of connection problems.

Distribution: Free 20-day trail.

Major features include:

✪   Multithreaded tracking of all routes for fast results

✪   The ability to print or copy test results

✪   Multi-language support

MySpeed Server

Developer Site: http://www.myspeed.com

Product Page: http://www.myspeed.com

Product Description: MySpeed is a Java applet that provides you with the ability to provide your visitors with a tool for testing speed and quality of service with your Web site. MySpeed easily installs on your Web server and does not require any client-side code.

Distribution: Online demo available.

Major features include:

✪   The ability to perform upload and download speed tests

✪   The ability to perform continuous connection speed tests

✪   The ability to rate quality of service for your Web site

✪   Built-in reporting

VisualRoute

Developer Site: http://www.visualroute.com/

Product Page: http://www.visualroute.com/

Product Description: VisualRoute is a traceroute application that you can use to analyze connectivity problems. The program offers a map of the world, which you can use to view the routes that your IP packets take as your compute over the Internet. VisualRoute is fast, allowing you to track all hops in parallel, making it work quicker than conventional traceroute programs.

Distribution: 15-day trial available.

Major features include:

- The ability to trace connection problems between a remote user and your Web server

- The ability to allow visitors to test their connectivity with your Web server

- Graphical representation of connections and connectivity issues

GLOSSARY

A

advertisement. On the Internet, an advertisement typically consists of paid and free banners as well as search engines and directory Web site listings.

affiliate. A member of a sales program in which the member receives payment for delivering customers to the Web site of the sponsoring the affiliate program.

affiliate program. On the Internet, an affiliate program is an agreement between a sponsoring Web site and member Web site in which member Web sites are paid for bringing visitors to the sponsoring Web site.

ALT Tag. An HTML tag that is used as a means of displaying text in place of graphics in browsers that do not support graphics. The ALT tag also provides an opportunity for Web publishers to reinforce keyword and keyword phrase relevance.

animated GIF. An animated image that uses the GIF89aa format.

ASCII (American Standard Code for Information Interchange). A standard encoding system for text.

ASCII file. A standard text file.

attachment. A file added to an e-mail message.

award. On the Internet, an award is an honor assigned to a Web site for excellence, exceptional presentation, or good content.

B

bandwidth. The amount of data that can be sent through a given communications circuit.

banner. *See banner advertisement.*

banner advertisement. An image used for advertising on the Web; the typical banner ad is a GIF image at 468 × 60 pixels.

banner exchange. A Web service in which member Web sites display other Web site's banners in exchange for displaying their own banner.

banner exchange ratio. The display-to-credit ratio offered by an exchange. The most common exchange is 2 to 1. If an exchange has a 2 to 1 exchange ratio, this means that for every two times that someone views a banner on your Web site, your banner will be displayed one time at a member site.

bookmark. A reference to a Web site stored by a browser.

browse. To window-shop on the Internet, wandering from Web site to Web site. See also *surfing*.

browser. A software application that is used to access and surf the World Wide Web.

C

case insensitive. A term used to describe software that treats uppercase and lowercase letters as equivalent.

case sensitive. A term used to describe software that treats uppercase and lowercase letters as distinct.

CGI (Common Gateway Interface). Defines how scripts communicate with Web servers.

CGI scripts. Programs that connect to a Web server and other applications. Also known as gateway scripts. See *CGI*.

click through. A count of the number of times that visitors click on a banner.

click-through ratio. The total number of clicks on a banner divided by the total number of impressions.

clickable image. An image that can be clicked on to access a link to a specified target resource, such as a Web page.

client. A computer that requests the services of another computer (or server).

comments. Hidden text embedded inside HTML pages, which is used by Web page programmers to document the contents of the Web page. Comments also provide an opportunity for Web publishers to reinforce keyword and keyword phrase relevance.

commercial online service. A commercial service, such as America Online (AOL), that connects people to the Internet. Most commercial services provide additional content and features for their users; these features generally distinguish a commercial service from an Internet service provider.

connection. A link between two computers for the purpose of communication.

contest. A marketing tool used to draw traffic to the sponsoring Web site with the promise of a chance to win a prize.

cool site. A Web site that has been awarded a status of "cool" by a Cool Site of the Day Web site.

copyright. The legal ownership of a given product or idea.

counter. A program used to track hits or page views.

crawler. See *indexer*.

D

database. A repository used to store and retrieve data. In the case of search engines, a database is used to store and retrieve information about Web sites crawled or spidered on the Internet.

dead link. A pointer to a URL on the Web that is no longer valid. Dead links are typically identified by the appearance of a 404- - File Not Found error message.

Description attribute. A Meta tag parameter that is used to specify a brief description for a Web page.

direct mailing. An e-mail message sent directly to an individual Internet e-mail address.

directory. On the Web, a service that provides a description of Web sites as well as links to the Web sites. Generally, you can browse a directory by category or search by keyword.

domain. The part of an address that identifies a Web site, such as tvpress.com.

download. To retrieve a file from a remote computer and store a copy of the file on your computer.

E

editor. A program used to edit a file.

e-mail (electronic mail). A service that provides the ability to send and receive messages on a network.

e-mail address. Used to identify the senders and recipients of an e-mail message. Created by combining a user name with a computer name, such as william@tvpress.com.

e-mail signature. Text that you can append into the end of your e-mail messages automatically.

exchange ratio. Generally pertains to the exchange ratio for banner ads; see also *banner exchange ratio*.

exclusion list. A list that identifies Web pages that should not be indexed by a search engine.

F

FAQs (Frequently Asked Questions). A list of frequently asked questions and their answers. Newsgroups, mailing lists, and other fun sites on the Web often publish a list of FAQs you can read.

frames. An HTML construct that defines a section or area within a FRAMESET as well as the content that is to be loaded into that section or area.

FRAMESET. An HTML construct that provides the ability to map out and represent the available space within a browser window.

freebie. Something given away by a Web site to its visitors with no strings attached.

G

game. A computer program that allows one or more players to compete against each other or a computer opponent.

GIF (Graphics Interchange Format). A compressed file format for images. The most widely used graphics format in Web pages.

.gif. A file extension used for GIF images.

giveaway. An organized effort to attract visitors to a Web site by offering to give visitors a freebie of some type.

graphic. An image displayed on a Web page, such as a picture, drawing, or other type of rendering.

guide. See *Web guide*.

H

hierarchy. Within newsgroups, the naming structure that helps computers track the various discussion groups.

hit. The number of file accesses at a Web site. Every file that is accessed to display a Web page, including each graphic, in a browser is considered a hit.

home page. The main page for a person's or an organization's Web site. Your personal home page is the page you see when you start your browser.

host. A computer that handles requests from clients.

hostname. The name of a host computer, such as tvpress.com.

.htm. A file extension used for Web pages.

.html. A file extension used for Web pages.

HTML (Hypertext Markup Language). A text-based computer language used to create Web pages.

HTTP (Hypertext Transfer Protocol). The protocol used to distribute information on the World Wide Web.

human-powered directory. See *directory*.

hybrid sites. A search Web site that combines qualities of both search engines and directories in order to provide visitors with results.

I

image. A name used to refer to a graphic.

image map. An image with multiple hot spots that link to different resources on the Internet; acts as a graphical menu of sorts.

impression. Describes the instances in which a banner is displayed.

indexer. For search engines, a utility that creates an index for all the pages at a Web site.

interface. Describes the mechanisms you can use to work with computer programs or the method by which programs communicate with each other.

Internet. A massive networked computing community or the system by which computers around the world communicate with each other.

Internet protocol address. A unique numeric identifier for a networked computer.

IP (Internet Protocol). A standard convention for passing information over the Internet; defines how data is packed and sent over a network.

IP address. See *Internet protocol address*.

ISP (Internet Service Provider). A company that provides access to the Internet.

J

Java. A programming language used on the Internet to deliver dynamic content to Web browsers.

JPEG. A standard for still-image compression that was developed by the Joint Photographic Experts Group.

.jpeg. A file extension used for JPEG images.

.jpg. A file extension used for JPEG images.

K

keyword. A word or phrase specifying words that represent information presented on a Web page.

keyword attribute. A Meta tag parameter that is used to specify keywords associated with the content of a Web page.

keyword list. A list of words or phrases that help identify the topic(s) covered on a Web site.

keyword loading. A spamming technique used to trick search engines into granting higher keyword ranking by repeating the same keyword and keyword phrases over and over again.

L

legal issues. Concerns that govern and restrict the actions and content of Web sites. Legal issues include local, state, national, and international laws and regulations.

link. An element that points to a resource on the Internet and provides the method for accessing that resource.

link farms. A spamming technique used to trick search engines into granting a high ranking to a Web site by making a Web site seem more popular than it really it is.

This is achieved by creating Web pages for the sole purpose of linking to a specific Web site.

list. A collection of links to Web sites.

log file. See *server log file*.

log file analysis. The process of examining the contents of a log file in order to extract data that is then used to create information that can be used to gauge visitor characteristics and behavior.

M

mailing list. A discussion group handled through a standard mail program, or a special type of e-mail address for distributing messages to a group of subscribers.

marketing campaign. An organized Web site promotion effort.

MetaCrawler. See *Meta search engine*.

Meta information. Data that is included in a Web page header but is hidden from the reader; generally contains instructions or special notes for Web clients.

Meta search engine. A search site that retrieves results by simultaneously querying multiple search engines and directories.

Meta tag. An HTML tag that provides the ability to specify information that search engines can use when creating listings for Web pages.

metro guide. A Web guide to a metropolitan area. See also *Web guide*.

moderated discussion. A discussion that has a moderator. Usually, all messages submitted to a moderated discussion are checked by the moderator before they are distributed or posted. See also *moderator*.

moderated mailing list. A mailing list that has a moderator.

moderated newsgroup. A newsgroup that has a moderator.

moderator. A person who manages a discussion and ensures it stays on track.

N

NCSA (National Center for Supercomputing Applications). Part of the University of Illinois, and the place where the original graphics-capable browser, called Mosaic, was developed.

network. A group of computers that are all connected in order to facilitate data sharing and communications.

news. Shorthand for newsgroups. See also *newsgroup*.

newsgroup. An electronic discussion group through which you can post and read messages.

newsreader. A program for reading and posting messages to newsgroups.

news server. A computer that stores discussion groups.

NOFRAME tag. An HTML tag that provides the ability to display content shown on browsers that do not support HTML frames.

O

off-page factors. Techniques used to help search engines determine a Web page's ranking using data collected from a source other than the Web page itself.

P

page. A document on a Web server.

page title. A descriptive statement defined in an HTML <TITLE> tag.

page view. A request for a Web page, which is normally in HTML format.

paid inclusion. Payment to a search engine made in exchange for an immediate listing in the search engine's database.

password. A security keyword used to protect your Internet accounts.

permission marketing. A process in which visitors are formally asked for permission to send them e-mail related to specific products and services.

poll. A small survey that gives individuals the opportunity to express their opinion on a specific issue or topic.

privacy policy. A formal statement regarding the operations of a Web site and the manner in which the Web site uses the information that it collects about visitors.

protocol. A set of rules for communicating on a network.

R

reciprocal link. A link placed on a Web site in exchange for a link back to the first site owner's Web site.

redirection. See *server redirection.*

registration. See *search engine registration.*

registration service. An organization that registers your Web site with multiple search engines and directories.

reindex. The process a search engine goes through when it returns to a Web site in order to validate its content or discover new links.

relevancy. For search engines, a term that is used to identify how strongly a Web site relates to the entered keyword query string.

repeat traffic generator. Any marketing technique that results in visitors returning back to a Web site. Examples of repeat traffic generators include games, online advice columns, and a Tip of the Day.

resource. A general term for a file on the Internet.

robots.txt. A file on your Web server that tells search engines which files should not be indexed.

S

scripts. A collection of programming statements written in a language such as JavaScript that executes within a visitor's browser.

search. The process of looking for Web sites by performing keyword searches using a Web search engine.

search engine. A Web service that assists Web surfers in finding Web sites on the Internet based on keyword searches.

search-engine registration. The process of applying for a listing at a Web search engine.

server. A computer that handles requests and provides resources.

server log file. A file stored on a Web server that is used to record events affecting Web pages.

server redirection. A technique used to point users at a new location.

signature. See *e-mail signature.*

signature file. A text file used to store an e-mail signature.

spam. An unsolicited message that tries to sell you a product or service.

spammer. Someone who distributes unsolicited commercial messages.

spider. See *indexer.*

standard. The widely accepted way to handle a process or technology; usually set by standards organizations.

statistics. Information compiled from a variety of resources, such as server logs.

stats. See *statistics.*

status code. A three-digit number that indicates the status of an HTTP request. The code 404 indicates that a file was not found.

stickiness. A term used to refer to the ability of a Web site to keep visitors interested enough to stick around and visit the site for a while.

surfing. To browse pages on the Web.

sweepstakes. A special type of contest in which prizes are donated by a third party in order to advertise or promote either the third party or its products.

T

T1. A type of digital communications line or the standard for distributing data at 1.44 million bits per second.

targeting. The selection of categories used when determining the appropriate Web sites where banners and other types of ads are to be placed.

thread. A unique subject or topic in a discussion group.

throughput. The measurement of the transfer rate between a server and client computers.

TITLE tag. An HTML tag that is used to specify a name or description for a Web page. The <TITLE> tag provides an opportunity for Web publishers to reinforce keyword and keyword phrase relevance.

top-level page. Another way to refer to a Web site's home page.

tracking software. A software application or Web service that tracks Web statistics and turns them into information that Web site owners can use to analyze the overall performance and success of their Web site.

treasure hunt. A special type of contest in which the hosting Web site hides clues throughout its Web site and challenges visitors to find those clues.

.txt. A file extension for plain ASCII text files.

U

upload. To transfer data from your computer to another computer.

URL (Uniform Resource Locator). Provides a uniform way of identifying resources on a Web server. Also referred to as a Web address or location. A typical URL looks like this: **http://www.tvpress.com/**

URL Analyzer. A software application or Web service that examines all of the links located on a Web site and reports on any that are no longer functional.

V

viewer. A program (helper application) for viewing files.

viral marketing. A marketing tool that leverages visitor opinion by encouraging visitors to pass on information provided by the Web site to friends and colleagues.

virtual launch. The act of promoting the opening or re-opening of a Web site for the purpose of attracting attention and bringing visitors to the Web site.

visit. The set of requests made by a single user in a single session; a collection of hits and page views that pertain to a specific person who requested files from your Web site during a specified time frame.

visitor. A person browsing a Web site.

W

Web address. The URL or location of a resource on the Web.

Web client. An application used to access Web-based technologies, such as a Web browser.

Web guide. A guide to the Web that tries to help you find the best Web sites.

Web master. The person responsible for administering a Web site or Web server.

Web page. A document on a Web server that is displayed when a Web surfer types its URL into a browser.

Web ring. A collection of related Web sites that are set up so that they point to one another under the direction of a central server that manager the ring.

Web server. A computer on the Internet that stores Web pages and allows browsers to access them.

Web site. A collection of Web pages on a Web server.

Web site statistics. A collection of data representing activities that have occurred on a Web server or for a specified Web site.

Web traffic analysis. The process of examining Web site statistics in order to extrapolate useful information that can be used to study visitor activity and assist in making decisions on how to improve the Web site.

What's New? directories. A special type of directory that is dedicated to storing and providing information about new Web sites on the Internet.

White Pages. A directory for finding e-mail addresses, phone numbers, and street addresses.

World Wide Web. A hypertext-based system for distributing information and resources. Also known as the *Web*, *WWW*, or *W3*.

Y

Yellow Pages. A directory for finding businesses on the Web and in the real world.

INDEX

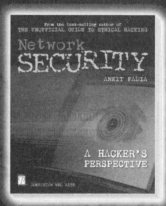